MEMBERS OF THE BRITISH CONSULATE AT KAUNAS.

Frontispiece.

LITHUANIA
PAST & PRESENT
By E. J. HARRISON
Formerly British Vice-Consul at Kaunas and Vilnius

NEW YORK

ROBERT M. McBRIDE & COMPANY

1922

Printed in Great Britain

G

PREFACE

In the following pages I have not attempted to do more than scratch the surface of a subject which, for adequate treatment, would require several large volumes. My main purpose is to arouse interest among English readers in a country and people whose glorious past and present renascence, under peculiarly moving conditions, are surely an earnest of great future achievement in all constructive activities. To this end I have tried to give a general outline of Lithuanian history, geography, economic position and possibilities, present-day political problems, cultural characteristics, etc., so that Britishers may no longer be able to plead ignorance as an excuse for their unfortunately apathetic attitude towards the legitimate aspirations of the Lithuanian people. Should the reception accorded this modest preliminary essay warrant it, I shall gladly hereafter embark upon a more exhaustive and ambitious handling of this fascinating subject.

For much of the material embodied in this book I am indebted principally to Stasys Šalkauskis' masterly study *Sur les Confins de Deux Mondes*, W. St. Vidunas' *La Lituanie dans le Passé et dans le Présent*, and Dr. Joseph Ehret's *Litauen*, which have rendered readily accessible many facts which otherwise might have eluded compilation.

I make no apology for largely employing the Lithuanian spelling of place names. The sooner we adapt ourselves to changed conditions the better. But for the reader's convenience, I have appended a short glossary giving the former Russian and present Lithuanian renderings of these centres.

A hint on pronunciation. The Lithuanian č is pronounced like our *ch* in church; the š like *sh* in shall ; and the ž like *z* in azure.

Authors' Club,
      Whitehall Court, London, S.W. 1.
          March 30, 1922.

CONTENTS

		PAGE
PREFACE	. . . .	5
GLOSSARY	. . . .	13

CHAPTER

I. INTRODUCTORY REMARKS 15

English Ignorance of Lithuania—Lithuania's Former Greatness—Chaucer's Reference to the Country—Early Commercial Treaty with England—Fatal Association with Poland—The Great War and German Designs—Proclamation of Independence—Polish Occupation of Vilnius—Lithuanian Retreat to Kaunas—Refusal of *de jure* Recognition by the Allies.

II. A TOPOGRAPHICAL OUTLINE 20

Historic and Ethnographic Lithuania—Area and Population—Vilnius, the National Capital—Testimony of Early Chroniclers—Other Provinces and Cities—Palanga on the Baltic Coast—Prussian Lithuania or Lithuania Minor—The Port of Memel—Configuration of the Land—Hills, Lakes and Rivers—Nature of Soil.

III. THE RISE OF LITHUANIA 37

The Lithuanian People not of Slavonic Origin—Lithuanian Language one of the Oldest in Europe Allied to Sanscrit—Aestians or Balts—Claim to Grecian Ancestry—The Early Grand Dukes—Struggles with the Teutonic Order—Prosperity of the Country under Gediminas, Keistutis and Vytautas the Great—Extension of Frontiers from the Baltic to the Black Sea—Beginnings of Polish Influence—Personal Union with Poland under Jagellon—Wars with the Tartars—Lublin Union with Poland in 1569—Partition of Lithuania and Poland at End of XVIIIth Century.

IV. PERIOD OF DECADENCE 49

The Reformation and Lithuania—Corruption of Catholic Priesthood and Lithuanian Nobility—Oppression of the Peasantry—Missionaries of New Doctrines—Nicolai Radvila, the Black—Re-introduction of Catholicism—Polonization of Upper Classes—Internecine Strife—Extinction of Independence.

V. UNDER THE RUSSIAN YOKE 55

Russification of the Country—The Iron Hand of Muraviev—Attacks on Lithuanian Culture—Closing and Dispersal of Vilnius University—Substitution of Russian State Religion for Catholicism—Manifesto of 1863 Prohibiting Lithuanian Tongue—Ban on Latin Alphabet—Victims of Muraviev's Rule—Abolition of Lithuanian Statute—Confusion in Administration of Justice—Russian Judges Ignorant of Lithuanian—Russian Confiscations of Lithuanian Lands—Wholesale Emigration.

8   CONTENTS

VI.   THE LITHUANIAN RENASCENCE   .   .   .   **62**

Neo-Lithuanian Movement—Secret Associations—Literary, Cultural and Political Activity—The Work of Basanavičius—Smuggling of Lithuanian Books and Magazines into Country—Decline of Polish Influence and Rehabilitation of Lithuanian Speech—Effect of Russo-Japanese War on Liberation Movement—Russian Revolution of 1905—Labours of Lithuanian Patriots—The Vilnius Memorandum—Congress of Vilnius—Historic Resolution—Russian Reaction —Development of Lithuanian Schools and Societies—Rise of National Press—Art and Literature—Economic Revival.

VII.   LITHUANIA DURING THE GREAT WAR   .   .   **75**

Lithuania as Battleground—Her Contribution to Allied Victory—Hostile Devastation of Country—Fall of Kaunas and Vilnius—The Land a Desert in the Wake of the War—Ravages of Disease—Deplorable Lot of Lithuanian Civil and Military Prisoners—Dispersal of Entire Families—Organization of Relief—German Military Occupation—Efforts at Germanization—Ober-Ost Administration.

VIII.   RISE OF THE NEW STATE **85**

Share of American-Lithuanians in National Movement—Congress of Chicago Declares for Self-Determination—Bureau of Information Established in Paris—First Berne Conference in 1915—Demand for Independence Raised in Russian Duma—Congress at Lausanne—Second Berne Conference Declares for Independence—Other Notable Gatherings—Conference of St. Petersburg—Diet of Vilnius in 1917—Election of National Council—Third Berne Conference—Recognition of Taryba as Lithuanian Constitutional Organ—Two Declarations of Independence—Stern Resistance to German Intrigues—Effect of Allied Victory—Appointment of Provisional Government—War against Bolsheviks—Polish Occupation of Vilnius in April 1919—Intervention of Supreme Council and Establishment of Demarcation Line—Election of Constituent Assembly—Lithuanian Political Parties—Lithuanian People Essentially Non-Bolshevik.

IX.   THE POLISH BETRAYAL **97**

Personal Observation of Polish Designs—British Commission for the Baltic Provinces—Branch Established at Kaunas under Colonel R. B. Ward—Author Appointed British Vice-Consul—Views of Former British Military Attaché on Polish " Prussianism "—Russo-Lithuanian Peace Treaty of July 12, 1920—Russo-Polish War and Lithuanian Neutrality —Polish Evacuation of Vilnius and Invitation to Lithuanians to Occupy City—Polish Treachery—Reds take Vilnius—Lithuanians Enter City—Transfer of Lithuanian Government to Vilnius—Conclusion of Suvalki Agreement and its Immediate Infringement—Colonel Ward's Aerial Visit to Warsaw and Polish Assurances—Polish Offensive against

CHAPTER — **PAGE**

Vilnius and Re-occupation of same, October 9, 1920—
Flight to Kaunas—Author's Return to Vilnius and Observa-
tion of Polish Methods—Complicity of Warsaw Government
in the Zeligowski Coup—Depositions of Polish Officers—
Intervention of League of Nations in Polish-Lithuanian
Dispute—Causes of League's Failure to Achieve a Settle-
ment—Termination of League's Intervention—Polish Viola-
tion of Four Demarcation Lines—The Unlawful Vilnius
Elections—Polish Pogroms of Lithuanian Institutions in
Vilnius—Lithuania Penalized for Sins of Poland—Denial
of *de jure* Recognition—Allied Failure to Settle Polish
Frontiers Largely Responsible for Situation.

X. THE MEMEL QUESTION 116

Defeat of the Borussians and their Gradual Germanization—
Teutonic Knights oppose Lithuanian Advance to the Sea—
Memel District—Ratio of Germans and Lithuanians—Memel
economically dependent upon Lithuanian Hinterland—
Allied Declaration of Predominantly Lithuanian Character
of Memel Region—Memel Port Lithuania's Sole Sea Outlet
—Provisional French Administration of the District for
Supreme Council—Franco-Polish Designs to Prevent Memel's
Reversion to Lithuania.

XI. LITHUANIA'S ECONOMIC PROGRESS . . . 122

Country's Favoured Position—Government's Abstention
from Issue of New Currency—Collapse of German Mark
Reacts to Country's Detriment—Lithuania Primarily an
Agricultural Land—Racial Percentages—Agricultural Yields
Before and After War—Capacity for Further Expansion—
Dairy-farming and Stock-raising—Current Prices often Lower
than Pre-War—Tendency towards Small and Medium
Farming—Lithuania's Timber Resources—Heavy *Post-
bellum* Demands—Need for Remedial Measures—Agrarian
Reform—Grants to Soldiers—Comparatively Mild Incidence
of Law with Recognition of Principle of Compensation—
Lithuanian Industries—Trade Figures—National Finances—
Credit Associations, Banks and Cooperatives—Lithuanian
Railways and Waterways—Government's Economic Policy—
Legal Reform.

XII. LITHUANIAN TYPES AND CHARACTER . . 145

Appreciations of Foreign Observers—Sexual Purity a
Notable Trait—Meeting of East and West on Lithuanian
Soil—Latent Capacity for Tremendous Effort—Physical
Aspects—Lithuanian Love of Nature—Democratic Senti-
ment—Belief in Religion—Lithuanian Superstitions often
Pagan Survivals.

XIII. IN THE COUNTRY 153

Description of Lithuanian Farm—Ubiquity of the Cross in
Lithuanian Countryside—National Dress—The "Juosta"
Worn by Women—Lithuanian Love of Song—Some Marriage
Customs—Rue as the Emblem of Purity.

CHAPTER   PAGE

XIV. LITHUANIAN MYTHOLOGY 163

Its Indo-European Origin—Lithuanians the Last to abandon
Paganism—Ancient Sacerdotal Caste not Unlike that of
Brahmins or Druids—Its Influence in both Religious and
Social Life—The Vestal Virgins—Fire Worship Practised at
Vilnius—Perkunas or God of Thunder—Myths of Sun and
Moon—Natural Phenomena Objects of Adoration—" Sventa
Ugnis " or Sacred Fire—Lithuanian Love of Symbolism
survives Paganism—Belief in Metempsychosis—Legends of
Giants—Interpretation of Dreams.

XV. LANGUAGE AND LITERATURE 173

Lithuanian Tongue part of Aestian or Baltic Linguistic
Branch—At One Time Identical with Lettish—The Two
Main Dialects—Resemblance to Greek and Latin—National
Existence Bound Up with Native Speech—Special Use of
Participle—The Genitive Attributive—Lithuanian uniquely
Rich in Diminutive and Caressive Forms—German Study
of Lithuanian Poetry in Eighteenth Century—Lessing and
Herder—The " Dainos " or Chansonettes—*Belles Lettres*
Proper—Duonelaitis, Mickiewicz and Vidunas—Drama
encouraged by the Jesuits—Modern Literary Revival.

XVI. ART AND MUSIC 185

The Work of Čiurlionis—His Fame in Russia and on the
Continent—Antanas Zmuidzinavičius—The Sculptors Rimša
and Zikaras—Modern Artists from the People—Peasant
Handicrafts—Lithuanian Ecclesiastical Architecture—
Churches of Vilnius—National Love of Music—Popular
Chants Reveal Greek Origin Homer's Hymn to Demetrius—
The Brothers Petrauskas—Simkus, Bražys and Naujalis—
Some Native Musical Instruments—Lithuanian National
Hymn.

XVII. THE PERSONAL EQUATION AND CONCLUSION . 196

Author's Early Association with Lithuanians—Journey
by Motor-Lorry from Riga to Kaunas in Summer of 1919—
A Night at Radzivilishki—Author Arrested by German
Soldiery—Meeting with Colonel Robinson and the German
Airman Rother at Keidany—Story of Rother's Dramatic
Rescue of Enver Pasha—Author's Entry into Kaunas—City
under Martial Law owing to Discovery of Polish Plot—
Life in Kaunas—Author's Visits to Vilnius—Impression of
the Poles—The Bolshevik Régime—Other Aeroplane Inci-
dents—Von Platen and his Russian Wife—Lithuanian
Leaders—Some Political Reflections in Conclusion.

APPENDIX 207

INDEX 225

ILLUSTRATIONS

MEMBERS OF THE BRITISH CONSULATE AT KAUNAS   *Frontispiece*

TO FACE PAGE

TWO VIEWS OF VILNIUS   22

INHABITANTS OF PALANGA GREETING LITHUANIAN TROOPS .   28

LITHUANIAN CHILDREN PRAYING FOR DEAD COMRADE   .   28

RED CROSS TRAIN AT KAUNAS   76

FIELD DRESSING STATION   76

VIEW OF KAUNAS FROM VYTAUTAS HILL   .   .   .   92

KAUNAS UNIVERSITY   92

LITHUANIAN BIVOUAC   100

ON THE FRONT   100

MONASTERY ON VILNIUS ROAD   112

MEMBERS OF BRITISH MILITARY MISSION AT KAUNAS   .   196

MAPS

MAP OF LITHUANIA ILLUSTRATING INFRINGEMENTS OF TEM-
     PORARY DEMARCATION LINES   .   .   *To face page*   14

ANCIENT MAP OF LITHUANIA   .   .   .   .   *At end*

Lithuania Past and Present

CHAPTER I

INTRODUCTORY REMARKS

My own experience is that, if we except certain business circles which before the war engaged in trade with the Baltic and to-day are making somewhat halfhearted attempts to resume these relations with the independent States that have succeeded to the old Russian régime in that part of the world, very few persons in England know anything at all about Lithuania. Spelling the name in syllables accomplishes little in the face of an abysmal ignorance extending to the very geography of the country. This unfortunate apathy goes to prove how very superficially the average citizen reads his daily paper, because for months past there have been repeated press references, long and short, to the Polish-Lithuanian dispute and the futile efforts of the League of Nations to settle it at Brussels and Geneva.

And yet at the end of the XIVth and the beginning of the XVth century Lithuania was the most formidable Power in the North, and the boundaries of this compact State extended from the Baltic to the Black Sea. On one occasion Moscow was almost taken by Algird, who spared it only in deference to the prayers of the Grand Duke Demetrius, thus unconsciously and naïvely revealing the boundless gulf which separates the simple barbarous mentality of that age from our own vastly superior conception of what is due to a military victor. The devastated regions of Northern France and East Prussia show conclusively how far we have advanced along the road of civilization since those primitive days. Few are probably aware that this period of Lithuanian power has found a place in English literature. In the *Canterbury Tales* Chaucer sends a brave English knight to that country, and in this connexion it is interesting to note that Chaucer calls Lithuania " Leetuwe " (Lietuva), which is the Lithuanian word for Lithuania, the latter being used only abroad. Historians also relate that in the XIVth century Keistut, or Keïstutis, the ruler of Lithuania, signed a commercial treaty with England. In Rymer's *Fœdera* there is also a document of Queen Elizabeth, written in 1560, giving a licence to a Lithuanian in the following terms :

He by Himself, his Servants, or Factors, maye or shall brynge in this our Realme of England within the space of one Monethe next hereafter following Thyrtic Tymber of Sabels and a Carkamet of Gold sett with Divers Pearles and pretiouse Stones without payinge Custome or Subsidie for the same

Lithuania has passed through many vicissitudes since that spacious epoch. Her disastrous association with Poland, of which more will be said elsewhere, involved her in the downfall of the latter in the XVIIIth century when the whole of Lithuania was attached to Russia by the sole right of conquest.

Although the Great War hit Lithuania hard and for a season led to the substitution of Teutonic tyranny for that of the Muscovite, its ultimate outcome proved on the whole favourable to Lithuanian national aspirations, which never ceased to be cherished in secret even during the darkest days of Russian and Polish oppression. During their period of military occupation, from 1915–18, the Germans tried in every way to suppress the national movement. They prohibited the publication of Lithuanian newspapers and threw the national leaders into jail. The object of the German Government was clearly to make Lithuania an integral part of Germany, but these efforts encountered a resistance which proved to be insuperable. Finally Lithuania succeeded in obtaining permission to call a convention at Vilnius in September

1917. This convention elected a State Council or Taryba, which on February 16, 1918, solemnly proclaimed the independence of the country. This day the young Republic annually celebrates as Independence Day.

After this came with bewildering swiftness the Allied victory, the German revolution, and the Bolshevik advance, which latter compelled the Lithuanian Government to withdraw from Vilnius to Kaunas, whence the defence of the country was energetically directed. The Bolshevik advance was checked at Koshedary, and the Lithuanians would again have entered Vilnius if they had not been deliberately forestalled by the Poles, who advanced from the south-east and occupied the city. The Polish occupation of Vilnius on this occasion lasted till July 1920, when the Polish defeat at the hands of the Soviet armies necessitated its abandonment, and the Lithuanian Government re-entered into possession.

Under the Suvalki Agreement, signed between the two States on October 7, 1920, Poland recognized the right of Lithuania to provisional administration of Vilnius and its territory, but this trifling fact in no way prevented her from flagrantly violating the agreement two days later, when the notorious General Zeligowski recaptured the Lithuanian capital. Thus the Lithuanian Government was again obliged to remove to Kaunas, and pending a settlement of the Vilnius question the affairs of the country are still directed from this temporary capital.

According to the Russo-Lithuanian Peace Treaty, concluded on July 12, 1920, Lithuania comprises an area of approximately 82,000 square kilometres (approximately 32,000 square miles), and the three governments of the former Russian Empire, Suvalki (Suvalkai), Kovno, (Kaunas) and Vilna (Vilnius), which is the ethnographical territory of the original Lithuanian Grand Duchy, and in past centuries was always recognized by both Poles and Russians as ethnographical Lithuania or Lithuania Proper. The population of this area numbers over 4,200,000, of which about 75 per cent. are Lithuanians by race and tongue, the rest being Jews, White Russians, Poles and others. Owing, however, to the loss of the

Vilnius region through the *force majeure* of Polish filibustering, the population actually under the jurisdiction of the Lithuanian Government at the time of writing is not probably much in excess of two millions, of which fewer than 3 per cent are Poles.

This, then, in brief, is the State which ever since the election of a Constituent Assembly, or Seim, in April 1920, by universal, direct, and secret suffrage, according to the system of proportional representation, has vainly sought for *de jure* recognition from the Allies, though this recognition has been granted by almost every other neutral country and former enemy state, large and small.[1]

Into the motives which have hitherto dictated so conservative a policy I propose to enquire later on in these pages. Moreover, I make no sort of apology for doing this frankly as a partizan. No man of spirit with any firsthand knowledge of the facts, such as I possess, could be otherwise. It was my inestimable privilege to live through the makings of history in the Baltic from the summer of 1919 to the winter of 1921, for the last fourteen or fifteen months of that period as British Vice-Consul at Kaunas, and for an all-too-brief interval at Vilnius, in which capacity I enjoyed unique opportunities of acquainting myself with the true inwardness of the situation. What at the outset was an objective investigation led me by inevitable stages to wholesale condemnation of the Poles and their *post-bellum* policy. Only an invertebrate degenerate could remain on the fence in such a quarrel. As a partizan, therefore, it shall be my special aim in the proper place to make as many other converts as possible by giving in some detail the reasons which in my own case proved so efficacious.

But before coming to that essentially controversial phase of my subject, I wish to excite public interest in

---

[1] Since these lines were written, the United States Government has granted unconditional *de jure* recognition to Lithuania. On July 13, 1922, the Ambassadors' Council in Paris offered *de jure* recognition on condition that Lithuania should consent to internationalization of the Niemen River. The Lithuanian Government accepted this condition in due course, and is therefore presumably recognized *de jure.*

other aspects of the Lithuanian problem, historic, geographical, sociological, æsthetic and cultural. Thus I hope to be the medium of removing from many British minds the reproach of ignorance of a country and a people with quite exceptional claims to our sympathy and support, not alone on grounds of international justice but equally on those of national expediency and self-interest. Indeed it is only to our proverbial middle-class and proletarian provincialism and indifference to foreign affairs, even when the latter have a vital bearing upon our destinies, that I can ascribe a popular attitude which has for so long tolerated Franco-Polish intrigues at our expense, and equally the very questionable *laissez-faire* policy of Great Britain herself in this regard.

If my own modest contribution to this branch of East European history helps, in however limited a degree, to disperse these clouds of ignorance and perhaps to galvanize the deadened national conscience into tardy recognition of its responsibilities, I shall not have laboured in vain.

CHAPTER II

A TOPOGRAPHICAL OUTLINE

IN any description of Lithuania we must distinguish carefully between the historic and ethnographic Lithuanias. What is called historic Lithuania or the Grand Duchy of Lithuania, comprises the territories of the former Russian governments of Vilna, Kovno, Grodno, Suvalki, Kurland, Minsk, Mohilev, and Vitebsk. During several centuries they formed, under the style of Lithuania, a political unit. When, therefore, we speak of old Lithuania up to the end of the XVIIIth century we mean this group of governments, which were not inhabited exclusively by Lithuanians but included various foreign ethnic elements which had been wholly absorbed in the energetic expansion of the Lithuanian State and passed under its dominion.

Ethnographic Lithuania, on the other hand, includes the old Russian governments of Vilna, Kovno, Suvalki, part of Grodno, and a small portion of the government of Minsk (Novogrodek). It embraces also the northern part of East Prussia with the districts of Memel, Tilsit, Heydekrug, Niederung, Ragnit, Pillkallen, Labiau, certain parts of Insterberg, Gumbinnen, Stallupönen, and Goldapp. The former Lithuanian territory is called Lithuania Major and the German territory Lithuania Minor.

If we include the Vilnius territory as an integral portion of ethnographic Lithuania and also the Memel district, at present administered by the French for the Supreme Council, we get an area of over 80,000 square miles, and a population which, in 1914, was estimated at 4,845,000. Thus in area and population Lithuania is larger than Belgium, the Netherlands, Denmark or Switzerland.

A large majority are of Lithuanian blood and speech. While much controversy has raged round this question, a fair estimate of the relative percentages appears to be Lithuanians about 75 per cent. ; Jews about 10 per cent. ; Polish-speaking element about 8 per cent. (for the entire district) ; Russians, White Russians and other nationalities 7 per cent. The population of the larger cities is approximately : Vilnius 214,600 ; Kaunas 90,300 ; Gardinas 61,600 ; Memel 32,000 ; Suvalkai 31,600 ; Šiauliai 31,300. These figures have been subjected to considerable modifications by the war. The present population of Kaunas, for example, owing to the tremendous influx of refugees from Vilnius and district in the wake of the Polish occupation is not far short of 120,000. The rural population constitutes 86·2 per cent. of the whole, indicating that Lithuania is essentially an agricultural country.

The Lithuanian province of Vilnius has a superficies of 42,500 kilometres, i.e. approximately the size of Switzerland. On the north it touches the province of Kaunas and the Vitebsk government ; on the east Vitebsk and Minsk ; on the south Minsk and the province of Gardinas ; on the west Suvalkai. It constitutes a plain traversed by a chain of hills. In view of the dearth of other means of communication the numerous rivers possess great importance. More than four hundred lakes cover 10 per cent. of the total surface, and lakes and rivers are surrounded by swamps. In the Trakai (Troki) district one marsh has a circumference of 85 kilometres. This province is divided into seven departments named after their respective capitals, viz. Vilnius, Trakai (Troki), Lyda, Šventionis (Svenciany), Vileika, Ašmena and Dysna.

The capital of the province and of the entire country is Vilnius, situated at the confluence of the Vilija and Vileika, at the foot of Mt. Gediminas, the name of the founder of the city. Before the war Vilna, as the Russians called it, was the capital of the General Government of the same name and was an important railway and commerical centre with a big trade in timber and cattle. Baedeker mentions that the history of the city stretches back to the earliest times, when it was a great centre of Pagan worship. A sacred fire was kept constantly burning at the foot of the hill upon which Gediminas (Gedymin), Grand Duke of Lithuania, built his castle when he founded the city in the XIVth century. In 1323 Vilnius was raised to the dignity of a town and was made the capital of Lithuania. The Grand Duke Ladislas Jagellon, who became King of Poland in 1386, introduced Christianity in 1387 and erected the cathedral of St. Stanislaus on the site of the heathen temple. Vilnius is afterwards often mentioned in the history of the struggles of the Lithuanians with the Teutonic Order, the Tartars, and the Russian Grand Dukes. During the XVIIth and XVIIIth centuries Vilnius was frequently pillaged by the Swedes, Russians, and Cossacks, and lost much of its former importance. In 1794 it offered a gallant resistance to the Russian army, but was captured on August 12th after a severe bombardment. At the opening of the war of 1812 Napoleon fixed upon the line of the Niemen as his base of operations and made Vilnius (at the point of intersection of the roads from Königsberg and Warsaw to St. Petersburg and Moscow) the strategic centre of the French line. On his retreat from Russia he again visited Vilnius, which he finally left in disguise on the night of November 24 (New Style December 6), 1812.

Vilnius's public edifices, her churches, and the memories which they enshrine, the palaces of the Lithuanian aristocracy, all have a great historical and national signification for Lithuania, and are the fruit of the work of many centuries, whose toil was accomplished under the hard conditions of bondage. Vilnius's other buildings are due to the work of the local labouring classes, composed for the most part of Lithuanian Jews. During the period of the Muscovite rule, the public edifices were constructed at the expense of the Russian Empire; but one seeks in vain for any evidence of such work by the Polish people.

During a period of over four and a half centuries Vilnius was the capital of the Grand Dukes of Lithuania, who were her national rulers. The capital of a State

VIEW OF VILNIUS.

VIEW OF VILNIUS.

To face p 22.

which in addition to the Lithuanian land properly so-called embraced vast Slavo-Russian territories, Vilnius, thanks to the autonomous rule of government which these latter enjoyed, served especially as the centre of ethnographical Lithuania (Lithuania Proper), which was composed of the principality of Samogitia and of the two palatinates of Vilnius and Trakai. The Government, the legislative and judicial administrations, constituted in the domain of Vilnius an indivisible whole, which was separated from the Slavonic regions of the Grand Duchy. Even after the Russian annexation, Lithuania Proper formed an administrative unit, composed of the three governments of Vilnius, Kaunas, and Gardinas, and designated under the general name of the " North-Western Country," with Vilnius as its capital, the seat of the central institutions of the whole land and the residence of the Governor-General.

Vilnius was the intellectual, artistic and religious centre of Lithuania, whose influence on the scientific and artistic development of Poland was considerable. However, even at that epoch, when the Polish language took the place of the Latin tongue, the University of Vilnius never lost its character as the home of Lithuanian culture.

During the whole of her existence as a sovereign State, and later, at the time of her struggle for independence, Lithuania, with Vilnius at her head, constantly asserted and defended with an untiring energy her real nationality and her right to absolute independence. In the same way, the unions with Poland were never an expression of free-will on the part of Lithuania but of combinations imposed on the country by Poland, who profited by the difficult situation of the Grand Duchy. The Union of Lublin, in 1569, was a striking example of this policy.

It was at Vilnius, at the time of the Russian dominion, that Lithuania experienced the most cruel losses in her struggle for liberty, and this city is the centre of the political and intellectual revival of Lithuania at the present day.

In view of the efforts made by the Polish delegation

at Brussels and Geneva before the Council of the League of Nations, in 1921, to disprove the Lithuanian origin of the Lithuanian capital Vilnius, it is interesting to recall that one of the oldest Polish chroniclers, i.e. Mathew Miechovita, himself states that the Lithuanians founded Vilnius (" *hi primum condiderunt oppidum Vilno* "). Miechovita even mentions a Duke Vilis (*dux Vilis*) who transported Lithuanians into that region and founded the city which from this Duke received the name of Vilnius. The Grand Duke Gediminas having transferred his capital thither assuredly maintained a Lithuanian garrison, as in the case of all ducal courts. There is no cause to doubt that at that time the inhabitants of Vilnius were Lithuanians, although there is no direct evidence available as to their precise nationality. The names of the children of both the Dukes Gediminas and Algirdas, as well as those of others, are Lithuanian of those times. Under Algirdas the nobles of his court Kiklis or Kuklejus, Miklis or Miklejus, and Niežila gained fame through their acceptance of the Orthodox faith about 1347 and their sufferings on that account at the hands of the Pagan Lithuanians. Even to-day they are revered as saints in the Orthodox Church under the style of Joannas, Antonius and Eustachius.

We have clear information about the nationality of the inhabitants of the town at the time of the introduction of Christianity into Vilnius by Jagellon in 1387. According to the testimony of J. Dlugosius (1415–80) Vilnius was then the capital of the Lithuanian nation (*caput et metropolis gentis*) and here the Lithuanians were baptized. Miechovita (1476–1523), M. Stryjkowskis and A. Guagnini, writing about the introduction of Christianity into Vilnius, say that the sacred eternal fires of the Pagan Lithuanians were then extinguished, their idols destroyed, the sacred mounds levelled, and 30,000 Lithuanians baptized. Moreover, as the Polish priests could not speak Lithuanian, the Lithuanian Grand Duke Jagellon himself explained their sermons to the baptized people. It appears from this that then the inhabitants of Vilnius, who were baptized *en masse,* were Lithuanians., That in the XIVth century the inhabitants of Vilnius were Lithuanians we know from other evidence, i.e. Count Kyburg, who, during the reign of Vytautas the Great, visited the latter in the summer of 1397 on a political mission, and testifies that the prevailing language in the palace and among the people themselves was Lithuanian, though already there were White Russians, Germans and Poles among the inhabitants. At a later epoch also the Lithuanian speech was used and esteemed in the Grand-Ducal palace at Vilnius. For example, Stryjkowskis clearly testifies that when on the death of the Grand Duke Zigmantas at Trakai castle in 1440 the Lithuanian nobles nominated Jagellon's son, Kazimieras, to be ruler of the country, the latter, who was born at Cracow, did not know Lithuanian and was therefore taught the language on his removal to Vilnius.

From writers of the XVth and XVIth centuries who travelled in Lithuania and visited Vilnius, such as Guillebert de Lannoy (1413–14) and Baron Herberstein (1517–26), we have mention of Vilnius, but no information about its inhabitants or their language. Guagnini (1538–1614) in his work *Sarmatiæ Europea descriptio*, briefly describes Vilnius, but is also silent about the nationality of its inhabitants. The Italian writer Jonas Boterius Benesius, whose work was translated into Polish and published at Cracow in 1659, superficially describes the Lithuanian people, and when mentioning Vilnius does not differentiate its inhabitants from other residents of the country who were Lithuanian.

It is a fact that as late as 1737 the Jesuits at St. John's Cathedral maintained preachers in Lithuanian, and it was only from that time that the Polonization of the Lithuanian inhabitants of Vilnius proceeded more rapidly till the majority lost their nationality. But even though denationalized the popular masses long retained the consciousness of their Lithuanian origin, as can be seen from the evidence of Father Hilarionas Karpinskis and M. Balinskis. The former of these writers, in his work *Lexykon geograficzny* (Wilno 1766, p. 602), speaks of the population, numbering 60,000, as Lithuanian and German, and that besides Catholics there were Orthodox, Lutherans, Calvinists and Jews, even Mohammedan Tartars, who had a mosque there. Balinskis in his work *Pisanie statystyczne miasto Wilna* (Wilno 1835), when describing the inhabitants of the city, makes no mention at all of Poles among them. He says only, " The inhabitants of the city of Vilnius are in their origin Lithuanians, Russians, Germans and Jews. There are so few inhabitants of other nationalities that in this respect they cannot make any distinction."

The town of Lyda with its 20,000 inhabitants (seventy kilometres south of the capital) still possesses some importance. From a historic standpoint the town of Trakai (Troki), twenty-five kilometres south of Vilnius, on the shore of the lake of the same name, offers some interest. Trakai Lake is dotted with several islets, on one of which may be seen the ruins of the ship *Königsberg* built by Keistutis, in which Vytautas the Great saw something of the world. Trakai, the capital of the Palatinate, formerly enjoyed great importance. Later its development was arrested and to-day it is only a small district town. On the upper course of the Vilija may be seen the château or castle of Verkai, where formerly the bishops of Vilnius resided during the summer months. To-day it is abandoned. At Birstonas are celebrated sulphur springs. Rodune has won an unenviable reputation as the scene of many conflicts with the Russians.

Forty per cent. of the total surface of this province is cultivated ; 19 per cent. consists of pasturage and meadow ; 28 per cent. of forests ; and nearly 11 per cent. of unculti-vated lands. The peasants of this region experience no little difficulty in drawing subsistence from the sandy soil, being in this respect worse off than the peasants of Suvalkai who, farther to the west, are better able to obtain necessary auxiliaries to agriculture.

The province of Kaunas, covering an area of 40,640 square kilometres, is thus almost equal to Vilnius in size. In the west it includes Samogitia ; to the north it is bounded by Kurland ; to the east by Vitebsk ; to the south by Vilnius and Suvalkai ; to the south-west by

Lithuania Minor. It forms a slightly undulating plain
with an altitude a little over 150 metres. Only in the
west are there any elevations, viz. the so-called mountains
of Satrija, Girgzduta, Medvegalis, etc. Among the navigable rivers are the Nemunas (Niemen), Vilija and Venta.
Lakes are also very numerous, the district of Zarasai
alone possessing four hundred of them. As in the province
of Vilnius swamps hinder communication. The great
swamp of Remygala, near Panevežis (Ponievezh), covers
136 square kilometres.

This province, like Vilnius, has seven districts, viz.
Kaunas, Telšiai, Šiauliai (Shavli), Raseiniai (Rossieny),
Panevežis (Ponievezh), Zarasai and Ukmergė (Vilkomir).
Kaunas, the capital, is situated at the confluence of the
Vilija and Nemunas, and before the war had between
ninety thousand and a hundred thousand inhabitants
but to-day is even more densely populated. In this
neighbourhood the banks of the Nemunas often rise to
a height of two hundred feet and are very picturesque.
Before the war Kaunas was regarded as a first-class
fortress, but this reputation was speedily exploded by
the German assailants who reduced it in a few days,
though treachery is supposed to have played an appreciable
rôle in this result. It is supposed that the town was
founded in the XIIIth century. In the XIVth century
it had already become a great bone of contention between
the Lithuanians and the Teutonic Knights. At the time
of the so-called " personal " union between Poland and
Lithuania, when Jagellon became king of the former
country, Kaunas began to serve as a centre for the export
trade from Poland and Lithuania to Russia. An English
trading factory was established here. In 1655 Kaunas
was plundered and burned down by a Russian army
under Tsar Alexis. At the Third Partition of Poland
in 1795 it was finally annexed to the Russian Empire.
On June 23, 1812, the French army reached the left
bank of the Nemunas, opposite Kaunas, and a hill near
the village of Ponyemon is still known as Napoleon's
Hill. Kaunas is the residence of the Bishop of Samogitia
and his chapter and also of the Lutheran Provost of

the Vilnius diocese. The Church of the Franciscans dates from the epoch of Vytautas the Great. The most remarkable of the Catholic churches is that of the Jesuits, which was built by Italians. The Jews, who are also numerous in Kaunas, possess four synagogues. The library of the Catholic seminary contains many very valuable manuscripts. Before the war Kaunas was well-known for its industries, one of the biggest iron foundries in Russia, that of Tillmann, doing a big business.

At Raseinial, a town of ten thousand inhabitants, the Diet of Samogitia formerly assembled. Kedainiai possesses a large Protestant church constructed in 1629 by the magnate Radvila, and it shelters the tomb of this princely house. The mortal remains of the Lithuanian historian Daukantas repose at Papilė. The Radvila family at one time had their residence at Kražiai, where there is to-day a well-known monastery. The Lithuanian poet Sarbiewski used to pursue his literary studies at the Jesuit college of this town, while at one time the Jesuit church possessed, according to report, Leonardo da Vinci's " Ascension."

Plungé, the home of the Princes Oginski, is the Lithuanian Jerusalem, the Jewish population being very large. On the banks of the Nemunas is the ancient fortress of Veliona, before which Gediminas died in 1341. Šidlava, in Samogitia, is a place of frequent pilgrimage, as also Kalvarija, which has a Calvary constructed on the model of the original at Jerusalem. The Biržai locality is known in history as the principal scene of Lithuanian opposition to Roman Catholicism and the headquarters of the Lithuanian Protestant Prince Nicolas Radvila the Black.

Under the Simpson boundary award between Latvia and Lithuania, the latter has acquired the watering-place Palanga on the Baltic, with valuable medicinal springs, and is considering plans for its development, together with Šventoji at the mouth of the river of that name, into an ocean port. There is indeed quite a mass of historical evidence available to show that there were in former years deep-sea harbours at both these places. During the XIIIth century, the Crusaders having taken

INHABITANTS OF PALANGA GREETING LITHUANIAN TROOPS.

LITHUANIAN CHILDREN PRAYING FOR DEAD COMRADE.

To face p. 28.

Prussia and the Knights of the Sword Latvia, the towns of Königsberg, Rusnis, Klaipeda (Memel) and Riga, which then belonged to the Germans, tried to seize the entire trade of Lithuania together with that of other regions. The Lithuanian Grand Dukes, on the other hand, did their best to thwart these schemes and to liberate Lithuanian trade from the German yoke. With this object, for example, Keistutis in 1842 concluded a commercial treaty with England. The trade of Lithuania at that time, in all probability, was conducted via Palanga or Šventoji. At any rate Vytautas the Great, wishing to open " a window into Europe " which should not be dependent upon Germany, restored those ports. It must therefore be supposed that they were situated very much where the present Palanga and Šventoji are to-day. Later, apparently, they were abandoned. The trade of Palanga-Šventoji even during the time of Vytautas had begun to decline. Lithuania having strengthened and improved her relations with Prussia and the Latvian Germans had revived the trade via the Nemunas and Dauguva (Dvina).

In the XVth century we find further information about Palanga port. From the XVIth to the XVIIth century the independent trade of Lithuania rose. Dutch and British vessels lay in Lithuanian harbours. In 1608 Šventoji still appears on a map of Lithuania published by command and at the expense of Radvila. From the XVIth to the XVIIth century, however, war and disorder detrimentally affected Lithuanian trade. According to one account it was in 1625 that the Swedish king Gustavus Adolphus, and according to another in 1701 that Charles XII, also of Sweden, at the instance of the Riga merchants, filled up Šventoji harbour with stones which were transported in nine vessels. There is information extant that in 1685 an English merchant named Horst opened his office at Šventoji. It is probable that the Swedes twice destroyed Šventoji port and that Lithuania restored it.

In the second half of the XVIIIth century the representative of Lithuania and Poland, Bukaty, in negotiation with

England on behalf of his Government, promised to restore Šventoji harbour; but as Lithuania dreaded foreign domination this project came to nought. The father of the present owner of Palanga, Tiskevičius, with the object of restoring the trade of Palanga, built a long pier alongside which his own and other vessels used to moor, but trade did not develop.

Now that the Lithuanian State has been recreated the importance of Palanga as a port will perhaps again be revived.

From an economic standpoint Šiauliai was formerly of considerable importance and should again become so, since it possesses some of the largest tanneries in the world and several confectionery factories.

Of the total provincial area 38 per cent. is under cultivation, 27 per cent. consists of meadows and pasture, 24 per cent. of forests, and 11 per cent. of marshes and uncultivated land. Lakes cover a surface of 400 square kilometres.

Suvalkai province, with only 12,300 square kilometres, is appreciably smaller than the other Lithuanian provinces. It is bounded on the north by Kaunas province, on the east by Vilnius, on the south by Gardinas, and on the west by East Prussia. In a topographical sense the country is divided into two distinct parts; the northern half is very fertile and possesses near Kazlų Ruda extensive forests, whereas the south-west, traversed by a chain of hills, is covered with innumerable lakes which abound in fish. The largest of these, Lake Vigrai, has an area of 10,000 hectares. Swamps are also numerous.

There are about 700,000 inhabitants in the province. There are seven district divisions known as Suvalkai, Augustavas (Augustovo), Kalvarija, Marjampolė, Seinai (Seiny), Vilkaviškis, and Naumiestis. During the Russian occupation of the province the capital, Suvalkai, had 25,000 inhabitants. The episcopal residence Seinai boasts a Roman Catholic seminary and is generally regarded with reverence by all Lithuanians as the home of Lithuanian religious culture. Augustavas is best known for its canal of the same name, which figured largely in the Great War.

Cultivated land constitutes 40 per cent. of the total, meadows and pasture 19.5 per cent., and forests 23 per cent. The rest is uncultivated.

The province of Gardinas has an area of more than 38,600 square kilometres and is divided into nine districts, i.e. Gardinas, Sakalė, Baltstoge, Brest-Lithuanien, Kobrin, Pružėnai, Slanimas, Vilkaviškis and Bielsk. On the north it touches Suvalkai and Vilnius, on the east the Minsk government, on the south Volhynia, and on the west Poland. Its configuration is also that of an undulating plain with a mean altitude of 160 metres. The highest hill, in the Slanimas district, reaches 280 metres. In the south-east are many swamps. The Lithuanian hills divide the country into two basins, that of the Baltic Sea and that of the Black Sea. This explains why some of the rivers flow north and others south. The Nemunas flows in the first-named direction and the Jasiolda and Pina, affluents of the Pripet, in the second.

The capital, Gardinas, is situated on the right bank of the Nemunas at the point where the river begins to penetrate a barrier of hills and forms a valley enclosed by sides one hundred feet in height. Gardinas is the point of bifurcation of several railway lines and possesses a land bank. Its efforts to improve agriculture are favourably known. Its fortress and environs were the scene of many sanguinary engagements during the war. Pružėnai and Vilkaviškis possess well-known distilleries. Slanimas has made a name for itself in apiculture. Balstogė contains many breweries and one of the biggest weaving mills in all Lithuania. Druskininkai is celebrated for its salt baths, and is very rich in radium.

Seventy per cent of the territory is a light soil. Cultivated land constitutes 39 per cent., meadows and pasture land 22 per cent., forests 25 per cent., and uncultivated land, marshes and moving sand 14 per cent. of the total area.

In the Minsk government, the district of Naugardukas, called also Naupilis, forms part of ethnographic Lithuania. Before Vilnius, Naugardukas was the Lithuanian capital, and ruins of the castle in which the Grand Duke Mindaugas resided may still be seen there.

No review of Lithuania would be complete without mention of Prussian Lithuania, which is generally now referred to as Lithuania Minor. Since 1422 it has been under Prussian domination. It was about that time, in fact, that Vytautas the Great ceded this part of the country to his enemies, the Knights of the Teutonic Order, in order to promote his far-reaching political ambitions elsewhere. Nevertheless, the greater part of this territory has preserved its Lithuanian character despite its secular dependence upon Prussia and the most persistent efforts to Germanize it. One can find in Prussian Lithuania Lithuanian customs, types, and, above all, the Lithuanian language. In 1654 the Old Prussians or Borussians renounced their Balto-Lithuanian idiom in favour of German. The Prussian Lithuanian does not differ essentially from his compatriot of Lithuania Major save in his religion, which is Protestant. The districts of Tilžé (Tilsit), Klaipéda (Memel), Ragainé (Ragnit), Pilkalné (Pilkallen), the eastern parts of the districts of Labguva (Labiau), Isruté (Insterberg), Gumbiné (Gumbinnen), Stalupénai (Stallupönen), and Goldape (Goldapp) are still in great measure Lithuanian.

The city of Klaipéda or Memel, situated at the entrance to the Gulf of Kurland, is a very important port for the future of Lithuania; but although, under the Versailles Peace Treaty, detached from Germany, together with the rest of the Memel territory, and recognized as Lithuania's sole sea outlet by the Powers in their reply to the German delegation on June 16, 1919, as already mentioned, the city continues to be administered by the French, very much to their own special advantage. In the Middle Ages, Memel was an object of fierce contention between the Lithuanians and the Teutonic Knights. To-day, in its national complexion, the place is largely Lithuanian. Tilžé (Tilsit), on the Nemunas, is the natural centre of Prussian Lithuania. Here was organized the contraband trade in Lithuanian books when the latter were prohibited in Russian Lithuania. Tilsit is also known as the scene of the Peace

Treaty of that name which Napoleon signed there in 1807. Gumbinė (Gumbinnen) on the Pisa and Isrutė (Insterberg) on the Pregel are two interesting localities.

The country is rich in meadow land, forests, and fertile soil. Agriculture and cattle-breeding form here, as they do in Lithuania Major, the principal occupation of the people. In certain regions, along the coast more especially, are less fertile lands and peat moors. The town of Trakėnai is famous for horse-breeding. Several small localities in the east, Palmininkai for example, are also known for their amber trade.

The climate of Lithuania varies according to the situation of the provinces. On the littoral it is influenced by the sea and becomes more and more continental as one advances into the interior. The mean temperature is 6.6 degrees centigrade. In July the mean is 18 degrees. In winter for four months the thermometer falls below zero. The rainfall is 580 millimetres annually, July and August being the wettest months. Westerly winds predominate, but in summer they blow from the north-west and in winter rather more from the south-west.

In the Vilnius province the climate is fairly continental. The summer temperature is generally higher than in Lithuania Minor (in July, for example, 18·6, whereas at Königsberg it is only 17·5 degrees). In winter, on the other hand, it is lower, the thermometer during five months (from November to March) falling below zero. The rainfall reaches 605 millimetres annually. Cloudy weather is frequent. At Vilnius, for example, there are on an average during the year only 68 bright days, 133 cloudy and 167 days of rain.

The climate of Kaunas province is strongly influenced by the sea. In July the average temperature is 18 degrees, while in winter it oscillates in the various districts between 3 degrees and 6 degrees. The atmospheric precipitation varies from 550 to 600 millimetres.

The province of Suvalkai has a mean annual temperature of 6·2 degrees. In July the average is 17·7 degrees; from December to March it is below zero. Suvalkai is not so rainy as the other provinces, the fall being from 500 to 550 millimetres.   The weather is very variable, especially in spring.   There are some 70 wet days in the year.

The province of Gardinas has the most continental climate.   The average temperature is in January 6 degrees, in July 20·9 degrees.   The annual rainfall does not exceed 335 millimetres, showing that Gardinas is the driest of the Lithuanian provinces.

In its generality Lithuania is a plain lightly inclined towards the sea and traversed by two chains of so-called mountains, the Lithuanian Hills and the Telšiai Heights. The Nemunas divides the Lithuanian Hills into two groups—to the left the chain of the south-west, to the right the chain of the south-east.   The latter crosses the Vilnius province and the north of Gardinas province.   The western chain, which is smaller, starts from the left bank of the Nemunas, extends to the province of Suvalkai and as far as Prussia.   Strictly speaking, these hills are merely light undulations with an average altitude not exceeding 200 metres.   The highest point is Mount Čiupiškiai (55 kilometres south-east of Vilnius), which rises 313 metres. In the valleys numerous lakes brighten the scenery.

The Telšiai Heights largely resemble the Lithuanian Hills.   They skirt the sea and traverse the districts of Telšiai and Raseiniai in the province of Kaunas.   Their lesser spurs extend as far as Prussian Lithuania.   The average altitude of the chain is 150 metres, the most notable peak being Mount Šatrija.   In Lithuania Minor is Rambynas, the legendary mountain of the Lithuanians. The region of Ober-Eysseln, owing to its charming scenery, is sometimes called the Lithuanian Switzerland.

Lithuania owes much of her scenic distinction to her rivers and lakes in which the country abounds.   This variety is caused by winds from the west which carry rain-charged clouds from the sea and also by the clayey soil which prevents the subsidence of the water.

The Nemunas is the great Lithuanian river.   Its course has the form of the latter Z.   The lower horizontal stroke corresponds to the line east-west which it describes from its source to the town of Gardinas ; there the river turns abruptly towards the north, but when several kilometres from Kaunas it resumes its east-west direction, which it keeps till it enters the Baltic a little below Tilžė (Tilsit). The Nemunas has cut for itself a deep bed and in places its banks are very steep, of cliff-like formation, while in others they are flat. In its upper reaches the Nemunas has been compared to the Rhine, but is less attractive in its lower reaches in Lithuania Minor, where it flows idly through a plain. Then for the last time it returns to the hills, piercing the Prussian spurs of the Telšiai Heights and winds round Rambynas, the mythological mountain of the Lithuanians.

The Lithuanian basin is formed principally by the Nemunas and its numerous affluents. On the right bank the Nemunas receives the Jura, Dubysa, Nevežes, Neris or Vilija, which comes from Vilnius, the Merkis, etc. Its affluents on the left bank are the Šešupė, Black Ančia, Zelve, Mulčia, etc. These affluents are not uniform and monotonous rivers : each has its distinctive aspect and passes through delightful country. The gilded waters of the Neris inspired the Lithuanian poet Mickiewicz. The Dane, which joins the Nemunas near Memel, is renowned for its beautiful shores. The Dubysa, which is certainly one of the prettiest rivers in Lithuania, acquired a melancholy notoriety during the war, many desperate engagements having been fought on its banks. The Venta, which traverses Kurland and directly enters the sea, often causes floods.

The lakes greatly contribute to the beauty of Lithuanian scenery. They exceed 2,100 in number. Corresponding to the two mountainous regions they may be divided into two groups. The greater number are in the Lithuanian Hills, i.e. about 1,500. The eastern chain, on the right bank of the Nemunas, is abundantly provided with them, notably Lakes Drukšė and Narutis (Narocz). On the left bank, in the region of the south-western chain, are Lakes Augustavas, Vigriai, Duse and Trakai. One of the eleven isles of the last-named contains the poetic ruins of a castle belonging to the epoch of Keistutis. The second group of lakes borders the littoral of the Baltic Sea and numbers about 600. The more important are Liepoja, Lukštas, Biršulas and Plateliai.

Geologically Lithuanian soil is in large measure the work of the glacial period. Glaciers from Scandinavia covered Lithuanian territory, and in their retreat left numerous morains and blocks of stone which they had brought in their course. Even to-day this plain traversed by hills affords sufficient proof of the diluvial formation of the country. The marshes, peat-bogs and valleys have an alluvial origin. The deeper strata, chalk for example, are products of the tertiary period.

The province of Vilnius is formed by tertiary strata which were mostly covered by diluvial formations. The quality of the soil is extremely variable. It is not rare to find sand close to the best black earth. Nevertheless sandy clay is most frequent in this province. Where clay, which is an impermeable stratum, predominates the waters remain stagnant and form swamps. Such is the case, for example, in the districts of Vilnius and Ašmena. In the district of Trakai, on the contrary, we find a very fertile black earth.

The province of Kaunas is of almost exclusively diluvial origin, although in places Devonian formation may be found (Šiauliai), also Jurassic and tertiary. The soil is in general clayey; but black earth exists in some districts of the north (Panevčžys, Šiauliai, etc.), moving sand in the Zarasai district. In certain places the marshes favoured by the clay soil have formed peat bogs.

The soil of the province of Suvalkai is in general a product of the glacial period. The valleys and marshes are of alluvial formation. By the side of these strata one meets here and there with chalk. The soil of the northern plains is of superior quality to that of the mountains of the south ; it is formed of clay mixed with chalk. The south has numerous swamps and, in places, a sandy soil. In general the soil here is much less productive than in the north.

The province of Gardinas is rich in clayey lands of a general diluvial formation. One finds some black earth in the south, but this is rather rare. It should be mentioned that there are moving sands in the districts of Pružėnai and Vilkaviškis and numerous peat bogs in those of Kobrin and Slanimas.

CHAPTER III

THE RISE OF LITHUANIA

For many years it was generally believed in Western Europe that the Lithuanians were Slavs. A similarly erroneous belief was entertained as regards the Estonians and Letts. The union of Lithuania with Slavonic Poland, then her dependence upon Slavonic Russia, have helped to create and foster this error.

Actually the Lithuanians together with the Letts and Old Prussians form a family of Aestians or Balts, who for centuries have preserved their own language and customs. They are part of the great family of Aryan peoples to which the Germans and Slavs also belong.

The Lithuanian language, however, conclusively proves the non-Slavonic origin of the Lithuanian people as a whole, for although it has borrowed individual words from the Slav vocabulary, as also from the German, in all other respects it is an entirely distinct and separate etymological unit. Slav and German borrowings no more make it German or Slav than our own Greek and Latin borrowings would make English Greek or Latin. Lithuanian is, in fact, one of the oldest, if not the oldest, language extant in Europe, and as such fully deserving greater attention from philologists. It is indeed very closely related to Sanscrit and possesses, according to the celebrated Russian philologist Fortunatov, more than 75,000 words. Intrinsically it is unquestionably a highly developed tongue which lends itself admirably to all nuances of literary and colloquial expression. No less an authority than Elisée Reclus, in his *Universal Geography*, says of it :

Of all languages of Europe, Lithuanian, which lacks augumentatives, is the one which possesses most affectionate and caressing diminutives. It has more of these than either Spanish or Italian ; it has more of them than even Russian, and can multiply them almost to infinity, applying them to verbs as well as to adjectives and nouns. If the value of a nation in the ensemble of humanity were to be measured by the beauty of its language, then the Samogitians and Litvines would occupy the first rank among the inhabitants of Europe.

A British authority, Benjamin D. Dwight, in his *Modern Philology* also writes :

This (the Lithuanian tongue) is a language of great value to the philologist. It is the most antique in its forms of all living languages of the world, and most akin in its substance and spirit to the primeval Sanscrit. It is also at the same time so much like the Latin and Greek as to occupy the ear of the etymologist, and in the multitude of words not otherwise understood, in the place of the interpreter, with its face fixed on Latin and its hand pointing backwards to the Sanscrit. It is like a universal interpreter, seeming to have the gift of tongues, since its tongue is so greatly like the rest in preserving the purse of prime model, from which they are all corrupt derivatives, as to seem, in whatever language you hear, the chime of that language, ringing loud and clear from ancient time.

The famous German philospher, Emanuel Kant, in his preface to *Mielke's Dictionary* says : " She (Lithuania) must be preserved, for her tongue possesses the key which solves the enigma not only of philology but also of history."

In the opinion of expert investigators this tongue affords proof of a primitive connexion between the Lithuanians and the Greeks. The cradle of the Indo-European races is generally located on the shores of the Caspian Sea ; and it is therefore not impossible that, after the dispersion of the ancient Aryan family, these two peoples for some time pursued a common route towards the west. Subsequently their paths diverged. The Eolians, Dorians, Ionians and Thracians, tribes of pure Hellenic race, drifted towards the south, whereas Aestians or Balts travelled north and established themselves on the shores of the Baltic.

It is generally admitted that at the dawn of the Christian era, or perhaps a little earlier, the primitive idiom of the Aestians disappeared in giving birth to two new languages

—Old Prussian (Borussian) and Letto-Lithuanian. The definite separation of Lettish and Lithuanian was effected only towards the end of the XIth century. In course of time the family of Aestian peoples was considerably reduced. It lost the Old Prussians who fell under the sway of the Teutonic Knights and were Germanized. Already in the XVIIth century the Prussians had abandoned their ancient idiom and adopted German.

In matters of civilization the Lithuanians came under the influence of the Finns, their eastern neighbours, but after the latter had migrated to the lands which they occupy to-day their influence ceased to make itself felt, and the Lithuanians have conserved their national character. Certain etymological analogies suggest a Gothic admixture or contact, as for example the names of some farming appurtenances, viz., " karvide," a cattle-shed, " avide," a sheepfold, etc., but this influence was not sufficiently strong to eliminate the ancestral customs of the Lithuanians.

To-day the ancient Balts are represented only by the Lithuanians and the Letts or Latvians. The two peoples, however, have developed along different lines. The Letts passed under the dominion of the Teutonic Order and became Protestants, whereas the Lithuanians formed an independent State and are Roman Catholics. Their languages also have drifted farther and farther apart, and to-day are two distinct idioms which, nevertheless, reveal a common origin.

Elsewhere in these pages the fascinating subject of the Lithuanian language is dealt with in more technical detail (*vide* Chapter XV, on Language and Literature).

Although nothing in the nature of an exhaustive historic survey of Lithuania's past is given here, since such an undertaking would require a volume or volumes to itself, even a superficial understanding of Lithuania's present would be impossible without noting the more important landmarks of her past.

The Lithuanian people, from almost time immemorial, have inhabited the shores of the Baltic between the Dvina and the Vistula. Their dwelling place was isolated from the main route of the nations from Asia into Europe by the plains of Southern Russia, intercepted by impassable swamps and forests. Thus the Lithuanian people in the past lived their own life in tranquil fashion, innocent of aggression against their neighbours. Until the XIth century very little reliable information about the origin of the Lithuanians can be found in the writings of other peoples.

Nevertheless the first actual reference to the Lithuanians appears in Tacitus, who lived in the Ist century A.D. Even at that remote epoch their territory was famous for its wealth of amber, which was sought by merchants from distant Rome. Tacitus speaks about the inhabitants of the land of amber and calls them Esti or Aestians, mentioning, too, that they spoke a language distinct from German. They used very little iron. They cultivated grain more carefully than the Germans. Later writers also refer to the Lithuanians as Aestians. In the VIth century Jordanes stated that the Aestians occupied an extensive area of the seacoast beyond the Vistula ; that they were people of peaceful habit, wherein they differed from the Germans, who more frequently migrated from place to place and came into collision with other races in consequence. In the XIth century Adam Bremeniskis speaks of the Aestians as a separate race, Pruri or Sambi, and styles them a humane people. He praises their customs and censures them only for one thing, i.e. that they were not Christians. Bishop Albertas was slain by them. Writers of various centuries give the dwellers of the Baltic coast the same name and write similarly about their manners and customs.

The Lithuanian language itself bears all the signs of extreme antiquity and hardly any indications of foreign admixture, thus showing that the Lithuanian race in its earlier stages had but little communion with other peoples but lived its own life in peace and contentment.

The name Lithuania (Lietuva) appeared for the first time in the chronicles of the XIth century on the occasion of the armed expeditions against Russian tribes. The Russian chronicler Nestor, a monk of Kiev, writes that the Russians, or rather the Ruthenes, victoriously fought the Lithuanians in the XIth century, but that subsequent epochs showed the great military superiority of the Lithuanians over the Russians. The Grand Duke Rimgaudas welded a congeries of warring tribes into a single more or less homogeneous principality, and battled successfully against the Russians to the east and the brethren of the Order of Sword-Bearers to the north in many decisive engagements. Ardvila succeeded Rimgaudas. This Prince or Grand Duke fought against the Tartars in 1242 to such good purpose that after a desperate struggle he achieved the liberation of both the Ruthenes and Ukrainians from the alien yoke. It is said that Ardvila founded the town of Naupilis, now known as Novogrodek, where the ancient ruins still exist. A little later began the Lithuanian wars against the Teutonic Knights.

Mindaugas, Ardvila's successor, reigned more than twenty years over Lithuania. In 1252 this Grand Duke was converted to Christianity with all the grandees of his realm. This fact is often passed over in silence, although it has an important bearing upon the conversion of the entire Lithuanian people some hundred years later. At the same period Mindaugas received from a Papal envoy a royal crown in his castle at Naupilis and in the presence of the Superior of the Order of the Teutonic Knights, proving that from that moment the Lithuanian rulers were invested with the kingly status. Mindaugas established a bishopric in the region of the present Vilnius and one of his sons even became a monk. The country, however, did not enjoy peace. The Lithuanians were soon obliged to oppose anew the encroachments of the Teutonic Knights, whom they severely defeated in 1261. At the same time the Prussians rose against the Order. Mindaugas fell a victim to assassination, and his death was followed by terrible internecine strife which lasted twenty years. At length Vitenis succeeded in winning power and in inflicting a decisive defeat upon the Teutonic Order near the river Treide.

The successor of Vitenis was Gediminas, perhaps the most powerful of the Lithuanian sovereigns. He it was who established his residence at Vilnius. This enlightened ruler pursued a different policy from his predecessors and threw open the country to the influx of Occidental civilization, inviting Western artists and artisans, the Franciscan and Dominican friars to co-operate in the task of educating the people. He favoured the extension of both the Roman Catholic Church and the Orthodox Greek faith. Yet he himself did not accept baptism, and under his tolerant and eclectic sway Pagan temples and Christian churches flourished side by side. In response to proposals that he should adopt Christianity Gediminas is reported to have made use of these words: " The Christians worship God in their own fashion, the Russians according to their usage, the Poles also, and we worship God in our own fashion. We have all one God, so why speak to me of the Christians ? Where can you find more crimes, more injustice, more acts of violence, corruption and usury than among Christians, and chiefly among those who are ecclesiastics as bearers of the Cross ? " There are bigots in the present year of grace who might profitably emulate this enlightened Lithuanian monarch of the XIVth century. Apparently the Lithuanians, always known for their religious tolerance, regarded religion as much more the private concern of individuals than did other neighbouring peoples.

The Teutonic Order continued its forays against Lithuania. Gediminas in 1323 complained to the Pope, but without result. He then had recourse to the sword and successfully repulsed the enemy. He further extended his dominion as far as the Dnieper to the east, and south almost as far as the Black Sea. He built a network of strong castles to safeguard his conquests, but failed to create a truly Lithuanian national culture. After his death civil troubles broke out afresh till his two sons, Algirdas and Keistutis, agreed to govern the country jointly. Algirdas, the elder, took over the eastern section, residing sometimes at Vilnius and sometimes at the castle of Mednikai. His court came to a certain extent under Russian influence, the wives of his second and third marriage having been Russian princesses. Nevertheless in a political sense Algirdas was far from being dependent upon Russia. On the contrary, he fought against the Russians on several occasions, and thrice entered Moscow as a conqueror.

Keistutis ruled Western Lithuania. His wife Biruté, the daughter of a Lithuanian noble, figures prominently in Lithuanian song and story. Tradition has it that before her marriage she was a vestal virgin who guarded the sacred fire on a hill near Palanga. When Keistutis met her he was so overcome by her beauty that he made her his consort. To this day this hill bears her name and is the bourn of many a popular pilgrimage. But in lieu of the ancient sacred fire there now stands a chapel containing an image of the Virgin, while on the northern slope of the hill is a grotto with a statue of Mary, made to the order of the present proprietor Count Tyszkiewicz, to resemble Notre Dame of Lourdes.

Keistutis resided at Kaunas and also at a castle on Lake Trakai which was erected by Gediminas. In marked contrast to his brother's court, here the Lithuanian language was alone spoken. His wife bore him six sons. Keistutis won the respect and affection of his people to a far greater extent than his brother, and to-day holds a place in the pantheon of national heroes. He was obliged to defend the country to the north and west against the Teutonic Order, though not always fortunate in these encounters, his opponent being the redoubtable Winrich of Kniprode. Once he was taken prisoner but escaped and sent his captor the following characteristic message: "Thanks for your kind reception. But if I should have the honour of welcoming you under similar conditions, I should know how to guard you better." His greatest misfortune was the loss of Kaunas. The defence was conducted by his son Vaidotas who, when he realized the hopelessness of his task, collected thirty-six of his bravest knights and tried to cut his way through the Teuton invaders, but was taken prisoner. The other defenders of the castle set fire to the latter and perished in the flames on Easter morning of 1352. Yet despite this loss, it was during the rule of the two brothers

Algirdas and Keistutis that Lithuania attained her greatest development, extending for the first time from the Baltic to the Black Sea.

After the death of Algirdas, in 1877, his son Jagellon tried to make himself master of the country with the help of the Teutonic Order. In 1882 he took Keistutis captive, as also his eldest son Vytautas, both of whom were incarcerated in Krevo castle. Several days later Keistutis was found strangled in his cell, but to allay the popular anger Jagellon conveyed the body to Vilnius where it was burnt, according to the national custom, seated upon an armoured horse.

Vytautas later escaped from captivity and proceeded, also with the support of the Teutonic Order, to challenge Jagellon's hegemony. When, however, Jagellon became King of Poland through his marriage to Hedwig, the Queen of that country, he effected a reconciliation with Vytautas, to whom he ceded a portion of the principality in the south. On ascending the Polish throne he left Lithuania to his brother Skirgaila, but the latter proved so incompetent that Vytautas had little difficulty in overthrowing him and assuming undivided control in 1392.

It was at this epoch that Polish influence began to make itself powerfully felt. The pious Queen Hedwig persuaded Jagellon to order the destruction of all the old Pagan sanctuaries and the extinction of all the sacred fires, while Jagellon himself embraced Christianity. Yet when Vytautas ascended the Lithuanian throne Polish influence sustained a check. Vytautas was the pupil of Hanno of Windenheim and was highly educated for those days, speaking both German and Latin. He had travelled widely in the west and south of Europe and had learned to know Occidental civilization. He sought to raise the standard of Lithuanian culture, but was greatly hindered by political complications. Lithuania was alternately exposed to Russian, German, and Polish influences, until finally the latter took the ascendant. None the less the rule of Vytautas synchronized with a notable extension of the power and prosperity of Lithuania. It was he who formed the project of expelling the Tartars from Europe, and although he did not entirely succeed in his self-appointed task his victories and his great prestige for many years checked the Tartar incursions into Lithuania and Poland. Tamerlane was then sovereign of the immense Tartar Empire. He dwelt in Asia and confided the government of his hordes in Europe to vassal khans. One of these, Toktamich, rose against his suzerain, and having been vanquished by another khan sought refuge in Lithuania and demanded aid from Vytautas. The Grand Duke first sent armed assistance and subsequently took command in person and inflicted a severe defeat upon the Tartars in the vast unexplored plains which extended beyond the Don.

The influence which Lithuania exercised over the Golden Horde and the Crimean Tartars dates from this moment. It is true that in 1399 Vytautas was defeated by Eudigne on the banks of the Vorskla, and had to beat a precipitate retreat, but this reverse did not discourage him and he continued the struggle with conspicuous ability. He intervened in the internecine feuds of the Tartars, played the rôle of arbiter, and was present at the election of two khans. These savage people entertained such respect for his justice that the entire Golden Horde beyond the Volga obeyed him. Twenty years after the battle of the Vorskla, the same Eudigne, who had previously defeated Vytautas, sent to Vilnius an embassy bearing rich gifts to solicit the friendship of the most powerful of European princes.

Vytautas possessed in his immense territories two ports—one, Palanga, on the Baltic, and the other, Odessa, on the Black Sea. It is narrated that on the day he vanquished the Tartar hordes established on the shores of the latter, he rode his horse into the water and proclaimed himself monarch of the ocean. The southern provinces of Volhynia, Ukraine and Podolia enjoyed a useful breathing spell under his régime. Fortresses established on the banks of the Dnieper and the Bobr were guarded by Lithuanian garrisons. Commercial caravans from the Orient could penetrate with their merchandise, and in perfect safety, into the heart of Lithuania. Vytautas built roads and bridges for the development of trade, and travelled the land in person to see that justice was dispensed and order maintained. No powerful subordinate ventured to oppress the people, because the Grand Duke was ever ready to listen to complaints and to punish the wrong-doers. His was of course the paternal form of government best suited to the times. Yet when circumstances seemed to dictate such a course he did not hesitate to take up arms. When, for example, the inhabitants of Novgorod, who had recognized Lithuanian sovereignty since Gediminas, refused obedience to Vytautas towards the end of his reign, the Grand Duke, although then eighty years of age, placed himself at the head of his army and reached the province of Novgorod with a cannon of giant size for that epoch, drawn by forty horses, the sight of which so terrified the recalcitrant Novgorodians that they promptly tendered their submission.

During the closing years of his prosperous reign, Vytautas wished to convert Lithuania into a kingdom and receive a royal crown. This idea was inspired by Sigismond, Emperor of Germany and of the Holy Roman Empire, who in his turn was actuated by the ulterior motive of wishing to shatter the alliance between Lithuania and Poland. There could have been none more worthy of the crown than Vytautas, but inasmuch as the Polish alliance united the two peoples under the same king, Ladislas Jagellon, the proposed coronation encountered insuperable opposition from the Poles and therefore came to nought.

Vytautas invited to his splendid castle at Luck the Emperor Sigismond, King Ladislas, and other monarchs, At this meeting they discussed not only the question of the coronation but also other important matters, such as means of expelling the Turks from Europe. Among other dignitaries present were the King of Denmark, Vassili, the Grand Duke of Moscow, the Pontifical delegate, the Grand Master of the Teutonic Order, envoys of the Greek Emperor, the Tartar Khan, several tributary princes, etc. Never before had Lithuania seen so brilliant an assembly. For the entertainment and feeding of his guests Vytautas ordered the daily delivery of 300 cows 600 sheep, 100 lambs, and 300 casks of beer. The festivities lasted fifty days, but no question of importance was settled. The coronation of Vytautas did not take place owing to the energetic opposition of the Poles, who feared that its effect might be the secession of Lithuania. Vytautas returned despondent to Vilnius, where he fell ill the following year. He was taken thence to Trakai, and when he felt his end approaching himself renounced his idea of being crowned. Ladislas did not abandon his cousin's bedside, and it was in the arms of Ladislas that Vytautas breathed his last at the advanced age of eighty-six. He was buried in Vilnius cathedral in 1430. The style of "Great" has been attached to the name of this distinguished ruler.

One of his most notable achievements, in conjunction with the Poles, was the crushing defeat he inflicted upon the Teutonic Order at Grunewald in 1410.

Notwithstanding this notable record, one measure of his, in the opinion of no less a critic than Vidūnas, contributed largely to the ultimate weakening of the Lithuanian nation. He sent the Lithuanian nobility to distant territories not inhabited by Lithuanians, where these emigrés, isolated from their countrymen, were soon absorbed by the foreign race and thus to a large extent lost to their own people. Polish influence gained correspondingly, and the Lithuanian nobility gradually adopted the Polish speech, Polish manners and customs.

With Vytautas ended the series of great Lithuanian rulers inaugurated by Gediminas. Among his successors some were men of talent who tried to govern the country in the spirit of their ancestors, while others endeavoured to retain their power by clever compromises. But none of them handled the marshal's baton more effectively than Keistutis ; none bore the sceptre with greater dignity than Vytautas.

Skipping, therefore, a succession of Grand Dukes whose administration witnessed the steadily declining power of the Lithuanian State, we reach the fateful year 1569, in which Polish-Lithuanian relations were regulated by the famous and disastrous Lublin Union. Nevertheless, under this treaty Lithuania retained her own treasury, law courts, and army distinct from those of Poland. At the end of the XVIIIth century Lithuania Major shared the fate of Poland, when the latter was partitioned, and thus fell under the Russian sway. Lithuania Minor had been annexed to Prussia before this epoch.

CHAPTER IV

PERIOD OF DECADENCE

IT is not strange that the great religious revolution of the XVIth century should have roused echoes in Lithuania. Documentary data dealing with the Reformation in Lithuania are still rare, but they prove that the country was powerfully moved by these new doctrines.

Contributory causes in Lithuania, as elsewhere, to this revulsion of feeling may be found in the corruption of the clergy. The bishops, more especially, abandoning the traditions of the Church, set the worst example to the nobility and people, which these were quick to imitate. At that time there were four dioceses in Lithuania, i.e. Vilnius, Samogitia, Kiev and Luck. The bishops were influential members of the Senate, participated actively in the political life of the country, and possessed considerable juridical competence. Every bishop received a minimum of five thousand florins gold annually, which in those days was a huge stipend. The Bishop of Vilnius enjoyed an annual revenue of forty thousand florins. The rents of the Bishop of Samogitia were not less than this sum. Possessing as they did episcopal, temporal, and senatorial power, these magnates of the Church speedily deserted the apostolic path and became infamous for their luxury, their ambition, their pride, and their excesses of every description.

These vices were shared in corresponding degree by the inferior clergy. Large numbers of priests were totally devoid of intellectual qualifications, many receiving Holy Orders without having passed through any school. Poland sent the most lamentable specimens as pastors to Lithuania. These worthies made not the slightest

4

effort to learn Lithuanian.   Disorganization and anarchy
in ecclesiastical affairs reached such a pitch that according
to contemporary evidence even Jews were appointed to
hold office as parish priests !

Contaminated by this example the Lithuanian nobility
presented a melancholy spectacle of deterioration.   Luxury,
effeminacy, and love of pleasure had become so deeply
ingrained in the aristocracy that venereal disease in the
Lithuanian tongue was styled "the court sickness."
Those who had not yielded to immorality in their own
country succumbed to the temptations offered by the no
less decadent courts of Western Europe, where the Lithuanian nobility made frequent sojourns.   The members
of the smaller nobility copied the manners of the magnates
and, perhaps, were even less discriminating in their choice
of relaxation.   One of their playful fancies was to undertake raids on the country and to massacre all who ventured
to resist them.

In such circumstances the peasantry suffered unspeak-
ably.   Treated as slaves they were steeped in ignorance.
The Church entirely neglected them.   The Lithuanians
had embraced Christianity in 1386, on which occasion
the various princes had assembled their subjects to be
sprinkled with holy water by Christian missionaries.   That
was the extent of their baptism, beyond which ghostly
teaching did not go, so that whilst the peasants had adopted
a few external signs of Christianity, inwardly for the
most part they remained Pagans.

Thus it was that the power of the Catholic Church in
Lithuania was largely illusory, and bound to collapse
at the first resolute attack.

Missionaries of the new doctrine began to preach in
Lithuania about 1530.   The two principal reformers were
Tortyllowicz, a parish priest of Samogitia, and Abraham
Culva, a member of the Lithuanian noblesse.   They were
sent by Duke Albert of Prussia who, in his zeal for
Reform, supplied the movement with money, books, and
preachers.   The new doctrine witnessed its full efflores-
cence during the reign of the Grand Duke Sigismond
Augustus.

Nicolai Radvila (Radziwill), known as the Black, was the central figure of the Reform movement in Lithuania. He belonged to a very wealthy and distinguished family of the Vilnius palatinate. Although enjoying the favour of the court, Radvila, in the midst of the prevailing degradation of manners, had preserved his moral integrity. Since Sigismond Augustus was without issue, Radvila was everywhere regarded as his successor to the throne. A Lithuanian of ancient stock, he was deeply indignant at seeing the Poles behave in Lithuania as though the country belonged to them and strongly opposed the union with Poland. Believing that the religious decadence of Lithuania was in great measure the work of unworthy Polish priests, he determined in this respect to detach his country from Poland by introducing the new faith. Thus he began to spread the Calvinistic doctrine about 1550. He brought foreign preachers into the country and sent Lithuanians to Switzerland in order to study the new religion at its very centre. So successful were his efforts that in 1555 almost all the nobles with their peasant subjects had become Calvinists. Indeed, the Calvinistic doctrines won a victory with almost unprecedented ease. Lulled into carelessness by their success, the Reformers took no steps to secure for their Church a legal foundation.

As long as Radvila the Black was alive and protected the Calvinistic Church nobody ventured to attack the new doctrine, but no sooner was he dead (in 1565) than the proud edifice of Calvinism fell even more rapidly than the previous Catholic Church.

The weakening of the Calvinistic Church was largely due to the multiplication of sects. Almost every great family had its own preacher and private chapel. As many as seventy-two different sects and churches are mentioned in statistics of the time. This Babylonic confusion between the various doctrines, in which the theories of present-day Bolshevism are said to have been formulated, ruined Radvila's work beyond salvation. The country people, who had never understood the Catholic faith, had no more comprehension of the Reformed belief, which they speedily abandoned to revert to the Pagan cult of their ancestors.

The conversion of Nicolas-Christopher Radvila to Catholicism was a severe blow for the New Believers. The Papal Nuncio Commendone and Cardinal Hosius greatly helped the Counter-Reformation in Lithuania, the former through his remarkable eloquence and diplomatic ability and the latter through his theological writings.

The new Church, already seriously undermined, miserably collapsed in 1569 when the Jesuits arrived in Lithuania to reconquer the country for the old faith. In this manner the vital work of Nicolas Radvila the Black, the great Lithuanian patriot, was destroyed in a few years, and one of the last efforts of Lithuania to escape from Polish influence was frustrated.

Ever-increasing checks and failures at this epoch bear witness to the baneful effects of the Lublin Union. Far-reaching projects of foreign policy were abandoned. The provinces of Poldachia, Podolia and Volhynia had been annexed by Poland and removed from the protection of Lithuania, who forfeited her rank among great Powers. The strength which had formerly been expended in expeditions and conquests was not employed to increase the internal prosperity of the country. Lithuania, accustomed to see her affairs directed by the Poles, became steadily more and more feeble in national will. And still another enemy had arisen. The Swedes invaded the country, which was now without a military organization, and the situation seemed desperate indeed.

The Polish union, which lasted two centuries, exercised a debilitating influence on the Lithuanian people. To speak Polish and to dress in the Polish fashion were considered the correct thing. Towards the end of the XVIIth century nearly all the Lithuanian nobility had ceased to speak Lithuanian. The clergy were rarely recruited in the country, but were imported from Poland and assisted the rapid Polonization of Lithuania. The upper classes of Lithuanian society, who went abroad for their education, became gradually strangers to the people who alone remained faithful to their native tongue and traditions.

In this manner the link between the head and members of the Lithuanian body was sundered. The nobility no longer took an interest in anything that was not foreign, whilst the people, doomed to live in wretchedness and poverty, were insensible to political affairs and the public weal.

A century after the alliance of Lublin had been concluded national sentiment awoke once more in Lithuania. On the occasion of a Swedish invasion of Poland the Lithuanian magnates Janus and Boguslav, scions of the virile Radvila race, proclaimed at Kedainiai, in 1655, the independence of their country and attached themselves to the Swedes. This bold stroke, however, won but few adherents and was the last evidence of Lithuanian life.

Thereafter the country fell a prey to the anarchy that had overtaken Poland. The right of brutal might everywhere prevailed. A vicious and dissolute nobility despoiled the people with impunity. The magnates, who jealously defended their privileges, maintained regular armies and fought among themselves. Under the government of the King of Saxony, Augustus (between 1733 and 1763), internal chaos reached its apogee.

The various national parties appealed for aid alternately to Prussia and Russia. Frederick II of Prussia, in conjunction with the two Empresses Marie Theresa of Austria and Catherine II of Russia, proceeded to partition the defenceless country. In 1793 there was a second and in 1795 a third and final partition of both Poland and Lithuania. The present provinces of Kaunas, Vilnius and Gardinas, i.e. the largest part of the country, were attributed to Russia ; the government of Suvalkai was attached to Prussia, who in 1815 ceded it to Russia.

Such was then the end of Lithuania, which failed to evoke a single effective protest. This ancient land, which in the past had subdued the power of the Teutonic Knights and repulsed the Tartar invasion, was sold into bondage like so much vile merchandise. At the debut of her history Lithuania had produced a Gediminas, a Keistutis, and a Vytautas ; at the time of the partitions nought remained save an enfeebled and a depraved nobility and a people who vegetated in misery and ignorance. The "Lietuvos Vytis" (Lithuanian Knight), symbol of a glorious past, was relegated together with the Polish Eagle to the dustheap. From that moment the Black Eagle of Russia spread its sombre wings over Lithuania, who was destined to retrieve her national dignity under the Muscovite claws.

CHAPTER V

UNDER THE RUSSIAN YOKE

ONLY sympathy and knowledge can help us to picture the sufferings of an entire people subjected to an alien yoke. For the Britisher the thing is but a dim historical tradition. But for thousands, nay millions, of members of the smaller peoples, not yet much beyond middle age, it is a dire personal reminiscence. And few among the resurrected nationalities of *post-bellum* Europe can entertain bitterer memories of such a past than Lithuania.

In 1795 the greater part of the country was attributed to Russia. It may be cited as one of history's little ironies that this subjugation of the Lithuanian people should have synchronized with the French Revolution and the fall of the Bastile, which put an end to the pleasing political maxim " *L'Etat, c'est moi.*" In 1793 Louis XVI. expiated the sins of his forefathers upon the scaffold.

But this national emancipation did not extend to St. Petersburg. True, the rights of Lithuania were confirmed on paper, but this was the last respite, and by 1793 the Russification of the country was begun with the governments of Vilnius and Gardinas. The Lithuanians were expelled from office and replaced by a horde of Russian functionaries. The government of Suvalkai alone enjoyed ostensible automony.

In 1831 the spirit of rebellion awoke in Lithuania, but it was suppressed with ruthless brutality. Suvalkai shared the fate of the other governments. The Russian Government decoyed the Lithuanian peasantry by the abolition of serfdom, so that they took but little part in the second insurrection of 1863. General Muraviev devastated the land. He asked only forty years to obliterate the Lithuanian national character. The Russian sword bit deeply into the Lithuanian flesh, and the Ukase of May 22, 1864, effaced the name of Lithuania from the map of the world, from which date all Lithuanians became subjects of the Russian North-West Provinces. Kalmucks and Tartars were let loose on the land to put down all manifestations of national sentiment. Only Russians took part in the administration of both governments and towns. In 1894 a secret edict bereft Lithuania of all remaining hope. To be eligible for employment on the railways, in the post offices, even to repair the roads, one had to be Russian.

Worse still, Russian tyranny extended to the intellectual and spiritual life of the people, for it was hoped the more easily to wean the Lithuanians, ever eager for education, from their national allegiance by compelling them to go to Russian sources for their mental pabulum.

After the first rebellion the university of Vilnius was closed down and its precious possessions were scattered among Kiev, St. Petersburg and Moscow. With the university fell also the higher schools. Eighteen institutions directed by the Jesuits, the Basilians and others were suppressed. There were left in Lithuania only three large seminaries, at Vilnius, Varniai, and Seinai, two normal schools, a few incomplete gymnasia at Vilnius, Kaunas and Suvalkai, while in these schools the Orthodox Russian reigned as master. Every high official received from the Government an allowance for the education of each of his children.

The suppression of the monasteries and the substitution of the Russian State religion for Roman Catholicism menaced the existence of the popular schools, which were directed by the monasteries and Catholic parishes. Private schools were strictly prohibited. On the other hand, a school was founded for every district with a population of from fifteen to twenty thousand inhabitants. Happy the district which possessed two or three of these schools. The well-to-do peasants and the landed proprietors sometimes engaged instructors who went from place to place to teach the children, but the school organization was notoriously inadequate. In bad weather many children could not travel the distance separating their homes from the schools, and the task of educating the children fell, as before, upon the family.

The Russian schools, moreover, could not entirely replace national instruction, since the families and the clergy secretly opposed their influence. For that matter the Russian teacher was not an educator, but simply the representative of a foreign bureaucracy, speaking a tongue scarcely comprehensible to the children and evoking no echo in their hearts. In order to prevent the diffusion of intellectual culture, in 1824 the peasant children were forbidden to attend the gymnasia. This prohibition was renewed in 1882 with a view to suppressing the Socialist danger. The only schools worthy of the name were the parochial schools in which the Lithuanian clergy taught the children their mother-tongue in a manner suited to the national sentiment. But these were closed in 1832, and thereafter the people had to make shift as best they could with books smuggled in from Lithuania Minor. The family, the hearth of Lithuanian life, had to replace the schools. In many cases the clergy took advantage of religious instruction to cultivate patriotic feeling among the children. As soon as the Russians got wind of this propaganda they subjected the clergy to a pitiless persecution, which reaped a lavish crop of martyrs.

But the most ruthless blow to Lithuanian intellectual life was dealt by the infamous Manifesto of 1863 which banished the native language from the schools altogether. The speech which every Lithuanian had learnt at his mother's knee was branded as a crime and the Lithuanian child was forced to learn an alien tongue. From that moment the popular schools were deserted. Only those seeking to curry favour and advancement attended them. The Lithuanian might not even pray in his native language. Suvalkai government, which had hitherto been allowed to teach the Bible in Lithuanian, now lost this privilege, and religious instruction had to be imparted in the privacy of the home. The well-known Lithuanian sculptor Petras Rimša, in a group entitled " Lietuvos Mokykla "

(the Lithuanian School), has left a touching symbol of
this sad period in Lithuanian history. It represents a
mother turning a spinning wheel and at the same time
teaching her child.

In 1865 Muraviev prohibited the use of the Latin
alphabet and circulated a Lithuanian grammar in Russian
characters.   Nothing more could be printed in Lithuanian
letters, since an exception made in favour of a restricted
scientific circle could not extend to the masses.   On the
other hand, the country was inundated with Russian
writings to replace the forbidden Lithuanian books.
Thus the world was confronted with an almost unprecedented spectacle, that of a nation of three million souls
dwelling on the soil of their ancestors, yet deprived of
the right to use their mother tongue.   The soft musical
sounds of the native idiom might not be pronounced save
behind carefully closed doors with the bolts drawn.
Lithuanian books crossed the frontier as contraband
during dark nights.   Russian police spies were posted at
the church portals to seize the prayer-books of the worshippers.   In return Lithuanian books printed in Russian
characters were gratuitously offered but scornfully rejected
by the people.

Muraviev ruled with an iron hand.   In less than two
years he sent 128 persons to the gallows ; 972 Lithuanians were condemned to penal servitude and 1,427
exiled to Siberia.   In all some 9,361 persons fell victims
to the fury of Russification.   To this number must also
be added the thousands who in some form or other
suffered from Russian persecution.   Muraviev, the hangman of Lithuania, was favoured by fortune, for although
his life was repeatedly threatened he managed to escape,
and on retiring from his congenial post, after two
years' tenure, received from the Tsar as a reward for
his services the title of count.   Later a monument in
his honour was erected at Vilnius, but all Lithuanians
carefully avoided its site, and to-day His Excellency
Michael Nikolaevitch Muraviev has disappeared from
the Lithuanian capital.   On the approach of the German
armies the retreating Russians appropriately passed a

cord round the neck of the notorious hangman and in this manner lifted him from his pedestal. Nor is it recorded that anybody wore crepe to commemorate his withdrawal.

Confusion in the administration of justice favoured the Russian domination. Before the introduction of any Russian legislation the country possessed a well-arranged body of law, which had been drafted in 1529 and bore the title of the Lithuanian Statute. This code contained laws and decrees promulgated by various Lithuanian sovereigns, and in course of time had been supplemented and revised. So practical of application was it that it even survived the partition and remained in force during part of the Russian régime. In 1848, however, the Tsar Nicholas I abolished it and introduced Russian law, which was not adapted to Lithuanian manners and customs. Nevertheless, notwithstanding this measure, the Lithuanian Statute persisted as common law and was accepted even beyond the Lithuanian frontiers, in White Russia and Little Russia—a striking proof of its suitability to the times. The Russian savant Speranski, a recognized authority in this domain, declared that it would be quite possible to modernize the Lithuanian Statute, but such a course, needless to say, did not commend itself to the Russian occupants, who preferred simply to rescind it.

The administration of justice became very complicated. In the Suvalkai government, which Napoleon had united to the Duchy of Warsaw, the Code Napoléon was in force. In the other governments, Vilnius, Kaunas, and Gardinas, Russian law prevailed, to which the landed proprietors and bourgeois alone were subject. Nobody bothered about the peasant. When serfdom was abolished in 1861 legislation should have been passed for the new free men, but nothing of the kind was done, and the Russian Government confided to each commune the duty of administering justice as it saw fit, so that each commune went to work in a different way. In the majority of cases recourse was had to common law. The judges were Russians, who understood hardly anything of the language of the country and were accessible to every kind of corruption. The Suvalkai government, which for a time had been attached to Poland, was deprived of jury trial. The inhabitants of the country were not equal in the eyes of the law, which constituted a grave defect, whilst the use of Russian, which many Lithuanian litigants did not understand, frequently operated to the detriment of the accused.

In this manner the Russians provoked hopeless confusion in the sphere of justice. It would have been infinitely simpler to adapt the Lithuanian Statute to the needs of the new régime and thereby avert the disorder which resulted from this triple melange—Russian law, the Code Napoléon and common law. But the Russian Government wished to have all Lithuanian law abolished. It was indifferent to the question of what sort of legislation took its place provided that it was not Lithuanian.

But this does not exhaust the list of measures adopted by the Russian tyrants for the exploitation of the country at the expense of the native inhabitants. In the wake of the loss of liberty and the mother tongue came the turn of agrarian wealth. Measures to this end were taken from 1795, when Russia seized the property of the Crown and the State domains. The insurrections of 1831 and 1863 provided the Russians with a convenient pretext for expelling many Lithuanians from their small patch of ground. If a single peasant revolted the entire village was punished, and the inhabitants in serried ranks set out on their long and weary march to Siberia.

After the suppression of the monasteries the wealth of the congregations reverted to the State. It amounted to millions. To the parish priests, professors, and teachers, who had received their salaries from the monasteries, ridiculous compensation was assigned. A parish priest might esteem himself fortunate if he could lay hold of 450 roubles annually, and a teacher getting 250 roubles was regarded as well paid. In order to gloss over this piece of barefaced robbery the Russian Government founded twelve scholarships of 300 roubles each for Lithuanians who should go to Moscow to study.

An Ukase of 1865 forbade the Lithuanian aristocracy to acquire landed property. In order to weaken the Catholic nobility they were allowed only to rent land,

and a lease might not be concluded for longer than twelve years.   The same measure was applied in 1894 to the Protestants and to Russians who had contracted marriage with Catholic women.

The peasant who wished to acquire land was obliged, in conformity with a decree of July 1868, to present a "certificate of patriotism," which the Government-General granted to those with whose political attitude the central authorities were satisfied.

In 1870 it was decided that no Lithuanian peasant might receive more than 60 hectares (about 150 acres) of land.   A decree of 1889 prohibited the cession of landed property to political and religious chiefs of Lithuania. In 1892 a new law interdicted the acquisition of land by all peasants who had opposed the closing of the churches and the destruction of the latter by dynamite.   All these decrees reacted disastrously on the country.   The peasant would no longer attach himself to his strip of ground, since he knew not at what moment his produce might be confiscated by the Russian chinovniks.   In these circumstances immense territories fell out of cultivation and the peasants migrated in thousands.   Lithuania became a land accursed, and accursed was he whose misfortune it was to dwell therein, since the Russian overlords regarded him as little better than a criminal and an outcast.

CHAPTER VI

THE LITHUANIAN RENASCENCE

FORTUNATELY for posterity the iron hand of Russia could bend but could not break the national spirit of the people. An interval of seeming despair gave way to the outbreak of a neo-Lithuanian movement largely directed by young Lithuanian students. Secret associations were formed. In 1875 a hectograph review entitled *Kalvis Melagis* (The Liar Blacksmith) made its appearance in St. Petersburg. At Moscow, through the same medium, was published *Auśra* (Dawn). Both these were written by students for students. All along the frontiers Lithuanian magazines cropped up. After Petersburg and Moscow came the turn of Tilsit, where in 1883 the indefatigable Dr. Basanavičius founded a monthly review styled also *Auśra*. Since 1887 have appeared successively, in 1889, *Varpas* (The Bell); in 1890, *Apźvalga* (The Review); in 1896, *Tevynės Sargas* (Guardian of, the Fatherland), in 1901, *Naujienos* (News), and *Ūkininkas* (Peasant). These periodicals represented various parties, but all pursued the same ultimate end—the creation of an autonomous Lithuania. Little by little these printed invocations penetrated into the soul of the people and set up vibrations by no means welcome to the Russians. Obsessed by the fear of losing the country the Russians began to organize their offensive. The Russian police agent insinuated himself everywhere, even into stables and cattlesheds, in the hope of there discovering the forbidden writings. Against smuggling Russia opposed a vigilant watch at the frontiers. Although thousands of these prints fell into the hands of the Customs guards, a highly-organized contraband system was able to diffuse a large number of the same among the people who read and re-read them surreptitiously. Thousands of journals, calendars, prayer-books and other pamphlets sent by secret press associations crossed the frontier, in spite of all the law could do to prevent it. Many of these publications were not printed but written by hand, and they circulated until they became illegible.

A keen sense of humour was not lacking among the authors of these broadsides. To mock the Russian Government, notoriously stupid as well as brutal, the larger part of them, actually printed at Tilsit, bore the name of Vilnius on their title-pages, together with the date 1863, the last year of freedom for the Lithuanian press.

These published incitements made the people bolder and bolder. Appeals were pasted on walls during the night, and in 1896 many were distributed in broad daylight. The struggle on both sides grew more and more embittered. From 1900 to 1902 the customs confiscated about 56,000 Lithuanian writings. Victory was scarcely in doubt from the start. On April 27, 1904, Russia capitulated : the interdict against Lithuanian printing was removed. Shortly afterwards the Russian Revolution extended to Lithuania, but the struggle was not violent, thanks to the concessions made by the Government on the question of the national language.

This impetus of Lithuanian culture led to an immediate development of national sentiment. Even before 1863 a literary renascence had begun. Prompted by belief in the greatness of his country Daukantas wrote a history of Lithuania in the Lithuanian language. The Bishop Valančius also wrote a history of the dioceses of Samogitia in the same tongue. His episcopal colleague Baronas composed Lithuanian poetry. All these men believed in the restoration of Lithuanian greatness. But in 1863 an icy blast passed over the land and withered these literary flowers. As the nobility inclined towards Poland the agricultural classes assumed the reins of government, and despite numerous obstacles the sons of the peasantry devoted themselves to study with fiery ardour. Even before 1875 they had formed secret associations and turned out some of the earliest national journals.

Cultivated Lithuanians no longer, as formerly, went to Russia in quest of positions, but remained in their own country and helped to sustain the national movement. A secret warfare against the brutish system applied by the Russians was conducted during many long years. At last in 1892 and 1896 revolt broke out openly. The people refused to recite Russian prayers in the churches, and on fête days absented themselves from the Orthodox Russian churches. Although Polish influence made itself very strongly felt in the country, Lithuanians step by step won a foothold in the normal schools and in the ecclesiastical seminaries. In 1870 the pupils of the seminary of Kaunas recalled their Lithuanian origin. Even at Vilnius, where Polish influence was very great, the Lithuanian students formed associations. Abroad they organized themselves even more rapidly. Lithuanian student societies were formed at Petersburg, Moscow, Riga, Odessa, and at Fribourg in Switzerland. In Russia these associations were secret.

They did not concern themselves solely with university questions. At the end of last century they launched appeals to the people. During vacations the students journeyed to distant villages in quest of fresh recruits. They established secret schools. The Lithuanian section of the Universal Exposition at Paris in 1900 clearly showed the activity of the Lithuanians. It contained nineteen journals and thousands of books, despite the printing prohibition.

The furious efforts of the Russian police to suppress these manifestations led to frequent collisions and many fatal casualties. The Russo-Japanese war afforded Lithuanian patriots an excellent opportunity for redoubled attacks upon the Muscovite knout policy. As we have seen, the first great victory was scored when Petersburg at last rescinded the insensate and dastardly prohibition of Lithuanian printing. This hardly-won concession opened the path to fresh objectives, and the newly-awakened native *intelligentsia* rallied to their large-scale offensive with increased ardour.

The stirring story of the Lithuanian Renascence must ever be associated with the name of Dr. Basanavičius, who devoted his whole life to the Lithuanian cause.

He was born in 1851 at Bartnikai, Suvalkai government, the son of well-to-do parents. He studied at the Mariampol gymnasium or high school, where he graduated with the silver medal award. Thence he proceeded to the Moscow university, where he studied philosophy and medicine. In 1879 he secured his medical diploma, and subsequently practised his profession off and on some twenty-five years in Bulgaria. After the Russian Revolution of 1905 he returned to Lithuania, where he still resides.

The value of his work for his country cannot be over-estimated. While the embargo on Lithuanian printing lasted he devoted himself to study of Lithuanian origins, collected the ancient Dainos or popular songs, historical reminiscences, etc., and immersed himself deeply in the national soul. In 1883 he went to Lithuania Minor, where at Ragainė and later at Tilžė (Tilsit) he published *Aušra* (Dawn) which did much to promote the Renascence movement. By devious and manifold contraband routes this paper found its way into Lithuania Major, where it met with a ready sale. The besotted Russian Government detected in this phenomenon a Bismarckian intrigue and tried to entrap the publisher. In 1885 Basanavičius was obliged to leave Germany, but he confided his work to his comrade Šliūpas. Basanavičius returned to Bulgaria, where he resumed his task of compilation, till he had prepared six large volumes on the Lithuanian people, which appeared in Lithuania Minor and America.

After the Russian Revolution of 1905 he renewed his activities in Lithuania Major. When the Diet of Vilnius assembled he was elected President in recognition of his tireless energy. He took advantage of the interval of calm succeeding 1905 to try to improve the moral and intellectual life of his countrymen. To this end he founded the Lithuanian Scientific Society, which published an organ called *Tauta* (Nation). He also opened a museum and library in Vilnius. In 1913 he visited the flourishing Lithuanian colony in the United States, which contributed large sums to help in the realization of his special objects, including the establishment of a theatre and a national museum.

Basanavičius has continued to live in Vilnius ever since, through all the upheaval of the Great War and subsequent unrest, never losing an opportunity of advancing the national cause. He attended the opening of the Lithuanian Constituent Assembly or Seim at Kaunas on May 15, 1920, when he was accorded a wonderful reception. It was my privilege also to be present on that occasion, and the scene made a deep and lasting impression upon my mind. Even Polish persecution of everything Lithuanian has hesitated to touch this noble veteran, and he lives among the books of his beloved Lithuanian library, occupying his leisure with his favourite studies.

Another notable name closely connected with Basanavičius is that of Vincas Kudirka, the Lithuanian national poet. For many years he remained under Polish influence till through *Auśra* he found the way back to his own people. After this paper had ceased to appear he secretly founded a students' society, which brought out a new paper, the *Varpas* (Bell). This organ was printed at Tilže, but edited by Kudirka from Lithuania Major, where the Russian police frantically sought to discover his identity. Besides the *Varpas* he also issued the *Ūkininkas* (Peasant), addressed more especially to the rural masses. He was responsible likewise for the clever satirical tales *Tiltas* (Bridge) and *Viešininkai* (The Officials). But the best of which he was capable is embodied in his many folk songs which brought consolation and hope to his countrymen in their darkest hours. His activity naturally aroused official hostility. On several occasions he had to don the garb of a convict, which by that time had grown to be regarded as an honourable distinction among Lithuanians. He was unhappily not destined to assist at the emancipation of the Lithuanian language in whose cause he had ruined his health in prison, for he passed away four years before the year of liberation deeply mourned by a grateful people.

The defeat of Russia by Japan evoked widespread

disorders, assuming the form of peasant risings in the country and strikes in the towns. The spirit of revolt speedily spread to Lithuania, where the panic-stricken Russian officials soon abandoned the field to Lithuanians, who lost no time in taking control of the local administration and the schools. In the autumn of 1905 the Tsar proclaimed freedom of person, press and assembly. Already in October of that year a number of Lithuanians had gathered at Vilnius and drafted a Memorandum addressed to the then Russian Minister, President Count Witte, demanding far-reaching autonomy, equal rights for all aliens in Russia, the recognition of Lithuanian as the official language in Lithuania, construction of Lithuanian schools, attachment of Suvalkai government, hitherto included in the Polish administrative system, to Lithuania, freedom for the Catholic Church, etc. This Memorandum was actually published in the Russian Government organ, *Pravitelstvennyi Vyestnik*. It naturally evoked a lively protest from the Poles, who feared lest the grant of autonomy should alienate their former allied State from Poland.

The initiative of the Vilnius Memorandum was the signal for a startling outburst of patriotic fervour and enthusiasm, all the stronger doubtless for its long suppression. In order to show that the foregoing Memorandum was not merely the handiwork of an isolated group of fanatics, the Lithuanian leaders decided to convoke a great National Lithuanian Diet or Congress at Vilnius.

The indefatigable fighter for Lithuanian freedom, Basanavičius, signed an appeal to all parties of the country to unite in Vilnius for the expression of the national demands. The land became a veritable beehive of political activity. Meetings were everywhere convened to choose delegates to the Vilnius Congress.

This Congress met in Vilnius on December 4th, admission being granted only by ticket. The congestion was tremendous, since more than two thousand delegates took part. All classes and callings were represented ; all governments, districts and communes had sent their nominees. With them sat numerous representatives of societies and clubs, officials of the various parties, and many delegates of Lithuanians abroad, notably from Petersburg, Moscow, Odessa, etc.   It was an All-Lithuanian gathering in the fullest sense of the word.

This Congress was followed by sittings of various organizations which adopted supplementary resolutions moved, for example, by the clergy of the three dioceses, the officials of the Peasants' Union, and the representatives of the Lithuanian Teachers' Body.

The decisions of this imposing national demonstration bore testimony to the readiness of the people for the coming test.   The event served as a warning, not only to the Russians but also to the Poles, to keep their hands off Lithuania in future.   How swiftly the Russian administrative apparatus could operate when it listed will appear from the example of the Governor-General of Vilnius, Froese, who on the day following the Congress issued a manifesto to the Lithuanian people in which he recognized the justice of their demands and promised to submit them to the Duma.   As a first step towards the fulfilment of the Tsar's Ukase of October 17, 1905, he permitted the employment of the Lithuanian tongue in the communal boards and schools.   The sequel, however, showed how insincere the Russian Government really was in its lavish pledges.

The following historic resolution was adopted by the Vilnius Congress :

1. RUSSIA AND LITHUANIA.

That Russia is the opponent of the rightful demands of the nationalities existing under her rule.   Since all Russia has now risen against this tyranny the Lithuanians also join the movement and decide to make common cause with the other nationalities.   To this end it is essential that every Lithuanian should be instructed in the importance of this step.

2. THE AUTONOMY OF LITHUANIA.

Only self-government will satisfy the aspirations of the Lithuanian people.   Lithuania must therefore be resuscitated within her ethnographic boundaries as an autonomous State in the Russian Empire.   Her relations with other Russian States must be established upon a federative basis.   Vilnius will be the capital of the country and the seat of parliament.   The latter will be elected by general, secret and direct ballot, in which women will also participate.

No means must be neglected to attain these ends. In the first place, all parties must be reconstituted and directed in a common action. The following are decided : Refusal of military service, and taxes, the closing of Russian schools and Russian bureaux, the boycott of all liquor shops, the threat of strike, etc.

3. LITHUANIAN LANGUAGE AND SCHOOLS.

The Lithuanian language is the official language. The schools must be the nurseries of the Lithuanian spirit and must be directed by teachers freely chosen. Good wishes for further success shall be expressed to all Lithuanians who, in the Vilnius government, are fighting against Polonization.

Unfortunately the fervent hopes aroused by the concessions won through the Russo-Japanese war were destined to sustain a serious setback. The realization of Governor-General Froese's programme speedily encountered exasperating checks. Another Russian official reaction led to renewed assaults on the Lithuanian language, which was again proscribed. The old horde of Russian chinovniks, but recently expelled, reappeared upon the scene to occupy their former posts. The right of land-ownership, ostensibly conceded to the Lithuanians, was so freely interpreted by Russian casuistry that in actual fact the Lithuanians received more paper than land. The fight against the Catholic Church was also resumed, and the anomaly was offered of Catholic priests and teachers obliged to go abroad to gain a livelihood. The former Russian muzzling order came into operation, and more inveterately than before the Russian police suppressed all public meetings of Lithuanians. Nevertheless this policy of pinpricks was now powerless to put back the hand of time ; its most obvious effect was to strengthen popular opposition and the resolve to win national independence sooner or later.

A very characteristic phenomenon of the epoch was the rapid development of the schools. Russian statistics, which cannot be accused of partiality to the Lithuanians, indicate that the percentage of illiteracy in Lithuania in 1897 did not exceed 45, whereas in Poland it was as high as 60, and in Russia 75 or 80. In 1905 a commission for popular education convened at Kaunas succeeded in establishing, partly at least, the Lithuanian language in the schools. Some Lithuanians were admitted into purely Russian institutions, the normal school of Panevežis for example. In localities where the State made no provision Lithuanian committees came into being. Thus the educational society " Saulė " (Sun) obtained permission to open a normal school at Kaunas, and so successful were its efforts that it established forty-five popular schools attended by more than a thousand pupils. This society shortly before the war comprised sixty-eight branches with 3,400 members, and in addition to schools had founded numerous communal libraries and reading-rooms which proved a veritable boon to the people. Three secondary schools were also created, together with a commercial school designed to train Lithuanians and thus better enable them to compete with the Jews, who had hitherto possessed a virtual monopoly of trade. Shortly before the War the society put up its own building at Kaunas at a cost of 200,000 roubles.

In the Suvalkai government the educational society " Žiburys " (Light) discharged similar functions. Its fifty-seven branches number 4,200 members, and it succeeded in opening seven popular schools, a school of agriculture, and a high school for girls at Mariampol. Further it established several asylums for the poor, and folk-halls, while libraries were opened in almost every parish.

Vilnius government also possessed its society of education styled " Rytas " (Morning). Its position, however, confronted by an active pan-Polish propaganda was very difficult and delicate. Yet it was able to form thirty-seven groups with a membership of 2,000, and thanks to its efforts reading-rooms were opened in several localities.

These three societies, " Saulė," " Žiburys," and " Rytas," will not soon be forgotten in Lithuania, where their splendid efforts in the cause of education and modern enlightenment have borne such rich fruit.

Analogous work on behalf of temperance was done by the society " Blaivybė " which was founded at Kaunas, and in 1914 had 40,000 members and 171 branches,

More than 25,000 pamphlets have been sent out by this association, and its labours have led to the closing of numerous pot-houses.

Equally symptomatic of the thirst for progress has been the wonderful expansion of the Lithuanian press of recent years. The Society of St. Casimir has done much in this direction. Its membership before the War rose to 10,000 and it established its own printing-office at Kaunas, whence issued a flood of educational and religious literature, together with reviews and magazines of all kinds. At Vilnius two daily papers, *Viltis* (Hope) and the *Lietuvos Žinios* (Lithuanian News), appeared, also many weekly and monthly publications. The same objects were pursued by the Society " Sietynas " which was established at Šiauliai and developed great activity.

Among student organizations a specially important rôle has been played by the Lithuanian Society for the assistance of Lithuanian students in the higher educational institutions of the city of Moscow, under the superintendence of Mr. T. Naruševičius (Naroushevitch). This society attained a membership of nearly five hundred and during recent years has expended a very large sum of money for the above-mentioned objects. Many members of this society now occupy very high official posts in Lithuania and elsewhere.

A comparison of the output of Lithuanian books during the three and a half centuries between 1500 and 1864 with the brief period from 1904 to 1914 will afford some idea of the national determination to make up for lost time. The figures are respectively 786 and 2,550. Not a village could be found without its subscribers to Lithuanian reviews ; not a district without its association for the development of the Press ; not a house without its calendar and religious books. It may be said without exaggeration that the entire people were obsessed with the desire for modern progress—the same people whom Muraviev the Hangman had undertaken to wipe off the map of the world in the space of forty years. There is nothing remarkable in the fact that science, art, and literature, in the real sense of those terms, came some-

what later in the day.   Political strife is not a favourable
medium for the cultivation of these refinements of life
which prefer to wait till the social structure is more or
less prepared.   In 1907 the Scientific Society of Lithuana
and the Society of Fine Arts were born in Vilnius.   The
former was founded by Dr. Basanavičius, and possessed
250 members.   It issued a yearly publication to which
all classes contributed.   Some time before the movement
began in Western Europe this Society proposed to investi-
gate Lithuanian folklore.   All the old songs, legends and
popular traditions were carefully collected and the Society
Annual began to publish them.   The yearly gatherings
of this society were formerly attended by more than five
hundred Lithuanians, and these occasions bore the character
of national fêtes.

During this comparatively placid period of Lithuanian
history poetry also was sedulously nurtured.   It was
customary for the villagers to assemble at the house of
a well-to-do peasant or landlord and there sing the old
popular ditties, the Dainos, which celebrate the glories
of the past, the joys of love and the plaintive nostalgia
of the Lithuanian people.

In the villages also popular plays were resuscitated.
The dedication of a church or the holding of a fair furnished
a convenient pretext for these popular representations
which, if they lacked somewhat in artistry, were replete
with rustic vigour.   In the towns theatrical unions were
formed which promoted the staging of Lithuanian and
also foreign pieces.   The Lithuanians have always enjoyed
a high reputation for their love of music.   In the village
choirs, conducted by the village organists, several artists
of note gained their first experience.   The names of
Šimkus, Sosnauskis and Brazys may be mentioned.   It
is to their credit that after perfecting their talent abroad
they returned to their native land to co-operate in the
further musical development of the country.

The Society of Fine Arts, with Žmuidzinavičius at
its head, has busied itself on the one hand with the preservation of valuable national monuments of the past,
and, on the other, with the encouragement of modern

artists and the creation of new works. This Society holds an annual exhibition at Kaunas which always contains numerous canvases of a high standard of merit, and never fails to attract a big attendance. It has even begun to excite attention abroad. One of the Society's cherished objects is to erect a national building to be designed by Lithuanian artists. The scheme meets with the lively encouragement of the general public who have liberally contributed to its realization.

The economic development of Lithuania in the past has encountered enormous difficulties. Enfeebled by mass emigration, the Lithuanians have had to fight against both the Russians and the Jews, although as regards the latter, my own personal opinion is that they are really a source of strength to the country at the present day. Economic debasement was a cardinal tenet of Russian policy as a means of maintaining their grip on the land. Even after 1905, when Lithuania had already begun to develop in all other branches of human activity, its economic life left a good deal to be desired. In the economic conflicts between Russia and Germany, Lithuania found herself, so to speak, between the hammer and the anvil. The Germans wished to take advantage of the weakening of Russia through her war with Japan to dump their products into the country. The Russians, powerless to compete against the Germans, avenged themselves by imposing heavy import duties upon German goods.

In many places, however, the primitive so-called " tryohkpolnyi " or three-crop tillage system of cultivation had given way to a more rational one which created a demand for new agricultural machinery. A more intensive culture was an immediate consequence of the political successes gained. The peasant attached himself anew to his plot of ground, and many Lithuanians who had emigrated returned to their native land. The passion for landownership is typical of the Lithuanian as of the Russian peasant. In spite of everything the Russian occupants could do, the native Lithuanian would resort to a thousand subterfuges to gain possession of uncultivated ground. The peasantry also acquired the land of impoverished proprietors. The Russian Government fought against this movement, by itself selling the land of ruined gentry and distributing it among Russian colonists who settled in the country *en masse*. These colonists were to be the Russian leaven designed to transform Lithuania into an Orthodox pasture, and needless to say they were liberally subsidized. Fortunately, these Russian plans miserably miscarried. The newly-created settlements disappeared as rapidly as they had sprung up, as soon as they had exhausted the official appropriations, and their holdings passed into Lithuanian hands. The latter, on their part, began to found societies for the purchase and sale of fields. In the Vilnius government the agricultural society " Vilija " thus functioned ; in Kaunas " Progress " ; in Suvalkai the societies " Ūkininkų Draugovė " and " Žagrė." The business turnover of these societies before the war had reached a total of a quarter of a million of roubles.

Concurrently with practical work theoretical instruction was not neglected. Agricultural courses were inaugurated and attended by the peasants, whilst the Government itself founded an agricultural school.

The situation became more tolerable, but was not yet such as to tempt the return of all the Lithuanian emigrants from overseas. Working hands were insufficient, and high rates of pay ruled for harvesters. But complete reorganization cannot be effected until the majority of Lithuanians abroad have returned to participate in this task. In this connexion it must be said that already the Lithuanians in the United States, who number not far short of a million, and are nearly all well to do, have generously co-operated to help their less fortunate compatriots in the homeland. More than one Lithuanian peasant owes the extinction of his mortgage to this source.

The women have taken an active part in the national development. Notwithstanding numerous difficulties, many of them have studied medicine and dentistry and are nowadays successfully practising their profession. Their services have been recognized from the first, and it was regarded as a matter of course that with Lithuania's acquisition of independence women should enjoy the franchise together with men.

CHAPTER VII

LITHUANIA DURING THE GREAT WAR

On the Eastern front Lithuanian territory was destined to bear the brunt of hostile attack, and in proportion to area and population no country has suffered more severely or made greater sacrifices; and that, too, I regret to say, with less Allied recognition than Lithuania.

Places like Kaunas, Gardinas, and Daugpilis were fortresses of the first rank, and as such naturally served as targets for the enemy's sledgehammer blows and as centres for the concentration of the Russian defence. Large bodies of troops were assembled in Lithuania and the country soon became one of the most important bases of operations. Owing to the slowness and insufficiency of means of transport, the Russian General Staff was obliged to requisition supplies on the spot for the needs of the Russian armies. More frequently than otherwise all these things, grain, horses, cattle, groceries, and raw materials of all kinds were confiscated without payment, so that early in the war the inhabitants were denuded of almost everything they possessed, not by the Germans but by their so-called protectors. As a typical example, in the village of Leipalingis the Russians seized 2,000 horses without any payment and left only two.

During the Russian offensive in East Prussia the Lithuanian provinces suffered terribly. Flourishing towns and villages were completely destroyed by artillery fire. Fifteen thousand persons, the majority Lithuanians, were deported by the Russians into the interior of the country, the brilliant idea underlying this policy being to leave the advancing Germans nothing but a desert. The first German advance into Lithuania took place in the autumn of 1914, when for the first time the Russians were driven out of East Prussia. At this time the districts of Suvalkai were mainly affected. Towards the end of 1914 some districts of the government of Kaunas, Taurage, Naumiestis, Palanga, and others shared the same fate. At the end of the winter of 1914–15 the Russian advance was again halted and the Russians after the battles of the Mazurian Lakes with heavy losses were compelled to fall back behind the Lithuanian boundaries. Later the German advance continued in the Suvalkai government, where, for six months, desperate fighting took place. In May the Germans succeeded in penetrating into Samogitia and Kurland. The banks of the Venta and Dubysa, behind which the enemy forces had entrenched themselves, were the scene of violent engagements, since the Russians did not yield ground without offering desperate resistance. At the beginning of July considerable German forces opened the attack on Kaunas, which was taken on August 18th. The Russians, entrenched in the region of the lakes, on the Kaunas-Vilnius road, made resolute efforts to protect the Lithuanian capital from capitulation; but Vilnius fell on September 8th. The Russians were pursued as far as Smurgainiai (Smorgon), where a fierce artillery duel caused the destruction of the town.

In the autumn of 1915 mobile operations gave place to positional warfare, and up to the peace of Brest-Litovsk the situation of the two armies changed very little.

Lithuania was speedily devastated. At the outset, as we have shown, she had to satisfy the requirements of the Russians for, as ill luck would have it, the German offensive coincided with the harvest season. During their retreat the Russians destroyed everything which they were unable to remove, with the result that the output of an entire year's hard work was lost to the inhabitants. Fighting raged all over Lithuania for several months, and artillery fire above all caused whole-sale devastation. The western districts of Kaunas and Suvalkai in many places resembled a desert. The towns of Kalvarija, Kibartai, Širvintai, Naumiestis, Sudarga,

RED CROSS TRAIN AT KAUNAS.

FIELD DRESSING STATION.

To face p. 76.

Šakiai, Šiauliai, Jurbarkas, Tauragė, Kretinga, Gagždai, and others were burnt or otherwise reduced to ruins.

The region of the Nemunas (Niemen), where the fortresses of Kaunas, Alytus, and Gardinas were situated, offered a frightful spectacle of destruction. In the parish of Kalvarija alone fourteen large villages with their estates were entirely obliterated. In the Liubavas parish only two or three houses were left. Many market towns were also destroyed, including Prienai, Simnas, Serijai, Druskininkai, and Liškevė. At Trakiškiai, of 56 estates one only was left intact ; at Dievogalas one out of 52 ; at Šilaliai and Pariečius one out of 40 ; while at Padainupis all were wiped out. Three-quarters of the town of Šiauliai were destroyed by fire, and this flourishing industrial centre of 80,000 inhabitants counts now only a few thousands. In the same neighbourhood, where there was much fighting, the majority of the villages, market towns, and farms were laid waste.

The western part of the Vilnius government and the district of Ežerenai (Zarasai) in the Kaunas government fared no better. These regions suffered severely under the tactics of the retreating Russians. Villages and farms were given to the flames, machinery and implements were carried off, and unspeakable miseries began for the inhabitants of these desolated areas.

This mania for destruction did not spare the churches, twenty-five of which were badly damaged. In many places these edifices were bombarded during divine service, and old men, women and children who had sought refuge therein were buried beneath the ruins. Even at Kaunas, the celebrated church constructed by Vytautas the Great, which had been converted into an Orthodox temple by the Russians, was badly shattered, and the Church of the Dominicans partially wrecked. Since the war, therefore, very heavy financial burdens have devolved upon the faithful in making good all this damage.

What with the inevitable devastation wrought by gunfire, and the deliberate plundering of so-called friends and open foes, Lithuania in the wake of the war was reduced to little better than a desert. The countryside, through lack of working hands, wore a wild and savage aspect. According to the testimony of Dr. Bartuška, who visited the country as an American delegate, Lithuania at that time seemed entirely ruined. He stated that he had called upon many ecclesiastics whose houses had been rifled literally of everything portable by the various passing troops. In the Suvalkai government, owing to the destruction of houses, the inhabitants were forced to dwell in the abandoned trenches.

In Kaunas province 144 mills were razed to the ground ; in Vilnius 285 ; in Suvalkai 87. The lot of the urban workers was no more enviable than that of the peasant. Hungry and poorly clad, they eked out a miserable subsistence, a constant prey to typhus, dysentery, influenza, and other maladies. Doctors and medicine were totally inadequate to meet the needs of the country. Unlike Belgium, Lithuania did not benefit from the liberal aid extended by the United States and Spain.

When, in accordance with the inhuman Russian policy, thousands of Lithuanian adults had to leave the country, entire families were broken up. The peasants first sought refuge in the towns, but were moved on farther by the Russian soldiery. Parents had thus to abandon their children, and were themselves transported into Russia in cattle trucks. At Vilnius, for example, thousands of children ran about the streets vainly seeking their parents. The Central Lithuanian Committee subsequently placed them in orphanages. But these institutions were without funds necessary to provide proper nourishment for the children, meat and milk being particularly scarce.

Meet objects of pity also were the Lithuanian civil and military prisoners. More than 30,000 Lithuanian soldiers were made prisoners in Germany and Austria, besides which the Germans seized 5,000 civilians as hostages as a reprisal for the behaviour of the Russians who, when evacuating East Prussia, had driven out 15,000 of the inhabitants, of whom quite half were also Lithuanians. The majority of these prisoners consisted of old men, women and children.

Very often civilians were thus carried off without cause

and merely on suspicion. The Lithuanian Aid Committee of Lausanne is in possession of authentic documents which show that sometimes enceinte women were torn from the bosom of their families, whilst women and children perished from hunger through the loss of the male bread-winners.

Thanks to the initiative of a priest named Strikas and a teacher named Velykas, who were among the prisoners at the Holzminden camp, a school for Lithuanian children was opened in the camp under their direction.

The majority of the military and civil prisoners received nothing from their families, as the latter were utterly unable to send them help. Even to-day many Lithuanians are in ignorance of what has become of their relatives. Besides the moral suffering inseparable from prolonged captivity, far from home and without news of their families, these unfortunates had also to endure terrible physical privations. The situation of the children was particularly lamentable ; many of them died through lack of proper care and food suitable to their years.

Praiseworthy efforts were made to lighten the sufferings of these unfortunates. The Lithuanians who remained in the occupied territories organized the Lithuanian Committee for the succour of war refugees, which is still functioning ; but its usefulness has been restricted by insufficient funds.

A similar committee in Russia Proper has had very extended activity. It established 175 branches, 293 schools, 84 workshops, and a large number of asylums and *pensions* capable of receiving 1,500 pupils. During three years it spent thirty-four million roubles. Through the efforts of this committee similar organizations were created at Stockholm and Copenhagen, the latter of which has been successful in ameliorating the lot of many Lithuanian prisoners of war Further help has been given by the Hispano-Lithuanian committee founded in 1916 at Barcelona.

Work undertaken in the United States has also been of considerable service to Lithuania. Congress decided to organize for November 1, 1916, a " Lithuanian Day," which was supported by a sympathetic appeal from President Wilson. A public collection on All Saints' Day produced more than a million francs, and this generous subscription proved of great value in extending the sphere of aid.

The Pope further co-operated in this commendable work. As far back as 1915 he personally contributed 20,000 lire to the Lithuanians, and he ordered for May 20, 1917 a collection in the churches for the same purpose. Although collections had previously been made on behalf of Poland and Belgium, a sum of 1,200,000 francs was raised. Switzerland served as intermediary between the various committees of Lithuanian aid, for it was at Lausanne that the Executive Committee for the organization of the world collection and the Central Committee of Lithuanian succour for the victims of the war had their headquarters. The former busied itself with the organization of the world collection ordered by the Pope, and the distribution of the amounts so raised.

The Central Committee of succour styled " Lithuania " was established at Fribourg on November 7, 1915. Its statutes were drafted in conformity with the Swiss Civil Code and were approved by the Government. The Committee operated in conjunction with the committees of Barcelona and Copenhagen. The first annual report showed 17,000 francs receipts and 18,000 francs expenditures, and the second 200,000 francs receipts and 50,000 francs expenditures. Up to November 1917 Switzerland, herself badly in need of food, could not permit the export of the latter in large quantities ; later, 10,000 and 15,000 francs monthly were disbursed for the despatch of foodstuffs. An American named Wood presented 25,000 dollars worth of clothing, but this gift could not be imported into Europe owing to the war.

With the German military occupation of Lithuania it became necessary to give the country a new organization, the old one having disappeared with the retreating Russian armies. The new administration was formed by Marshal Hindenburg in August 1915 ; its headquarters were at Tilžė (Tilsit), and it embraced a portion of the Kaunas and Suvalkai governments. At the head of this administration was placed Prince Isenburg. After the conquest of new parts of Lithuania by the Germans, the military government transferred its seat to Kaunas in April 1916, and there assumed the name of the Vilnius-Suvalkai Military Administration. The limits of this administration were again extended by a decree of Marshal Prince Leopold of Bavaria, who, as Governor-General of the East, in April 1917 removed his headquarters to Vilnius. This enlarged jurisdiction was styled the Military Administration of Lithuania. It formed merely part of an administration which extended from the Gulf of Riga to the line Brest-Litovsk—Warsaw comprising a territory of 212,000 square kilometres known as Ober-Ost. The authorities assigned to Lithuania constituted a central and district administration.

The central administration was divided into a central department, a department of justice, an economic department, a forestry department, and a department of commerce and raw-materials. Each of these departments dealt with matters that could not be entrusted to the district administrations. The central administration had at its disposal the military gendarmerie, which had groups at Vilnius, Kaunas, Panevėžys and Šiauliai. In addition, under the central administration, functioned an Imperial Commissary of the Committee of War Indemnities. In all, the personnel of this administration numbered 4,000 soldiers, without counting some twenty commissariat companies and several engineering units.

To the central administration were subordinated two urban districts and 82 rural districts, with an area varying from 1,500 to 4,000 square kilometres. These districts were administered by captains, with the assistance of other officials, i.e. a steward, justice of the peace, a district doctor, commissariat officers, a military detachment and a company of military gendarmerie.

The districts were divided into sub-districts administered by prefects, who were usually officers of commissariat. They were helped by a staff and a detachment of covering troops.

6

The Central Forestry Department had divided the country into seventeen military inspectorates, the superintendence of each of which was assumed by a Chief Inspector of Forests. For inspection of schools the country was divided into eight districts, at the head of each of which was an inspector.

The Department of Justice of Vilnius had three district tribunals in the country (Vilnius, Kaunas and Suvalkai). To the Kaunas tribunal were subordinated 21 peace circuits; the Vilnius and Suvalkai tribunals each had seven of these.

Upon the military authorities of Vilnius devolved the administration of the country. While the Eastern front existed, a purely military administration was necessary for the security of military transport and the rear of the army fighting against Russia. Much also was done to ensure the proper sanitation and health of the troops; very little similar solicitude was exhibited on behalf of the civilian population.

Lithuania suffered greatly from the German occupation. Enormous quantities of timber were removed from the country. The forests bordering the lakes, roads, and rivers were almost completely razed to the ground. Many long years and vast sums of money will be necessary to restore these devastated regions. In the same manner the land was denuded of horses and cattle through constant requisitioning not only for the needs of the army of occupation but for purposes of export to Germany. The value of this form of loot, reckoned at the present exchange, would run into billions of marks. True the authorities of occupation nominally paid for these requisitions, not in money, however, but in exchequer bills with which the peasants' coffers were congested, but which were devoid of all practical utility. Many of these bills bore inscriptions injurious to the bearer, of whose ignorance of German the donors took advantage. A favourite sentiment was: "The bearer of this bill is condemned to a hundred blows"; another ran: "The bearer is a fool and, should he complain, should be put in prison." Nor were these merely idle pleasantries; on the contrary, they were often carried into execution, and many peasants were forcibly incorporated into the labour battalions.

Much could be written about the efforts of the military administration to Germanize the country. A beginning was made with the names of places and families. Suvalkai became Suwalken ; Kaunas, Kaunen ; Širvintas, Schirwindt ; Klikeli Klickeln, etc. The theatres played only German pieces, and the cinematographs showed only German films.

German papers made their appearance in great number, among them being the *Zeitung der 10 Armée*, the *Liebesgabe*, *Kownoer Zeitung, Wilnaer Zeitung, Libauerzeitung, Zeitung von Grodno, Nachrichten von Suwalki, Bialistocker Zeitung*. In Lithuanian *Dabartis* was printed at the rate of 20,000 copies daily. Lithuanian papers proper were not viewed with any favour by the authorities, and *Viltis* and *Lietuvos Žinios* were suppressed. A complaint submitted to Berlin by a delegation of the Lithuanian National Council in the United States brought no amelioration. To appease the literary hunger of the Lithuanians sheets like *Laisvė* (Freedom), and *Laisva Lietuva* (Free Lithuania) were hectographed and spread broadcast. The *Kvailas Prusas* (Stupid Prussian) was issued as a satirical journal, the editor and readers of which the German authorities vainly tried to discover. The barristers Jonas Vileišis and Janulaitis, suspected of collaboration in this paper, were arrested and interned in Germany. Many other Lithuanians on similar suspicion were also detained for a long time in captivity.

In the newly-organized schools the German language was introduced as a compulsory subject from the first year. When, too, in June 1918 the Vilnius teachers opposed an increase in the hours for German their schools were closed.

These efforts at Germanization were the natural outcome of the German policy as a whole, which insisted upon the necessity, from military, political and economic considerations, of annexing Lithuania to Germany. In the light of these aims one can understand why the German Government did not abolish the Ober-Ost administration even after the peace of Brest-Litovsk, when a state of war with Russia ceased to exist. On this subject responsible Lithuanians addressed petitions and energetic protests to the German Government. The Eastern front fell in February 1918, but the military command continued, and the free and independent Lithuanian State was still subjected to military control. In January 1918 Prince Isenburg retired from his post as Administrator of Lithuania. The pan-German papers congratulated him on the successful discharge of his mission, and the university of Fribourg-en-Brisgau conferred upon him the title of doctor *honoris causa* for services rendered to the German cause.

CHAPTER VIII

RISE OF THE NEW STATE

The great Vilnius Diet of 1905 marked an epoch in the reawakened national consciousness of the Lithuanian people. It exacted at least a verbal recognition of autonomy from Russia, though, as we have seen, the concessions ostensibly granted were realized only in part. During the years that followed, however, the great progress of Lithuanian culture served still more to strengthen the national sentiment. The Lithuanian people more imperatively than ever demanded freedom, and a repetition of the events of 1905 could not have been far off when the war broke out in 1914. The Lithuanians were not slow to understand that the moment had come to present their claims anew.

The Lithuanians in the United States have always displayed considerable activity in everything concerning their native land. So in this case they were the first to make themselves heard when from October 21 to 28, 1914, in Chicago, they convened a national congress which was attended by three hundred delegates. The gathering declared itself in favour of the reorganization of the Lithuanian State in conformity with the principle of self-determination. Further, this State was to be independent of Poland, and besides the Lithuanian territory of Russia was to embrace the Lithuanian region of East Prussia and the Suvalkai government. The Lithuanian Bureau of Information in Paris was entrusted with the task of diffusing knowledge of Lithuania among the general public. Moreover, J. Gabrys was commissioned to treat with the belligerents on behalf of Lithuania. A national fund was created to cover all expenses in this connexion.

In America a national council was established for the protection of Lithuanian interests. This council represented all Lithuanian organizations, those of the latter numbering more than a thousand members nominating one delegate and those with over five thousand members two delegates each. The American Lithuanians followed events in Europe with keen attention, more particularly in the Motherland, and held themselves in readiness to intervene should a favourable opportunity offer itself.

In the wake of America the Lithuanian colony in the neutral countries of Europe laboured ceaselessly for the promotion of national aspirations. Thus on August 8 and 4, 1915, the first Berne conference was held. This assembly was of exceptional importance as affording occasion for the formulation of Lithuanian demands for a free and independent State, in the folowing terms :

1. The Lithuanians and the Letts form, in the great family of Indo-European peoples, a parallel branch not subordinate to that of the Germans and the Slavs. To the number of seven millions they oecupy a territory of 250,000 square kilometres situated between Russia and Germany, on the shores of the Baltic Sea, in the basins of the Nemunas and Dauguva (Dvina).

2. The Lithuanian people oecupy, by reason of their intellectual culture, the first rank among the peoples subject to Russia.

3. The Lithuanian State extended, from the XIIIth to the XVIth century, from the Baltic to the Black Sea and rendered great service to the rest of Europe in its struggle against the Tartars.

A few days later, August 30, 1915, the Lithuanians demanded their independence from the Russian Duma. The Lithuanian deputy, Januskevičius, in a memorable speech traced the material and moral sufferings endured by the Lithuanian people. He closed his remarks with this appeal : " Come to the aid of our unhappy country, and give us the assurance that our just demand for national autonomy will be fulfilled."

This was the second time that the Lithuanian question had come before the Russian Duma. Previously, in August 1914, a Lithuanian deputy, Mr. Yčas, from Kaunas, had spoken in favour of autonomy and the annexation of Prussian Lithuania to Russian Lithuania.

Lithuania was represented at the congress of oppressed nationalities held at Lausanne in February 1916. Here the Lithuanian delegates made the following declaration :

The issue of the war is uncertain. Whatever it may be, Lithuania does not wish to return to political servitude or to revert to a situation which would permit Russia or Germany to impose their yoke upon the country. A free Lithuanian people occupying the entire national territory, and having free political, intellectual, and economic development—such are the demands of the Lithuanians of all parties.

This declaration clearly expressed the end proposed by the Lithuanians ; it was articulated still more clearly at an exclusively Lithuanian assembly which took place at The Hague ; here the Lithuanians, conscious of their rights, acted on their own initiative.

Shortly afterwards, from March 1-5, 1916, Lithuanian delegates from Lithuania, the United States and Switzerland, assembled for the second time at Berne to discuss the situation in Lithuania which was then under German military occupation. This conference pronounced in favour of the organization of a free and independent Lithuanian State, and justified its demand as follows :

1. Lithuania was for many centuries an independent State.

2. The Lithuanian people have never ceased to demand their lost liberty.

3. Lithuania possesses a very clear ethnographic character, and a national culture, and she forms a distinct political organism.

4. Only an independent Lithuanian Government will be able to repair the immense damage which the War has caused to Lithuania.

5. The creation of a free and independent Lithuania will favour the establishment of a durable peace.

6. At the outbreak of the War the Allies proclaimed the liberation of oppressed nationalities as the object of the War.

7. The German Government also, through the Imperial Chancellor, has declared that the German troops have " delivered " Lithuania.

The delegates further declared that the alliance between

Lithuania and Poland had been *ipso facto* and juridically abolished through the partitions of the two countries among Prussia, Austria and Russia in 1772 and 1795, and that the Lithuanian people desired to be masters within their ethnographic boundaries and protested against any encroachment on their rights by Poland.

The latter portion of this declaration was inspired by the consideration that the Poles were representing Lithuania as a Polish province; that the Poles wished to usurp the legitimate rights of the Lithuanians; and that they were everywhere posing as the representatives of Lithuanian rights.

Moreover, it was declared that the university of Vilnius, which the Poles pretended to regard as a Polish institution, was actually Lithuanian. Founded in the capital of the Grand Duchy of Lithuania, the university of Vilnius wished to become again Lithuanian, while respecting the rights of national minorities.

Lithuanian conferences succeeded each other almost uninterruptedly. That held at The Hague from April 25th to 30th had considerable importance; the resolutions there adopted have the value of a programme of action. The representatives of the Lithuanian people declared that Lithuania, after having escaped from Russian domination, did not wish to exchange its reconquered independence for a fresh yoke. This resolution was based upon the following considerations :

1. Russia oppressed Lithuania during one hundred and twenty years (since 1795); had despoiled her of her name and in lieu thereof had given her the style of "North-West Russia."

2. The national administration and the Lithuanian Statute have been set aside and in their stead foreign institutions have been imposed upon the country.

3. The Russian Government has suppressed the university of Vilnius (1831), closed the schools, and persecuted the Lithuanian language and literature.

4. The Russian Government has done great damage also to the Catholic Church; in persecuting Catholics it has not recoiled before the spilling of blood.

5. Under barbarous governors (Muraviev the Hangman, for example) the country has suffered a setback of half a century at least in the development of its civilization.

6. The forty years' prohibition of printing (1864–1904) grievously injured the country, notwithstanding which the intellectual level is higher than in Russia (52 per cent. of the population can read and write, whereas the proportion in Russia is only 29 per cent.).

7. Besides the robbery of her culture Lithuania has also had to endure that of her soil which the Lithuanians by their labours of several centuries have rendered fertile.

8. Since the beginning of the War some hundreds of thousands of Lithuanians have fought in the Russian army ; despite this, Russia has not promised to the Lithuanians the political autonomy which she has accorded to the Poles.

9. During their retreat the Russian troops massacred young and old in the country and carried off thousands of Lithuanians.

At this time two different opinions were entertained by Lithuanians regarding the future of their country. One party desired an autonomous Lithuania under a Russian protectorate, whereas the other, and the more numerous, demanded complete independence. In the long run the latter won the day. To promote their object all the political parties of Lithuania and of the Lithuanian colonies abroad created a High National Council upon which devolved the duty of representing the Lithuanian people in all matters concerning the country. This Council chose Switzerland as its domicile so as to enjoy the necessary freedom for the exercise of its activities, which soon became greatly extended. For some time previously there had existed at Paris a Lithuanian Bureau of Information which was now transferred to Lausanne, where it entered upon a new sphere of usefulness.

The Lithuanian deputies had formerly demanded autonomy from the Duma. With the fall of the Tsarist Government the situation changed ; the many Lithuanians who had been deported from their own country into Russia by the Russian troops began to concern themselves vigorously with the future of their native land. In June 1917 they convoked a special conference at St. Petersburg. This was attended by three hundred authorized delegates, besides some two thousand other Lithuanians who were present by invitation as an auditory. The congress adopted a resolution which, in its general outline, coincided with that passed some weeks later by the Lithuanian Diet at Vilnius. But a minority of the Left, composed for the most part of Socialists, quitted the conference to hold a meeting of their own which assumed the style of " democratic," and passed a resolution differing somewhat from that of the general congress. This schism somewhat hampered the political action of the Lithuanians in Russia, and in the party of the Left hostile groups were speedily formed which fought among themselves. Unity of aim was thus impaired. In this emergency the Lithuanians of Russia decided to convoke an assembly of their compatriots from both Lithuania and the colonies at Stockholm.

The next really epochal event in the history of the struggle for independence was the Diet of Vilnius which sat from September 18 to 22, 1917, attended by two hundred and twenty delegates. Owing to the German occupation of the country it proved impossible to choose the delegates through a general vote, but they were all prominent and well-known men, representatives of the various parties, classes and professions. This Diet was therefore a faithful organ of the Lithuanian people. The most important work of this Diet was the election of a National Council (Taryba) and the adoption of an historic resolution. The latter reads as follows :

1. In order that Lithuania may be able freely to develop it is necessary to make the country an independent State, based upon democratic principles and having ethnographical frontiers which shall take into consideration the interests of economic life.

The national minorities of Lithuania shall be given every guarantee for their cultural needs.

In order to fix definitively the bases of independent Lithuania and her relations with neighbouring countries, there shall be convoked at Vilnius a Constituent Assembly elected in conformity with democratic principles by all the inhabitants of Lithuania.

2. If, before negotiations for a general peace are entered into, Germany should declare herself ready to recognize the Lithuanian State and to defend Lithuanian interests in the peace negotiations, the Lithuanian conference would then admit the possibility for the future Lithuanian State of entertaining with Germany relations which remain to be determined, but which shall not prejudice the free development of Lithuania. The conference makes this declaration in consideration of the fact that the interests of Lithuania, in normal times, are rather in the direction of the West than the East or South.

In the election of a National Council the conference gave evidence of considerable political ability. Although, for example, the Catholic Nationalist Party possessed a large majority in the Diet, it welcomed representatives from the Left, two Catholic Democrats already elected actually retiring to make room for two Socialists. The special aim of the Diet was to form a Council which should be truly representative of the entire country. Four ecclesiastics, several landed proprietors, lawyers, professors, peasants and workers were elected. The total membership of this Taryba was twenty, consisting of the following prominent Lithuanians : Dr. J. Basanavičius, M. Biržiska, S. Banaitis, H. Bizauskas, Pr. Dovydaitis, St. Kairys, P. Klimus, D. Malinauskas, Doyen Mironas, S. Narutowicz, Petrulis, Dr. A. Smetona, J. Smilgevičius, J. Staugaitis, A. Stulginskas, Dr. J. Šaulys, K. Šaulys, J. Vailokaitis, J. Šernas, Dr. Jonas Vileišis. The Vilnius Diet of 1917 recalled the tradition of the great Diet of 1905, and all subsequent conferences have worked on the lines foreshadowed by this historic gathering.

On the initiative of many Lithuanians from Russia, the Stockholm conference assembled from October 18 to 20, 1918, the Lithuanians from Russia being the most numerous. The Centre was strongly represented at this conference, whilst the extreme Right and Left were comparatively weak. The Lithuanians of Switzerland and America also sent delegations. The conference received a report on events in Lithuania and on the

Vilnius Diet of whose resolution it took cognizance and to which it declared its adhesion.

About this time a third conference was held at Berne to elaborate, with the cooperation of the Taryba, a detailed programme of foreign and domestic policy. A delegation from the Taryba therefore attended, with President Smetona at its head. This assembly adopted a large number of decisions, of which the most important was one which declared adherence to the resolution of the Vilnius Diet recognizing the Taryba as a properly constituted organ of the Lithuanian people. The conference further adopted the national boundaries as fixed by the Vilnius Diet, embracing the former Russian governments of Vilnius, Kaunas, Suvalkai and Gardinas, and the district of Naugardukas (Novogrodek) in the government of Minsk. Vilnius, the ancient capital of the Lithuanian kingdom, was to be the federal capital. The conference also declared that a port on the Baltic was absolutely necessary to Lithuania for her economic development. On this occasion the Berne assembly discussed the opening of a national university at Vilnius and the suppression of the German language as a compulsory branch of study in the primary schools.

The Lithuanian Taryba on December 11, 1917, first proclaimed the liberty and independence of Lithuania, but a more authoritative proclamation was that of February 16, 1918, which is now regarded as the official date. Inspired by very obvious ulterior motives Germany was the first foreign State to recognize Lithuanian independence *de jure* on March 24, 1918. In spite of this recognition, signed by the then Kaiser himself, the powerful pan-Germanic Party subsequently made desperate efforts to effect the annexation of Lithuania to Germany, and failing that some sort of " personal " union first between Lithuania and Prussia and then between Lithuania and Saxony. All these efforts, however, were sternly resisted by the Lithuanians themselves who, with dearly bought knowledge of the disastrous consequences of the union with Poland, were in no hurry to repeat the experience with Germany. In the course of this remarkable

VIEW OF KAUNAS FROM VYTAUTAS HILL.

KAUNAS UNIVERSITY.

To face p. 92.

struggle the Taryba, which meanwhile had assumed the title of State Council on July 11, 1918, with a view to checkmating German intrigues, actually proclaimed Lithuania a democratic monarchy and offered the crown to the Duke of Urach, a descendant of the ancient Lithuanian dynasty of Mindaugas. Fortunately for the future of the country this verbal pronouncement was never implemented in fact, and Lithuania has remained a republic.

The Allied victory favoured the rapid development of events in favour of Lithuania. The Taryba adopted a provisional constitution ; a Directory of three members for the exercise of executive functions was appointed ; and Dr. A. Smetona served as the first President of the State Council, in this capacity officially representing the Lithuanian State until the supercession of the Taryba by a Constituent Assembly (Steigiamasis Seimas) on May 15, 1920. But before that date Lithuania was doomed to undergo many vicissitudes. The Provisional Government had been established at Vilnius, but when the German front collapsed the Bolsheviks began to advance early in January 1919, and the Lithuanian administration had perforce to be removed to Kaunas, which, with a brief interlude in 1920, has since been the temporary capital of the State.

Driven out of Vilnius, the representatives of the young Lithuanian State did not despair, but embarked vigorously upon the task of organizing an army, with such success that the further advance of the Soviet forces was checked, a severe defeat being inflicted upon them at Koshedari. In April 1919 the Lithuanian troops were closing in on Vilnius when the Polish army advancing from the direction of Lyda deliberately forestalled them and entered the town on April 20th of that year. To prevent an armed conflict between Lithuania and Poland the Supreme Command of the Allied and Associated Powers established a line of demarcation on April 26, 1919, which was promptly violated by the Poles, as also the second line laid down by Marshal Foch on July 27, 1919.

As stated briefly above, the old Taryba or State Council,

which had done such yeoman service, was superseded in
May 1920 by the Constituent Assembly (Steigiamasis
Seimas) elected on April 14th and 15th of the same year,
by universal, equal, direct and secret suffrage, according
to the system of proportional representation. Of the
inhabitants who had attained their majority (twenty-one
years) 85 per cent. took part in these elections ; in certain
of the electoral districts the number of votes was as high
as 92 per cent., thus plainly evidencing the high degree
of political consciousness prevailing among all classes.
Owing to the Polish occupation of Eastern Lithuania,
the elections could be held only in twenty non-occupied
districts. The electoral unit was one representative to
about 15,000 inhabitants. There were elected in this
way 112 representatives who, according to parties, are
thus classified :

Christian Democrats	59
Social Populists	29
Social Democrats	18
Jews	6
Poles	8
German	1
Non-partizan	1

As regards education, 58 of the foregoing (52 per cent.)
have had a university education ; 25 (22 per cent.) secondary
education ; and 29 (25·5 per cent.) a primary education.

The Constituent Assembly was convened at Kaunas
on May 15, 1920. Its first act was to ratify the proclamation of the independence of the Republic of Lithuania.
The Assembly recognized and approved all the acts of
the Provisional Government, and having announced the
republican form of government, elaborated the fundamental
principles of the State Constitution. The Assembly also
formed a fully authorized executive Government which
took the place of the former provisional administration.

As will be seen from the above list of parties the strongest
numerically is the Christian Democratic Party, which has
an absolute majority. It is recruited largely from the

rural districts where religious influence is powerful, but also numbers adherents among the working classes of the towns. In the domain of domestic politics and social questions its tendencies are moderate. On the agrarian reform question, however, it supports the policy of dividing up the big estates to provide for the landless and the insufficiently landed, soldiers more particularly, but recognizes the principle of compensation and private property.

The Social Populists represent more or less the same elements of the nation as the Christian Democrats, but differ on religious questions. They favour nationalization through gradual evolution rather than through revolution. They are a thoroughly patriotic group.

The Social Democrats are largely compounded of urban dwellers and industrial workers, and are advocates of socialization. In the assembly they form the opposition; nevertheless in moments of crisis they cooperate with the other parties in work of positive organization. Between them the Christian Democrats and Social Populists constitute a bloc disposing of 88 votes out of a total of 112. It is understood that as soon as a definitive State Constitution can be drafted and agrarian reform completed (this has only just been announced—February 1922), the present Constituent Assembly will deem its task accomplished and give place to an ordinary assembly or parliament, which will then be elected.

Lithuania being essentially an agricultural country, as has been shown elsewhere, possessing a peasantry passionately attached to the land, Bolshevik propaganda has never stood the slightest chance of gaining a real hold upon the popular imagination. This fact was most strikingly shown during the contact between Lithuanian and Russian troops in Vilnius at the time of the joint occupation following the withdrawal of the Poles. The Soviet "Revkoms" (Revolutionary Committees) made desperate efforts to undermine the strong national feeling of the Lithuanian common soldier and by meetings and pamphlets appealed fervently to his "class consciousness," but in vain. The native wit of the simple ranker was

proof against these blandishments.   Kipras, Juozas, Stasys
and the rest had an inconvenient habit of contrasting their
own well-clad and well-fed condition with the often
dilapidated state of the Red Guardsman, with the result
that the Lithuanian troops emerged from the ordeal
rather more " boorzhui " than when they went into it.
Superficial observers, profoundly ignorant of the real
principles of Communism, have made the mistake of con-
fusing popular insistence upon division and distribution of
the big estates in the Baltic countries with "Bolshevism."
Of course it is nothing of the kind, but actually a movement in absolutely the reverse direction.   True Communism
denies the right of land-ownership, whereas no government
in Lithuania which sought to abolish this right could hope
to survive twenty-four hours.   There could, in fact, be
no better earnest of national stability and prosperous
development than the manifestation of this very land
hunger which guarantees to the country permanent
sources of wealth.   Elsewhere in these pages the latest
available data on the attempt so far made to deal with
agrarian problems are given, and the foregoing remarks
are merely prompted by what has gone before.

CHAPTER IX

THE POLISH BETRAYAL

As largely an eye-witness of later events in Lithuania I feel entitled to speak with some authority about the unprecedented international scandal which, for the time being at least, has terminated in the triumph of Polish military might over Lithuanian right, without eliciting anything more effective than feeble verbal protests from the League of Nations to which the dispute was relegated for settlement.

In May 1919 I was fortunate enough to be appointed secretary to the British Commission for the Baltic Provinces (*sic*) under its distinguished Commissioner, Colonel S. G. Tallents, C.B., C.B.E., with whom I travelled via Switzerland, Austria, Czecho-Slovakia, Poland and Germany to Libau, Riga and Reval in the early summer of that year. During this period I participated in stirring incidents which do not properly form part of the present recital. It should be said, however, that on the occasion of a conference between Colonel Tallents and a Lithuanian delegation at Libau in June 1919, I for the first time began regretfully to realize that the Poles, with whom hitherto I had ever sympathized in their picturesque struggle for freedom, were proving false to all their loudly vaunted principles, and were indeed doing their best to extend to their weaker neighbours the self-same treatment from which they had only just succeeded in emancipating themselves with the indispensable aid of the Allies. This discovery was a bitter disillusionment, but I would not permit sentiment to weaken an objective judgment, and inasmuch as all subsequent first-hand knowledge has but served to increase the counts of my indictment against Poland, which dates from this moment, I have not the slightest hesitation in putting my name to this open confession of political faith.

At the end of August 1919 I was sent from Riga to Kaunas under Colonel R. B. Ward, A.F.C., R.A.F., to establish a branch of the British Commission at the temporary Lithuanian capital. Later, however, this branch was converted into a consulate, and Colonel Ward's appointment as Acting British Consul for Lithuania by the Foreign Office synchronized with my own as Acting British Vice-Consul, a post which I held up to the early part of 1921. From this it will be clear that I enjoyed exceptional opportunities for gaining " inside " information of what was going on both openly and behind the scenes. Possessing a very sound knowledge of Russian, both written and spoken, to which I have since added a growing acquaintance with the fascinating Lithuanian tongue, it was easy for me to communicate direct with all the principal Lithuanian actors on the political stage during this period, totally dispensing with intermediaries.

My own personal views of the merits of the Lithuanian-Polish controversy are fully shared by my former chief, Colonel Ward, as also by the various members of the British Military Mission then in Lithuania, who never overlooked an opportunity of investigating every " incident " between Poles and Lithuanians of which we had an over-supply during those strenuous times. In this context a remark once made to me by a former British Military Attaché in Kaunas so aptly sums up the case against Poland that I cannot refrain from quoting it here. He said : " I am out to oppose Poland in Eastern Europe for much the same reasons that I opposed the Boche in Western Europe during the war, because the Poles as they now behave are the Prussians of Eastern Europe minus the Boche efficiency." I do not think it would be possible to express the sane, considered judgment of a typical British military man in fewer or more effective words.

On July 12, 1920, the Lithuanian Government, with the entire approval of our own Foreign Office, concluded a

Peace Treaty with Soviet Russia which gave Lithuania her ethnographic frontiers, with Vilnius as her capital. The Poles were then at war with Russia and in very bad case, for the Reds were rapidly advancing on Vilnius. It should be added that throughout this conflict Lithuania preserved the strictest neutrality, the mendacious charges of the Polish Government to the contrary having been entirely disproved by our own military investigators, and the Military Control Commission of the League of Nations.

Conscious of the necessity for evacuating Vilnius under Bolshevik pressure the Polish High Command hurriedly resolved to invite the Lithuanian army to occupy the city in preference to the Reds. For this purpose one Colonel Rylski was sent to Kaunas early in July, and I had the good fortune to be present with Colonel R. B. Ward at the conference between him and the members of the Lithuanian General Staff, headed by Colonel Klesčinskas, the Chief of Staff, and Colonel Žukas, the Lithuanian Minister of Defence, when the terms of this transfer were discussed. In accordance with the understanding thus arrived at, the Lithuanian forces moved forward with a view to forestalling the Red Army and entering Vilnius before them. Almost incredible as the sequel may seem to those even yet unfamiliar with the incorrigible treachery of the Polish official temperament, despite the express invitation and promise given, the Lithuanian echelons were suddenly attacked by the Poles near Vievis on July 14th, and although they succeeded in repulsing this totally unexpected onslaught, their advance was inevitably delayed some twenty-four hours, with the result that the Russians occupied Vilnius before them.

The Lithuanians, however, entered the capital on the following day, July 15th, and for some days held the city in conjunction with the Russians, who eventually, in accordance with an agreement concluded between the two High Commands, withdrew and left Vilnius in sole possession of the Lithuanian authorities towards the end of August.

The Bolsheviks had not been in the town twenty-four hours before, with their usual energy, they had started a daily paper for the spread of Communistic principles, and eloquent comrades from Moscow and Petersburg were promptly imported to give frequent lectures to the troops and citizens. Many of these lecture notices still adorned the walls of the city when we first entered it on the withdrawal of the Bolsheviks. The so-called " revkoms " or revolutionary committees also sprang up like mushrooms overnight wherever the Soviet troops were quartered. I was subsequently told by Colonel Žukas, the Lithuanian Minister for Defence, that so far from discouraging contact between Lithuanian and Russian troops during the period of joint occupation, he was entirely in favour of it as the simplest and cheapest form of anti-Bolshevik propaganda, because on comparing his own well-fed, well-clad and well-shod condition with the decidedly nondescript wardrobe and lean, hungry look of the average Red Guardsman, the Lithuanian Tommy felt less inclined than ever to interfere with the established order in his own little peasant republic. Apropos of this brief period of Russo-Lithuanian military intercourse, Colonel Žukas reported to me an actual conversation that once took place between a Lithuanian and a Russian soldier. Asked what he was fighting for the Lithuanian replied, " For my country." " For your country ? " the Russian echoed ; " I'm fighting for something far better than that. I'm fighting for a programme ! "

In due course the Lithuanian Government transferred its seat to Vilnius, all the foreign diplomatic missions and consulates removing at the same time. The British Consulate secured excellent quarters in one of the main thoroughfares, the well-known St. George's Boulevard, and the individual members of the Staff were just settling down to useful work and a reasonably comfortable existence in this ancient and picturesque city, when a further manifestation of Polish faithlessness upset all their well-laid plans.

It is or should be a matter of history that, according to the terms of the famous Suvalkai agreement, signed by the Lithuanian and Polish representatives on October 7, 1920, in the presence of the Military Control Commission of the League of Nations, Poland formally

LITHUANIAN BIVOUAC.

ON THE FRONT.

To face p. 100.

recognized the validity of the Lithuanian occupation and provisional administration of the Vilna (Vilnius) region, including the city of that name. Yet not even this solemn written pledge could bind the Poles once they saw an opportunity of retrieving their position with the relaxation of the Bolshevik peril. They were perfectly willing to make use of the Lithuanians to serve their own ends, but equally ready to sacrifice them for the same motives. Hardly had the ink had time to dry on the Suvalkai agreement than Polish troops under the notorious General Zeligowski attacked Vilnius and occupied it on October 9th, just two days after the signature of the said agreement.

Several days before this development signs were not wanting that something of the sort was in the wind, and great uneasiness prevailed among the inhabitants in consequence. It was in this emergency that Colonel R. B. Ward, the British Consul, anxious to allay the popular anxiety, undertook an aeroplane flight to Warsaw for the purpose of obtaining formal official assurances that the rumoured intentions of the Poles were unfounded. He had an interview with Prince Sapieha, the then Polish Minister for Foreign Affairs, and also with the Polish military authorities, who solemnly declared that the Polish Government had absolutely no intention of reoccupying Vilnius. Colonel Ward returned to the Lithuanian capital bearing these glad tidings which were joyfully received, but their tranquillizing influence was not permitted to last long.

So marked had become Polish military activity south of Vilnius that a mixed military delegation, consisting of the British Military Attaché, Major Pargiter, the French Captain Pujol, and the Latvian Consul Ozol, proceeded to Yachuny on October 6th in order to obtain from the Polish Command nearest to Vilnius an explanation of these movements. The members of this delegation, particularly Major Pargiter, were treated with scant courtesy by the Poles, and were forced to return to Vilnius with the report that the Poles denied all knowledge of the orders for a suspension of hostilities under the Suvalkai agreement and were awaiting instructions. The delegation itself had no further doubt it was only a question of hours before the Poles would again be in Vilnius. I well remember a conversation which I had with Major Pargiter at the time, and he was very emphatic on the subject.

Sure enough on October 8th, the day after the signature of the Suvalkai agreement, superior Polish forces launched an offensive from south to north against Vilnius, which at the time was defended by three Lithuanian battalions and one battery, which were quite inadequate to repel the Polish advance. The order for evacuation was therefore given and carried out on the night of the 8th. During the entire day and night a violent engagement developed south of the city.

In this emergency, upon me devolved the disagreeable duty of leaving Vilnius by one of the last outgoing trains on the evening of the 8th, bearing with me, in addition to my own personal hand baggage, a bulky, sealed sack containing the British official ciphers. The train was packed and we had to travel in total darkness. The exodus from·the doomed city was tremendous. The thousands of persons who could not possibly be carried by rail, sought safety in flight on foot, or in horse-drawn vehicles, for the most part in the direction of Kaunas. A very large proportion of these refugees were of course Jews, who knew full well the fate likely to overtake them if they were caught by the Polish soldiery.

We ourselves arrived at Kaunas, after a long and tiring journey, in the small hours of the morning, and experienced great difficulty in obtaining any sort of accommodation for the night. I myself had paired off with an acquaintance who held a responsible official post and whose *bona fides* there seemed no reason to doubt. In fact, without his assistance, it would have been physically impossible to convey my belongings from the train to the congested horse tramcar which carried us from the station to the hotel, for needless to say no porters were available at such a time. I am happy now to bear unsolicited testimony to the great kindness and perfect loyalty of this particular individual, for the simple reason that he was subsequently found to be a Bolshevik agent who, in the ordinary way, would have been only too ready to filch the official secrets of a foreign State hostile to his employers. It is true that I took every possible precaution against this sort of interference, but amidst the confusion and Cimmerian darkness of this sudden departure from Vilnius it would have been the simplest thing imaginable, had he been so minded, to relieve me of both my personal and official possessions without exposing himself to any danger of detection. I must perforce conclude, therefore, that a certain measure of personal regard for me was responsible for his welcome restraint.

Some days after these events, the various foreign missions, including the remainder of the British consular staff, were evacuated from Vilnius by a special train for the despatch of which, under the protection of the Control Commission of the League of Nations, I was fortunately able to arrange with the Lithuanian General Staff.

On October 19th I myself returned to Vilnius in the capacity of special correspondent for a certain London paper, to ascertain the exact position of affairs. Owing to the fighting then in progress between the forces of the legitimate Lithuanian Government again established at Kaunas, and those of the so-called Central Lithuanian Government, controlled by General Zeligowski, it was impossible to travel by the more direct route viâ Vilkomir, and I therefore drove through Preny, Olita and Orany in the neighbourhood of which I passed the last Lithuanian outposts. I made the trip under abnormally difficult conditions. Direct communication had of course ceased, and had it not been for the lucky chance that Mr. S. B. Kaufman of the American Joint Distribution Commission wished to return to Vilnius on business connected with his committee and kindly placed his Ford car at my disposal, there would have been scant likelihood of my securing transport.

I found Vilnius little changed outwardly since I left it in such a hurry. There were comparatively few troops to be seen in the city itself, the majority being at the front. Superficially life seemed to be running in normal channels, but further investigation led to considerable

modification of this impression. From non-Polish inhabitants I ascertained that since the Polish occupation
there had been 9 murders and 104 armed robberies.
Seven of these murdered victims were Jews, but two
were sons of a Russian priest and had been shot in cold
blood by armed robbers. I found all the Jewish residences
strongly barricaded, so that one had to effect an entry
by the back staircases; and regular watches had been
established, the male inmates keeping guard duty throughout the night. Nobody ventured out after sundown.
One evening, I was told, a band of thirty or forty armed
men surrounded a huge block of buildings in the Uglovaya
Street and called upon the inmates to open the courtyard
door, announcing that they were soldiers come to make
a revision. They were told to return in the morning.
To this they replied by trying to batter the door down,
and opened rifle fire. Immediately by preconcerted
arrangement the inmates of the building, men, women and
children, rushed out into the courtyard and in chorus
raised a sustained cry for help which could be heard all
over the city. Finally the assailants withdrew. The
following morning thirty-five genuine Polish troops headed
by an officer appeared and declared that they had been
fired on from this building the previous evening, and
therefore proposed to search the premises. In the course
of the search the officer found in an attic a quantity of
cocaine valued at a million marks, which he promptly confiscated and retired with his men, declaring himself satisfied
that the inmates were innocent! Nearly every Jew with
whom I talked stated that, not to speak of the short-lived
Lithuanian régime, which had seemed almost too good to
be true, even under the Bolsheviks, life and property had
been infinitely safer than under the Polish flag.

During the brief interval that had elapsed since the
withdrawal of the Lithuanians and the entry of the Poles,
prices of various food products had doubled, trebled,
and quadrupled. This unhappy city had already changed
hands seven times, and the inhabitants pined for peace,
order, and cheap food.

From a military standpoint Central Lithuania was then

stronger than when Zeligowski entered the town on October 9th, and from a qualified British expert, and ex-officer established in business, I obtained very satisfactory evidence of the close connexion between General Zeligowski and the Warsaw government. For that matter, the Polish flag flew over official buildings, and the militia wore Polish brassards. Only Polish money circulated. The first decree of General Zeligowski defined the territory of Central Lithuania as embracing all districts of the Vilnius government, save Vileika and part of Disna district, also almost all Gardinas (Grodno) district. The national emblem was the eagle and epaulettes, taken from a historic tablet on the walls of the famous belfry of St. Casimir attached to the cathedral. This emblem decorated the red flag of the "Republic." The provisional governing commission comprised departments of Foreign Affairs, Regional Defence, Interior Trade and Industry, Ways of Communications and Public Works, Labour, Finance, Provisioning and Agriculture, State Properties, and Justice. This administration was to continue only till the convocation of a Constituent Assembly which would have to determine the ultimate form of government. I obtained several interviews with leading officials, including Mr. Jerzy Iwanowski, Director of Foreign Affairs, and Engel, the Director of Department of Justice, who naturally insisted that the *coup de force* was inspired by local patriotism.

One significant little incident which helped to satisfy me personally of the close connexion between the Zeligowski adventure and Warsaw was my chance street encounter on this occasion with none other than Lieutenant Wonsowicz, whom I had known previously in Kaunas as Polish liaison officer. Wonsowicz, himself a naturalized American citizen of considerable private means, was one of Pilsudski's most trusted secret agents, and his presence therefore in Vilnius at such a time could hardly be misconstrued. He had suddenly left Kaunas some few weeks before to escape arrest by the Lithuanian police for ceaseless plotting against the existing administration.

On the return journey to Kaunas our car broke down

ten versts from Preny, and we had to accomplish the rest of the route on foot and in a prehistoric stage-coach packed with good-natured Jews.

Unfortunately for the pleasing fiction of a mutinous General (Zeligowski to wit), and Polish innocence of complicity in his coup, we have the signed depositions of Polish officers, including Lieutenant Grodski, Captain Buczynski, Captain Javorski, and Lieutenant Slovikovski, to prove that the entire plot was engineered by Marshal Pilsudski himself, in conjunction with other highly placed military officers, who held a conference in the Marshal's train at Gardinas (Grodno) on October 1st and 2nd to concert plans for the reoccupation of Vilnius.   General Zeligowski was selected to command the enterprise because he was a native of Central Lithuania, and could therefore rather more gracefully father the theory of a purely local movement than some outsider.   The Polish officers whose names are given above further testified that money and munitions for the Zeligowski troops came solely from Warsaw, all settlements of accounts being effected direct with the Ministry of Military Affairs at the Polish capital.

Incidentally Lieutenant Grodski deposed that the centre of the Polish secret military organization in Western Lithuania, known as the P.O.W. (Polska Organizacija Woiskowa), was at Warsaw, its head being Section No. 2 of Information of the Polish General Headquarters, the Chief of which was Lieut.-Colonel Matczynski. The latter's substitute, Major Kieszkowski, was Commander-in-Chief of the entire P.O.W. organization.   This organization was directly connected with the 2nd Information Section, which in turn was subordinated to the Chief of the General Staff.   The P.O.W. organization possessed at Vilnius its sections P.P.S. and P.O.W., equally directed by the 2nd Section of Warsaw.   The Chief of the 2nd Section at Vilnius was Major Koscialkowski, ex-Commander of the Sharpshooters of the Niemen.   At Kaunas the Chief was an old Starosta of the Troki district, Lieutenant Staniewicz, who had charge of the Sharpshooters of the Niemen and of the " Bojowki " (a preparatory fighting organization) in Lithuania.   At the head of each bojowka was a Polish officer, the chief of these bojowki at Kaunas being an ex-officer of the Russian Army, Antzierovitch. The same witness testified that the Polish Government had fully decided to overthrow the Kaunas Government at all costs, and it was to this end that it was deemed necessary to give a solid organization to the P.O.W. Important funds were actually devoted to this purpose ; unlimited credit exempt from all control was guaranteed. Lieut.-Colonel Matczynski had charge of these credits, which he transferred to Major Kieszkowski, who in turn sent money by courier to the various chiefs of the bojowki. One project on foot at the time was to unite all these subversive groups into a single organization of the Niemen, but I am not aware whether this project has been realized. Those curious to learn further details of these Polish intrigues I would refer to *The Lithuanian-Polish Dispute*, published at the instance of the Lithuanian Legation in London by Eyre & Spottiswoode in 1921.

The intervention of the League of Nations in the Lithuanian-Polish dispute dates from September 1920, and formally terminated in January 1922, after a series of futile conferences at Brussels and Geneva under the auspices of M. Paul Hymans, the President of the Council. To my mind, this intervention was from the first foredoomed to failure by the obstinate and mysterious obsession, whereof M. Hymans was a victim, that some sort of "special tie" must be effected between Lithuania and Poland. This obsession, coupled with the wholly unwarrantable transformation of the Vilnius territory from an object of litigation into an object of exchange, helps to explain the failure of M. Hymans to bring the two parties to an understanding. It seems incredible that any British representative on the League Council should have been able to share the conviction of M. Hymans that his final project of agreement offered a fair solution of the dispute. Quite irrespective of numerous minor objectionable features, it contained several clauses so dangerous to Lithuanian integrity that no Lithuanian Government dare accept them.

For example, Article 11 of the proposed agreement

requires Lithuania to grant Poland at all time the free use of Memel as well as the Niemen for the transport of all classes of goods, including munitions and implements of war. This clause blissfully loses sight of the fact that Lithuania is already bound under her treaty with Russia to observe strict neutrality in the event of war involving that country. Acceptance of the clause would thus invalidate that neutrality from the start, and would be doubly dangerous seeing that the entire trend of Poland's foreign policy renders another conflict between Russia and herself inevitable sooner or later.

Article 9, concerning conditions for a defensive military agreement between Lithuania and Poland, besides being of a far-reaching character wholly unjustified by Lithuania's international position, actually contains a proviso that in case of disagreement on the obligation on either side to come to the assistance of the other, the question shall be submitted to an arbitrator, appointed in advance by the Council of the League of Nations with their consent ! The suggestion that a sovereign State should blandly surrender one of the most important attributes of statehood in the shape of the right of determining for itself an issue involving the lives and liberties of its own citizens is really so monstrous that I do not like to express my true opinion of the class of mind capable of fathering it. Whilst no doubt the possible surrender of this attribute is on paper reciprocal, in practice it would obviously be unilateral, for the simple reason that Lithuania, unlike Poland, harbours no aggressive designs against her neighbours, and with a guarantee of her neutrality by the Great Powers and an honestly defensive union with the other Baltic States, can very well dispense with so potentially perilous a pact with so very questionable a friend as Poland has hitherto shown herself to be.

Article 6 declares that both the Lithuanian and Polish languages shall be official languages throughout the whole Lithuanian State. Now, whilst the Lithuanian Government was fully prepared to make Polish a concurrent official language with Lithuanian in the Vilnius territory, at the request of the Vilnius Diet, it could not properly permit it to be thus extended to Western Lithuania, where the Polish element hardly exceeds 2½ per cent. of the total population, and, moreover, speaks Lithuanian.

Again, in Article 8 the provision made for coordination of the foreign policies of the two States would in practice inevitably have led to a complete subordination of Lithuanian to Polish interests.

It is noteworthy that although Lithuania went so far as to accept even this ill-contrived project as a basis for discussion, Poland declined to make a similar concession, thus revealing an inordinate political appetite incapable apparently of being satisfied with anything less than the entire absorption of Lithuanian into the new Polish State.

In an address before the League of Nations Union on January 27, 1922, Mr. Naroushevitch, the Lithuanian Chargé d'Affaires in London, made the following reference to the Zeligowski *coup de force* and the League of Nation's failure to find a satisfactory solution of the Polish-Lithuanian dispute :

Taking advantage of their military superiority, the Poles dictated conditions to Lithuania, and when subsequently convinced that their forcible occupation of Vilna would enjoy the support of certain Powers, calmly infringed the Suvalki Treaty.   It is indeed a matter of history that only two days after the signature of this agreement the Poles, acting through the " rebel " General Zeligowski, seized the Lithuanian capital of Vilna and subsequently occupied the Vilna territory.

The League of Nations has not failed to inflict upon General Zeligowski's adventure well-merited blame. M. Leon Bourgeois, then President of the Council of the League, in a letter addressed to M. Paderewski on October 4, 1920, specially declared : " The Polish Government, after having appealed to the League of Nations on the subject of its difference with Lithuania, accepted the decisions of the Council—immediate cessation of hostilities ; neutrality of the territory occupied by Lithuania to the east of the line of December 8th, with reservation of respect for this neutrality by the Soviet authorities ; formation of a Control Commission which is now on the spot and charged with taking the necessary steps to stop or avert any conflict, without prejudging in any way through its action a definite territorial settlement. The occupation of Vilna is thus a violation of the engagements *accepted vis-à-vis the Council of the League of Nations, and the latter is compelled to demand of the Polish Government what immediate steps it proposes to take to ensure respect for engagements."*

In these circumstances, M. Leon Bourgeois, realizing the danger which General Zeligowski's act constituted for the prestige of the League of Nations, deemed a fresh hearing of the parties by the Council necessary. "The question at issue to-day," he wrote to the latter, "is really not only the determination of the rights and obligations of each of the two Governments concerned, but above all of the right that belongs to the Council of the League of Nations not to allow that decisions which it has taken and the effect of proceedings which it has advised, after a solemn agreement concluded before it between the interested parties, to be checkmated. *It is for the future of the work of the League a question of essential importance which necessitates deep deliberation."*

The foregoing citation will make it clear that Poland has been guilty of violations of her engagements not only towards Lithuania but also towards the League of Nations itself. Four separate occasions may be recalled in this context. On September 20, 1920, she infringed the so-called Curzon line, and twice before violated the Foch line. Finally she committed a flagrant breach of the Suvalki agreement by occupying Vilna and the Vilna territory. Her offence against the League will be made clearer to the lay mind by reference to Article 12 of the Covenant of the League, which reads : "The Members of the League agree that if there should arise between them any dispute likely to lead to a rupture they will submit the matter either to arbitration or to enquiry by the Council, and they agree in no case to resort to war until three months after the award by the arbitrators on the report by the Council."

Unfortunately, in spite of so palpable an infringement of the Covenant on the part of Poland, it must be stated that the League so far has not seen fit to apply to the latter the measures specially provided under Article 16 of the Covenant, with a view to enforcing obedience to the obligations undertaken by all members of the League. Article 16 reads :

"Should any member of the League resort to war in disregard of its covenants under Articles 12, 13, or 15, it shall *ipso facto* be deemed to have committed an act of war against all other members of the League, which hereby undertake immediately to subject it to the severance of all trade or financial relations, the prohibition of all intercourse between their nationals and the nationals of the covenant-breaking State, and the prevention of all financial, commercial, or personal intercourse between the nationals of the covenant-breaking State and the nationals of any other State, whether a member of the League or not. It shall be the duty of the Council in such cases to recommend to the several Governments concerned what effective military, naval or air force the members of the League shall severally contribute to the armed forces to be used to protect the covenants of the League."

It is not too much to say that the failure of the League of Nations to exact respect for its authority from a recalcitrant member, Poland, lies at the root of all subsequent inability of the Council of the League to solve the dispute between Lithuania and Poland. We have had frequent occasion to point out to the Council of the League that withdrawal of Zeligowski's troops from the contested territory is an indispensable preliminary condition to any peaceful settlement of the dispute, for while Poland continues to ignore the engagements which she deliberately assumed under the Suvalki agreement, profound distrust of her good faith in all future negotiations must remain deep-rooted in the mind of the Lithuanian people, and thus constitute an insuperable obstacle to a satisfactory *modus vivendi*.

Early in January 1922 the Council of the League of Nations, in view of the rejection of its recommendations by both parties, formally terminated its intervention, and gave notice of the withdrawal of the Military Control Commission, while at the same time it proposed the acceptance of a fifth demarcation line to take the place of the present neutral zone between the contending parties. Hitherto the Poles have violated four lines, viz. that established by the Supreme Command of the Allied and Associated Powers in April 1919, the second line laid down by Marshal Foch on July 27th of the same year, the line established under the Suvalki agreement of October 7, 1920, and the so-called " Curzon " line fixed by the Supreme Council as frontier between Poland and the provinces of the old Russian Empire. In these circumstances, the Lithuanian Government not unnaturally failed to see what good purpose could be served by the merely nominal provision of yet another demarcation line which the Poles would overstep with the same gay insouciance as heretofore the moment this should suit their purpose.

The Poles have given additional proof of their keen regard for their international engagements and their respect for the League of Nations, of which they are a member, by holding elections early in January 1922 for the so-called Vilnius Seim, in open defiance of the warning of the League of Nations Council that no such elections could be recognized under existing conditions of Polish

military occupation of the region, and while the entire
question of the attribution of the district remained *sub
judice*. These elections followed an ostensible withdrawal of General Zeligowski from Vilnius, but not of
the Polish bayonets, which continue to control the
situation, and under whose stimulating protection the
elections were held.

It is symptomatic of the fundamental falsity of the
Polish position that the Lithuanian, White Russian,
and Jewish inhabitants, who, according to pre-war Russian
statistics, constitute some 90 per cent. of the population,
refused to take any part in these farcical proceedings.
The result is that of the 106 members composing the Diet
or Seim, only four are non-Poles, and virtually all the
members are pledged to vote the Vilnius territory into
Poland. Such is self-determination as she is determined
in these spacious *post-bellum* days.

In October 1921 the Polish authorities of Vilnius
organized a systematic pogrom of Lithuanian cultural
institutions, including the well-known Lithuanian gymnasium or high school, orphanages, banks, etc. The
school children were brutally beaten by the Polish police
and soldiery and compelled to seek refuge in the neighbouring woods, where classes were subsequently held. In the
wake of the refusal of the Lithuanians and White Russians
to participate in the January elections, the Polish
authorities gave further evidence of their deliberate
resolve to exterminate everything Lithuanian in the
occupied territory. With this object in view, on January
20th and succeeding days, they raided a large number of
Lithuanian and White Russian institutions, including the
offices of the Lithuanian National Committee, White
Russian National Committee, the Lithuanian and White
Russian newspaper offices, as also many private residences
of Lithuanian and White Russian leaders. The pretended reason was that these leaders were implicated
in espionage and Communist activities for the overthrow
of the existing administration. It goes without saying
that not a tittle of incriminating evidence could be found
to support this charge, but failing such evidence the police

MONASTERY ON VILNIUS ROAD.

To face p. 112.

did not scruple to confiscate the private property of the victims, such as money, gold and silver articles, linen and clothing. Moreover, twenty Lithuanian and thirteen White Russian leaders were summarily arrested, and after being kept in solitary confinement for several days, were expelled from the region on February 5th of the same year. All these exiles are residents of Vilnius, many of life-long standing, and own property and businesses in that city. The majority, too, left behind them wives and families destitute of the means of support.

The Lithuanian Government lost no time in lodging emphatic protests with both the Military Control Commission and the Council of the League of Nations against these acts of Polish tyranny, but at the time of writing there seemed scant likelihood of anything being done to secure redress for the unfortunate victims beyond the customary verbal expressions of avuncular disapproval from the League, which have about as much practical effect on the pachydermatous hide of Polish officialdom as the time-honoured water on the time-honoured duck's back.

Meanwhile poor Lithuania continues to be penalized for the sins of her more powerful neighbour by being denied *de jure* recognition pending a settlement of the Vilnius question between them. England was the first of the Allies to grant *de facto* recognition to Lithuania, and this step aroused hopes which have not since been fulfilled. On the contrary, the world is regaled with the anomalous spectacle of the very Powers which fought the Great War, avowedly to win liberty for the smaller peoples, declining to grant *de jure* recognition to one of those very peoples, whilst the particular State hitherto regarded as the embodiment of the opposite principle, i.e. Germany, long ago accorded such recognition, and has since been followed by virtually all the neutral Governments of Europe, including Russia, Estonia, Finland, Latvia, Sweden, Denmark, Holland, Switzerland, Czecho-Slovakia, Brazil, Argentine, and other South American Republics. And yet *de jure* recognition has already been extended to Estonia and Latvia, the two other Baltic States, whose claims to same are not one whit

8

superior to those of Lithuania. To those " in the know," it is clear that Franco-Polish intrigue is at the bottom of our failure to do belated justice to Lithuania. France is committed to the policy of a Greater Poland to serve as a Buffer State between Germany and Russia. To this insensate object Lithuania would cheerfully be sacrificed. Why Great Britain should tamely permit herself to be dragged at the heels of this reactionary movement is more than I care to say at the moment, but it is quite certain that our policy in this respect in no wise reflects the true wishes of the English people, but is merely an expression of the arbitrary opinion of permanent officials. Of such stuff are our modern democracies made.

With reference to the question of the *de jure* recognition of Lithuania, I should like to point out that this issue, remote as it may seem to many unfamiliar with the facts, has none the less a very important bearing upon the welfare of this country. It is therefore on grounds not only of international justice but also of national expediency that I appeal for fulfilment of an obligation already long overdue.

That the Allied and League policy hitherto pursued of penalizing the weaker party to the dispute, Lithuania, for the sins of the stronger, Poland, has directly contributed to the prolongation of disorder and unrest in Eastern Europe, and therefore to the increase of unemployment here at home, can easily be demonstrated.

Article 87 of the Versailles Treaty requires the Allied Powers to determine the Polish frontiers. This so far they have not done, and Poland, as we see, takes advantage of the conveniently fluid condition of her boundaries to extend these in many directions at the expense of her weaker neighbours, of whom Lithuania unfortunately happens to be one. Had the Allies been fully alive to their responsibilities as sponsors for the new Poland which their victory brought into being, they would never have tolerated such a state of affairs, but would have invoked the powers which the Covenant of the League of Nations confers upon its signatories to compel their unruly ward to observe those international engagements which she has deliberately assumed. Yet in face of Poland's repeated violations of these engagements, including infringement of four demarcation lines, a flagrant breach of the Suvalkai agreement, and later still the holding of elections in the Vilnius region, not only have the Allies taken no action, but they have even perpetrated the grave inequity of making the innocent party a scapegoat for the transgressions of the guilty.

To such a pitch has this biased treatment of the two countries been carried, that whilst the Allies helped to create the Polish army and have supplied it abundantly with munitions, since largely employed for purposes of aggression, they have refused to sell and to allow others to sell to Lithuania arms required solely for purposes of self-defence. Comment on this discrimination is needless.

But the vital consideration for ourselves is that, so long as such a situation of unrest and uncertainty, due to Polish Chauvinism and our own direct encouragement of the same, is permitted to continue, just so long must the reconstruction of Eastern Europe be delayed, and just so long must the repercussions of this situation express themselves in terms of economic stagnation among ourselves. Poland's aggressive attitude constitutes a constant menace to peace. And once peace is seriously disturbed in that part of the world, it will not be easy to set bounds to the spread of the succeeding conflagration ; whilst the ever-present possibility of a disaster of this nature is bound to act as a baneful deterrent to all constructive effort and thus indefinitely retard the complete economic recovery of Europe, in which England is more deeply interested than any other first-class Power.

Our *de jure* recognition of Lithuania would be one of the most effective methods of letting Poland know that her policy of Imperialism towards that young State no longer enjoys the tacit approval of the Allies, and that she must in future content herself with what rightfully belongs to her. That, coupled with the prompt carrying out of Article 87 of the Versailles Treaty, would go a long way towards restoring those conditions of political stability in Eastern Europe without which it is vain to look for any permanent amelioration of our own economic miseries here at home.

CHAPTER X

THE MEMEL QUESTION

As stated in an earlier part of this book, the ancient Litho-Baltic races from time immemorial have dwelt on the shores of the Baltic Sea, between the River Vistula in the south-west and the stream of the Šalis in the north, near the Frisches Haff, the Kurisches Haff and the Gulf of Riga. The Borussians or Old Prussians occupied the region between the Vistula and Pregel in the south. The Letts lived in the north and occupied the lower basin of the Dvina. The Lithuanians lived along the Nemunas between the Borussians and Letts.

The Borussians, although supported by the Lithuanians, were nevertheless unable to resist the attacks of those sturdy professional scrappers, the Teutonic Knights, and after three centuries of struggle were overcome. But although the Teutons concentrated all possible means to denationalize the Borussians, it took about four hundred years to Germanize the latter. To-day, however, the Borussians are German in speech and in spirit.

The campaigns of the Teutonic Knights against Lithuania Proper began in 1274, their object being to keep the Lithuanians away from the Baltic. The Teutons succeeded in conquering the neighbouring Lithuanian provinces of Sudavia, Nadrovia, and Salavia, including the present Memel district. This territory is situated north of the Rivers Laba, Pregel and Angerop. From the year 1422 these Lithuanian provinces were under Prusso-Brandenburgian rule. The greater part of the Prussian Lithuanians in Sudavia, Nadrovia and Salavia, however, still retained their old customs and language, and to-day desire to be reunited with the rest of the Lithuanian people.

The north-eastern portion of these provinces constitutes the Memel district.

Memel district (Memel-Gebiet), situated between the Nemunas River and the former Russo-German frontier, was detached from Germany by the Treaty of Versailles, and is more precisely defined in Part II, Article 20 of the Treaty. The district has an area of 2,410 square kilometres of solid land and 426 square kilometres of water. The population is composed of Lithuanians and Germans, whose relative proportions have never been established by reliable statistics. According to descent, however, we may regard 80 to 90 per cent. as Lithuanians. If, on the other hand, we base our definition of nationality upon the use of language, a smaller percentage would probably result. The German Peace Delegation, which was not over-scrupulous in its compilation of statistics affecting the Lithuanians, commented thus on the peace conditions for the Memel territory :

> The Memel territory is predominantly German as regards the number of inhabitants. There are about 68,000 Germans against only about 54,000 inhabitants *speaking* Lithuanian.

According to statistics contained in the German Clerical Almanac (Pfarr-Almanach) of East Prussia, 1912, there were among 138,524 evangelical inhabitants 71,810 Lithuanians. But these German statistics include many elements not native to the country, such as officials, troops, etc., who, with the fall of the German hegemony, must naturally withdraw and give place to local inhabitants.

If we examine the position of Memel on the map we see that its sole hinterland is Lithuania. The unnatural separation of the district from this hinterland in the past has therefore had the result that Memel port, notwithstanding its freedom from ice, its greater depth than Königsberg and other favourable conditions, has not developed, but has remained quite an insignificant town on the Baltic coast, with a population of about 32,000. Through the connexion of the Kurisches Haff with the sea a natural harbour basin many kilometres in extent is formed alongside the city. The city of Memel is crossed

from east to west by the River Dauge, which flows into the
Memel Tref, i.e. the confluence of the Haff and the Baltic.
Another natural advantage is proximity to the Nemunas,
which is navigable up to Grodno (Gardinas) through
Lithuanian territory rich in natural resources.

In view of the foregoing, the Allies, in their reply of
June 16, 1919, to the German Delegation, made the following statement :

> The Allied and Associated Powers reject the suggestion that
> the cession of the district of Memel conflicts with the principle
> of nationality. The district in question has always been Lithu-
> anian. The majority of the population is Lithuanian in origin
> and speech, and the fact that the city of Memel itself is in large
> part German is no justification for maintaining the district under
> German sovereignty, particularly in view of the fact that the port
> of Memel is the only sea outlet for Lithuania.

The soil of Memel territory is largely sandy. Although a
high standard of cultivation has been attained, the export
of foodstuffs is none the less entirely insufficient to cover
the total expenditure of the territory on administration,
and the upkeep of public and Government institutions.
The local industry, consisting chiefly of wood manufacture,
and based also upon other agricultural products imported
almost exclusively from Lithuania, is thus entirely dependent upon the latter. The same must be said about
commerce. In that which concerns economic conditions,
it may be taken as proved during the year 1920 that
the Memel district cannot be self-supporting. The budget
of about 60,000,000 marks, as drafted by the local
administration for that period, appears to be sufficiently
high for a region with a population of approximately only
140,000.

Considering, too, that according to the Versailles Treaty
a certain percentage of the German Imperial and State
debt will have to be assumed, and that German Imperial
and State property remaining in the district to the
estimated amount of 232,387,000 marks will have to be
made good, it is obvious that a financial burden will have
been heaped up under which the little country must
eventually break down.

The provisional administration of the Memel district, in an effort to cover its deficit, has sought to increase its revenue by imposing duties upon all goods entering the country from Lithuania. But this measure is at variance, firstly, with the accepted obligation to admit goods in transit entirely free of duty, and, secondly, must have the effect of diverting goods traffic to other rival ports such as Libau and Königsberg. Such a policy, therefore, cannot improve the well-being of the district, but, on the contrary, may conceivably lead to its utter impoverishment.

From what has been said it will be clear that the Memel territory, owing to its restricted area and population, as well as its geographical situation, cannot support an independent economic existence, but must either revert to Germany or be attached to Lithuania as a natural former component part of the latter. There is no other alternative. The Danzig analogy does not hold good here. Danzig is already a well-developed port with an extensive trade and a considerable indigenous population. Danzig, by virtue of its geographical position, serves the needs of both Polish and German territory by which it is encompassed, whereas Memel, by virtue also of its geographical position, is solely a Lithuanian port, the requirements of Prussia being fully met by Königsberg.

The Memel territory continues to this day to be pre-eminently a Lithuanian country. To declare it either independent or Memel a free port would evoke profound dissatisfaction alike amongst the inhabitants of Prussian and former Russian Lithuania, which in turn would detrimentally affect the development of the port, because in that case the Lithuanian people, in view of the political instability and uncertainty of the position of this small stretch of territory, would not expend any effort upon its improvement, which they would surely do if, through mutual consent, this territory were to receive the status of an integral part of Lithuania. The independence or freedom of Memel territory, on the Danzig model, would foment ceaseless political intrigues among certain German elements which pursue a policy of reversion to Prussia. It is equally certain that Polish groups would also lose no opportunity of creating complications with a view to gaining control over the region. Mindful, therefore, of the economic, political, geographical and national factors in the case, it will scarcely be possible to find any other solution of the Memel problem than that proposed by the Powers in their reply to the German delegation.

Pending a just settlement of this question in favour of Lithuania, as foreshadowed by the Treaty, the region is being administered by the French on behalf of the Supreme Council. All familiar with the trend of French *post-bellum* policy will understand quite well what that means, viz. that they are administering it entirely in their own interests. Incidentally, a somewhat remarkable anomaly may be detected in the details of this French administration. For the time being, incredible as such a statement must seem as it stands, the policy of the French tends to strengthen German influence. The explanation, however, is simple. Confronted by a choice of what it must deem two evils, i.e. the German and Lithuanian elements, French policy is reduced, despite French hatred of all things German, to favouring the old German officialdom and the German party generally, because it is inflexibly hostile to the desire of the Lithuanian majority for inclusion of the Memel territory in the adjacent State of Lithuania. Undoubtedly, too, this tendency is encouraged by the Poles, who, with no economic justification for the outlay, have established a consulate at Memel to promote purely political ends, and are working tooth and nail to prevent the natural gravitation of the region towards Lithuania. Thus, Franco-Polish policy, frankly Germanophobe elsewhere, is ostensibly Germanophil in the Memel region.

General Odry signalized his advent in the winter of 1920 by enlisting Germans only in the local administration, to the bitter disappointment of Lithuanian-speaking citizens who had looked forward with hope to the arrival of the French as heralding the dawn of a brighter era for Lithuanian aspirations. At the present moment there is only one Lithuanian—and a fully Germanized one at that —in the Direktorium as against four Teuton Germans. The clerical staff of the Direktorium is also rarely recruited from natives of Memel territory; usually it is imported from Germany, as in the case of the higher officials.

Notwithstanding repeated petitions from the Lithuanian inhabitants, the Lithuanian language is not taught in the higher schools. Both General Odry and M. Petisné, the French Prefect, have rejected numerous requests that Lithuanian should be recognized as an official tongue with German.

In commercial matters the same orientation is observable. The advice of German merchants, and more especially of the former Memel Ober-Burgermeister, Altenberg, preponderates. This policy reacts to the detriment of Memel territory, because while it continues, the neighbouring Lithuanian State naturally will not enter into any commercial or customs treaty with the region.

The consensus of opinion amongst the Lithuanian population of Memel territory appears to be that under the existing form of administration Germanism bids fair to become stronger than in the halcyon days of the Kaiser.

CHAPTER XI

LITHUANIA'S ECONOMIC PROGRESS

OF all the Baltic States Lithuania enjoys the most favoured financial and economic position. This is very largely owing to the caution and prudence of her fiscal policy, which from the first led her to avoid recourse to the printing press for the replenishment of her exchequer.

In common with Poland and part of Latvia she found herself at the close of the German occupation in possession of the so-called Ost currency issued by the German Treasury for circulation exclusively in the occupied territory. But whereas the other States and Poland, in their natural eagerness to exercise all the attributes of independent nationhood, lost no time in issuing their own paper currencies, Lithuania, looking farther ahead, wisely decided to retain the Ost money until such time as she should be in a position to introduce her own coinage with an adequate gold guarantee behind it. The result of this far-sighted policy is that whereas Poland, Latvia and Estonia to-day are saddled with vast depreciated note issues, the unit of which in every case now stands at four figures to the pound sterling, and continues to decline, the Lithuanian " auksinas " or mark, until quite recently, when the slump of the German mark set in, retained comparative stability, its fluctuations being almost exactly determined by those of the German mark proper. The later collapse of the mark has naturally reacted unfavourably upon the Lithuanian economic situation, and may indeed be said to have imposed upon the Lithuanian people a share of German reparations. The new Lithuanian Government is alive to the situation thus created, and in its latest declaration foreshadowed the liquidation of the

Ost currency, and its replacement by a national money backed by an adequate gold reserve or funds equivalent to gold. The total volume of Ost paper money in circulation to-day is estimated at about two milliard marks.

Lithuania is, *par excellence*, an agricultural country. Both pre-war and post-war figures establish this fact conclusively. She thus produces within her own borders everything necessary to a self-contained independent existence. True, she has no great mineral resources, but not being a manufacturing country she is in no absolute need of them. On the other hand, Russia is not vitally concerned in anything that Lithuania produces. It is not meant to suggest that Lithuania could lead a healthy existence merely as a " peasant republic," such as the former Boer republics of South Africa. On the contrary, her full cultural development demands active intercourse with other countries. But merely as a question of existence Lithuania's position is as favourable as that of any country, and more so than, say, that of a land like Switzerland, which has, nevertheless, managed to maintain its independence during a period when larger and more powerful States have been broken up or absorbed by their neighbours.

Lithuania, including the Memel and Vilnius districts, has an area of about 34,000 square miles, more than Belgium (11,373 square miles), the Netherlands (12,650 square miles), Denmark (13,580 square miles), or Switzerland (15,976 square miles). Lithuania's area and population are approximately the same as those of Bulgaria before the war. The population of this territory in 1914 was 4,345,000, greater than that of Denmark (2,775,000), Norway (2,393,000), or Switzerland (3,781,000). As we have already seen, however, the Polish betrayal has temporarily deprived Lithuania of a considerable area of territory in the Vilnius region, so that the actual population at present under the rule of the Lithuanian Government is not much in excess of two million (actually 2,750,000), confined mainly to the Kaunas and a bit of the Suvalkai Government.

A large majority of the population is of Lithuanian blood and speech. For the entire area claimed the percentages are approximately: Lithuanians, 75 per cent.; Jews, 10 per cent.; Polish-speaking element, about 8 per cent.; Russians, White Russians and other nationalities, 7 per cent. The pre-war population of the principal cities was: Vilnius (Vilna), the capital, 214,000; Kaunas (Kovno), 90,300; Gardinas (Grodno), 61,600; and Šiauliai (Shavli), 31,300. The rural population for the entire area claimed is about 86·2 per cent., but in the area now under Lithuanian jurisdiction it is even higher, falling not far short of 90 per cent.

AGRICULTURAL YIELD.

Of the twenty-three million odd acres claimed, the actual area at present administered by the Lithuanian Government is about thirteen millions. The country for the most part is level and possesses a fertile soil. The staple crops are rye, wheat, barley, oats, peas, potatoes and flax. I give below for purposes of reference the average annual production before the war for the whole of Lithuania (excluding Memel, then part of Germany), and for 1920 for that part of Lithuania under the administration of the Lithuanian Government. It will be noted that as to wheat, peas and potatoes, there is a relative increase in the 1920 crop over the pre-war figures. There is also a great increase in flax production, the area planted in flax in 1921 being 50 per cent. greater than the pre-war.

	Pre-war Averages (for Entire Country).	1920 (say Five-eighths of Total Area).
Rye ..	40,000,000 bushels	20,000,000 bushels
Wheat	3,680,000 ,,	2,760,000 ,,
Barley	11,500,000 ,,	6,900,000 ,,
Oats	31,500,000 ,,	17,500,000 ,,
Peas	2,400,000 ,,	2,200,000 ,,
Potatoes	57,000,000 ,,	36,800,000 ,,
Flax	—	40,000 tons
Flaxseed	—	1,400,000 bushels

The approximate quantities of these crops exported during 1920–21 were : Rye, 600,000 bushels ; wheat, 736,000 bushels ; barley, 1,115,000 bushels ; oats, 2,450,000 bushels ; flax, 20,000 tons.

I give below the number of animals in 1913 for the whole of Lithuania and for that portion which is now administered by the Lithuanian Government, also the number in 1920 for the latter territory. The actual increase in the quicker breeding animals, sheep and swine, and the relatively small diminution in the number of horses and cattle, are notable when one considers the destruction wrought by the war and subsequent enemy occupation. It must be remembered that the Germans during their nearly four years military control of the country (the Ober-Ost régime) fairly bled it white. Huge quantities of foodstuffs and raw materials were exported to the Fatherland at purely nominal prices. That the post-war figures should show so comparatively small a falling-off as compared with the pre-war figures says much for the national powers of recuperation.

	1913 (all Lithuania).	1913(Five-eighths Lithuania).	1920(Five-eighths Lithuania).
Horses	762,000	495,000	380,000
Cattle	1,481,000	998,000	865,000
Sheep and Goats ..	1,055,000	720,000	730,000
Swine	2,000,000	1,350,000	1,400,000

Calves and lambs are not included in the above figures.

Further notable progress in agricultural development has been made since 1920, but complete statistics are unfortunately not available at the moment. It can be said, however, that the area now under grain cultivation is nearly four million acres, and that the annual crop reaches nearly two million tons. The annual milk supply is reckoned at a hundred million pails. Large as are these figures, they are capable of very considerable expansion. It is estimated that with proper rotation of crops it would be easy to increase the yield 15 to 20 per cent. Moreover, much of the so-called unsuitable land could be made productive, thus raising the output of the area under cultivation by some 40 per cent. The introduction of more modern fertilizers would still further enhance the yield per acre. In the opinion of the Lithuanian Minister of Agriculture, Dr. Alexa, the measures indicated would bring the total crop to 150,000,000 poods (say 2,500,000 tons) instead of only some million odd tons, which would mean a surplus for export of some hundreds of thousands of tons.

There is still ample scope for the development of dairy-farming and stock-raising in Lithuania. Even slight improvement under the former head would provide 150 to 240 million eggs annually for export, and between 5 and 7 million poods of first-class butter (between 80 and a 100 thousand tons). Pig-breeding is another very promising branch of stock-raising, and with a little development Lithuania could easily export annually 10 to 15 million poods live weight (up to some 250 thousand tons).

The position during 1921 with regard to livestock was difficult, owing partly to bad management, but chiefly to the unprecedented drought, which caused a shortage of fodder everywhere. None the less, the quantity of stock in Lithuania has appreciably increased. The Ministry of Agriculture is devoting attention to the question of importing agricultural machinery and implements duty free, and to improved facilities for the extension of agricultural credit.

With reference to current prices, it can be shown that in many cases these are actually lower than before the war. Rye, for example, can be bought for 90 marks the pood (36 lbs.), or half a dollar, about the pre-war price, whilst cattle are much cheaper. Before the war a cow in Lithuania cost from 30 to 40 American dollars, and a very good one 60 dollars, say from 5,500 to 11,000 marks, whereas to-day it costs less than half that amount. Similarly with horses and swine. The latter cost only a third of the pre-war price.

An analysis of the principal categories of agricultural

activity to-day in Lithuania gives small farms of from 12 and 15 acres to 25 and 37 acres ; medium farms from the last-named area to 75 and 100 acres ; and big communal farms from the last-named area to 150 and 200 acres. Then come the estate farms. Of these categories, the smaller farms produce in the first place two lines, swine and poultry, some cattle, but absolutely no grain for sale. The medium-sized farms, as compared with the first, provide fewer poultry products, some cattle products, and are beginning to provide grain for sale. The big communal farm, in proportion to its area, produces much fewer eggs and swine, perhaps a little cattle, more horses and more grain products. The estate farms furnish no poultry or swine products, little cattle in comparison with their area, and much grain.

In Lithuania to-day taxation tends to protect the communal in preference to the estate farm. Speaking generally, poultry and livestock are more profitable than grain-growing. This means that the most intensive farming in the country is devoted to cattle and poultry products, i.e. small and medium farming, rather than to large-scale or grain-growing agriculture. Prices also favour this tendency. Under normal conditions, especially, the highest prices comparatively are for cattle and poultry products, whereas grain prices are lower. These conditions are more favourable to small- than to large-scale farming. Consequently, by introducing agrarian reform and creating small and medium-sized farms, Lithuania should increase the output of the more profitable branches of agricultural activity.

LITHUANIAN FORESTS.

After agriculture, the most important source of national wealth is timber. The area under forest for both Eastern and Western Lithuania is some 19 per cent., but if we take the region now actually under the administration of the Lithuanian Government, the proportion is only 17 per cent., or say roughly about two million odd acres. In the same context it must be recalled that military operations conducted on Lithuanian soil during the war, and the subsequent enemy occupation of the entire country, naturally tended to impoverish the originally abundant timber resources of Lithuania.

The principal species are pine, oak, fir, birch, maple, lime, etc., needed for the manufacture of wood-pulp, paper, railway sleepers, furniture, etc. The normal annual production is 8,475,840,000 feet board measure. At the present time the export of both timber and flax from Lithuania is greatly impeded by the unsettled question of the port of Memel.

The Ministry of Agriculture has drawn attention to the necessity for prompt remedial measures if the premature depletion of the national timber supply is to be averted. In the wake of the war the needs of reconstruction all along the line have become so enormous that a quite disproportionate demand for timber has arisen, and great difficulty is experienced in coping with the irregular felling of the forests. The Ministry of Agriculture is taking steps to introduce a system of quinquennial periods for timber felling. Should more than a fifth of the specified quantity be cut in any one year proportionately less would be cut in the following year. Taking the cutting of a normal year State institutions require more than a third, or up to 40 per cent., which is very high. The biggest consumers are the railways for fuel purposes, and owing to conditions of external unrest the Ministry of Defence has to make very frequent use of the lines for the conveyance of troops. Failing the possibility of using coal upon a large scale, owing to its high price as compared with wood, it is hoped that more extensive use can be made of peat in order to relieve the present disproportionate consumption of wood. Lithuania's peat supplies are virtually unlimited. Furthermore, the Ministry of Agriculture has urged the necessity for employing brick and stone as universal building materials, instead of wood, as at present, if the country's timber resources are to be rationally conserved. The value of Lithuania's timber exports for the first ten months of 1921 was 165,413,566 marks.

AGRARIAN REFORM.

Agrarian reform in Lithuania has now been under way since 1919, although the formal enactment dealing with this subject was adopted by the Constituent Assembly only in February 1922. The special objects of this law are to provide land for the landless and to increase the holdings of those who at present possess an insufficient quantity ; to create conditions favourable to the development of rural economy, more particularly small and medium-sized farms ; and to place under State control those national resources which in private possession tend to be wasted.

To this end the State will appropriate the so-called " majorats," or entailed estates, and lands granted by the former Russian Government either in fee simple or on privileged conditions ; certain lands belonging to the former Peasants' Land Bank and Nobles' Bank ; lands of private persons who own more than 375 acres in the first place, and more than 200 in the second place, leaving to such persons 200 acres, the site of which they are free to choose. These lands will be alienated with all immovables, with the exception of industrial and commercial establishments.

Majorat estates and lands granted by the former Russian Government as gifts or on privileged conditions, and the lands of the former Peasants' and Nobles' Banks are taken over by the State without indemnity ; the rest are bought by the State at a pre-war price. The State assumes the mortgage debts with which these latter are encumbered, and deducts such sums from the price to be paid to the former owners. The larger and more neglected estates will first be dealt with, whilst properties not exceeding 375 acres will be appropriated at a later date. The law allows foreign owners to liquidate their holdings during three years.

Alienated lands will serve to create farms of from about 20 to 50 acres, which will be given to the landless and insufficiently landed citizens. Nevertheless, care will be taken not to cut up lots, the preservation of which,

9

for local reasons, is deemed necessary. In addition to the creation of farms, alienated lands will be utilized for urban needs—the extension of towns, parks, kitchen gardens, experimental farms, agricultural schools, charitable institutions, etc.

For the lots which they thus receive the new owners are required to pay the State sixteen quintals of rye per hectare (say two and a half acres), or the value of such quantity. Should the owner be unable to do this at once, he is granted a delay of thirty-six years in consideration of an annual payment of from half to three poods (one pood equals 36 lbs. avoirdupois) of rye per hectare, with interest at the rate of 5 per cent. on the amount outstanding. Families of men who have fallen in the defence of their country, wounded soldiers, and certain volunteers receive free grants. Moreover, all the military recipients of land enjoy for ten years a free of interest grant of 80 poods of grain and 100 trunks of timber for building purposes.

For the realization of agrarian reform there is created a Central Office with special organs in the districts. It is proposed to acquire the requisite funds to implement the reform through the sale of lots not liable to division, and the organization of an agrarian hypothec bank designed to furnish loans to small and medium holders over and above the general State resources.

Agrarian reform further contemplates the rational control of the work of splitting up villages into separate farms, already under way ; the suppression of survivals of serfdom in the form of common pasturage, servitude, etc.

It is estimated that agrarian reform will affect some 2,300 to 3,000 landlords, and an area, for the part of Lithuania free from Polish occupation, of about 2,500,000 acres, whereof a million acres consist of forests and 1,500,000 acres of fields.

On the basis of 200 acres per capita, 3,000 landlords will need 600,000 acres, leaving some 900,000 acres available for appropriation, out of which it is estimated between 25,000 and 30,000 farms can be created. Considering that small proprietors will receive only supplementary lots below the average in size, it is expected that with the disposable land fund it will be possible to settle between 35,000 and 40,000 families.

The area accruing from distributed estates and cut-up villages was about 38,000 acres in 1919, 92,000 acres in 1920, and more than 225,000 acres in 1921. Of the last-named figure, about 75,000 acres were parcelled out of estates, and the balance from cut-up villages. In 1921–22 4,362 lots were made out of cut-up villages, and from divided estates 1,400 lots were bestowed upon soldiers, 900 lots upon the landless, and 1,800 lots upon those with insufficient land. On the whole, during 1921–22 the work of agrarian readjustment affected 8,000 families.

Thanks to the larger number of land-surveyors now at work and steadily increasing, it is anticipated that the area distributed will be proportionately augmented. The Minister of Agriculture's estimate for 1922 was about 525,000 acres, and the work, if continued at this rate, should be accomplished in seven or ten years.

The present number of farms is estimated at 200,000, which, with the realization of agrarian reform, will probably be increased to 240,000.

The Department of Agriculture now has under its jurisdiction about 1,100 estates and subsidiary estates, with a total area of about 325,000 acres, which are rented to a considerable number of small holders, several thousands in all, the balance having been already divided and allotted to the soldier owners, to landless and insufficiently landed persons. Besides these 325,000 acres, the Department of Agriculture has under its jurisdiction land appropriated for military needs, and not yet divided, also monastic and former colonists' land. The total quantity of land taken over by the Ministry of Agriculture is not less than a third of the total land appropriated. But it has to be borne in mind that this land constitutes the sole source for the further work of achieving agrarian reform. During 1921–22 the military received 1,400 farms; in 1922–23 they will probably receive some 3,000. This means that for soldiers alone a very large quantity of grain must be appropriated. If the Ministry of Agriculture did not possess this source, it would be necessary to allot a considerable sum in the Budget for the purchase of grain, which in turn would involve a very elaborate organization, while, too, such wholesale purchases would greatly raise the price of grain.

Of all the Baltic States it is safe to say that the Lithuanian Agrarian Law is the mildest in its incidence. In the wake of the Russian Revolution and the emancipation of these Border States, no government refusing to satisfy the peasant land hunger could have survived twenty-four hours. As I have already shown elsewhere, the recognition of the necessity for land reform is not even a party issue in Lithuania ; on this all parties, Right, Left and Centre, are entirely agreed. Even the Social Democrats, who in principle do not recognize private land-ownership, have bowed to expediency and reconciled themselves to the realities of life. But the Agrarian Law applies the principle of compensation for all land thus appropriated.

LITHUANIAN INDUSTRIES.

Whilst in no sense an industrial country, Lithuania before the war could boast 5,140 industrial establishments of various kinds, with a productive value of 62 million Russian gold roubles. Of these 35 per cent. manufactured food products and beverages, 12 per cent. were for the working up of hides, bones and other animal by-products, 10 per cent. for wood-working, 25 per cent. for clay products, 3 per cent. for weaving, 4 per cent. for manufactured chemical products, and 11 per cent. for other miscellaneous products. Incidentally, one of the biggest iron foundries in Russia, that of Tillman, is at Kaunas. During the war the larger industrial establishments were dismantled or destroyed by the Russians themselves, but are gradually recovering. At Šiauliai (Shavli) are several tanneries which before the war ranked amongst the biggest in the world. These are now being restored to working order.

It goes without saying that the most prosperous future awaits those branches of both commerce and industry associated more particularly with agriculture. The weaving of flax fibre affords a case in point. If only 40 per cent. of the present annual output were woven in Lithuania, it would represent a value of several hundreds of millions of marks.

Referring to this subject, the new Lithuanian Prime Minister, in a declaration made before the Constituent Assembly on February 8, 1922, said that the Government proposed to devote attention to those branches of trade and industry which work up the raw products of agriculture and prepare the worked-up products for export, the Government considering that such branches should occupy the first place among the various classifications of Lithuanian trade and industry.

The Lithuanian peasant is undeniably skilful in the sphere of handicrafts. Members of the family weave linen and woollen clothing of excellent quality, and make wooden articles of every description, some of these being of high artistic value, in this respect recalling the " kustarnaya rabota " of the Russian villages. It is not, therefore, at all unreasonable to anticipate that with the introduction of capital a flourishing textile industry might be built up in Lithuania, seeing that the people both like and understand this sort of work.

The amber industry should not be overlooked. The Baltic coast is the only area in the world where the collecting, digging and manufacture of amber constitute a practical industry. The amber is found in the so-called " blue earth " layers of the Tertiary period (the layers are from 2 to $3\frac{1}{2}$ feet thick), not only on the beach, but farther inland. Even before the time of Herodotus, as shown by excavations of Greece, Italy and Egypt, Baltic amber was known to the ancient world. In our times the value of amber has diminished, but even so the industry continues to exist in Lithuania Minor. All products of amber, such as necklaces, buttons, buckles, cigarette-holders, etc., which are displayed in the windows of the jewellery stores, come from Lithuanian soil. In the future this industry could be greatly expanded.

Besides agricultural products and timber, there are other resources for the potential increase of the country's production—such as large deposits of peat, chalk, quartz, and sand suitable for glass manufacture, clay for the pottery industry, and mineral springs in Birstona and Druskenikai containing a large percentage of radium, etc. Prospecting has also revealed the existence of oil-shales and coal seams rich enough to repay exploitation.

There are not many waterfalls in Lithuania, but the Nemunas(Niemen) River offers quite a head along its course, so powerful, indeed, that the strongest swimmer cannot make the slightest progress against the current. No doubt this force will be utilized in the future. For example, were the two bends of the river near Birstona straightened, the project would develop enough power to run many large industrial plants as well as electric railways. There are also many other swift currents that can be harnessed.

TRADE FIGURES.

Turning to trade, exports and imports in 1913, exclusive of Memel, showed the following figures. Exports about £4,000,000, imports about £2,500,000. Exports were composed chiefly of breadstuffs, cattle and their products, and timber ; imports, coal, iron, textiles, and metal manufactures, including machinery.

For 1921 exports totalled 631,964,118 marks in value, in round figures. The biggest individual items are : Eggs, 75,762,185 in number, valued at 147,580,576 marks ; timber of all kinds, 195,610,618 marks ; flax-seed and tow, 184,885,016 marks ; pig bristles, 21,933,102 marks ; and hides, 20,393,953 marks. In percentages, timber represented 32 per cent., flax about 30 per cent., eggs and chickens 25 per cent., livestock 9·1 per cent., and rags 1 per cent.

Of these exports in 1921, Germany took 51·3 per cent., England 27·1 per cent. (chiefly eggs, amounting to 135,389,000 marks), and Lithuania Minor 14 per cent. Very much smaller percentages went to Latvia, Czecho-Slovakia, Russia, Sweden, Denmark, and America.

Imports for 1921 amounted to 879,881,980 marks in round figures. Of these the most important group consisted of textiles, representing 31·5 per cent. of the total value. Iron and metal products constituted 18·4 per cent., sugar 9·5 per cent., herrings 3·5 per cent., salt 1·3 per cent., and tobacco and tobacco goods 2 per cent. of the total. Among countries of origin, Germany heads the list with 70·72 per cent.; Lithuania Minor follows with 11·95 per cent.; then comes Danzig, 6·79 per cent.; Holland, 3·38 per cent.; America, 3·06 per cent.; Latvia, 1·6 per cent.; and England, 0·85 per cent. Czecho-Slovakia, Italy, Russia and Esthonia, and Japan furnished inconsiderable quantities.

To show the expansion of Lithuania's purchasing power, it may be pointed out that her imports for April 1921 alone, i.e. 70,000,000 marks in value, exceeded by 10,000,000 marks the total for the first quarter of 1920, which was only 60,000,000 marks. In 1920 the imports totalled 428,728,541 marks, and the exports 501,797,168 marks. Given better political conditions, especially the removal of the constant Polish menace, greater production and larger exports and imports would be assured.

LITHUANIAN FINANCES.

Reference has already been made to the Ost currency and to the Government's intention to get rid of this as soon as possible in favour of a purely Lithuanian money suitably guaranteed with gold. In spite of numerous economic and political difficulties, ordinary revenue is now sufficient to cover ordinary expenditure, and were it not for the exigencies of national defence, more particularly, coupled with extraordinary outlays required for construction (railway stations, workshops, bridges, rolling-stock, etc.), there would be no deficit. The direct taxes levied by the State are: Real property tax, tax on private forests up to 8 per cent. of sales of timber, patents for commerce and industry, progressive inheritance tax. Indirect taxes are: Customs duties, taxes on matches, tobacco and alcohol, export licences, registrations and stamp taxes. A liquor sale monopoly, not only for revenue, but as a means of coping with intemperance and secret distilling, and a tobacco monopoly are contemplated.

Under the Russo-Lithuanian Peace Treaty of 1920, Russia has paid Lithuania the sum of 3,000,000 roubles gold, which will probably be utilized in connexion with the scheme for an emission bank to help in the extension of credit upon reasonable terms to commerce and industry.

The total State expenses in 1920 amounted to 422,329,000 marks against a population of 2,500,000, or about 170 marks *per capita*. The expenses in 1921 were 801,523,000 marks against a population of 2,750,000, an average of 291 marks *per capita*. Revenue for 1920 amounted to 422,329,209 marks, and for 1921 to 766,472,729 marks.

Lithuania's foreign indebtedness is inconsiderable. The principal items are :

To the American Treasury, 882,136 dollars, dating from June 30, 1919, for various products, medicines, aid rendered to poor children by the American Red Cross. Interest, at 5 per cent. ; redeemable June 30, 1922.

To the American Treasury, 4,159,491 dollars, from June 28, 1919, for merchandise received from American stocks in France (sugar, tinned goods, medical instruments, pharmaceutical supplies, etc.). Interest, 5 per cent. ; redeemable June 30, 1922.

To Great Britain, £16,811 12s. 4d., for tonnage for transport of above supplies from France. Interest, 6 per cent. ; redeemable January 1, 1925.

On June 1, 1920, the Government floated the so-called " Liberty Loan," which was covered chiefly by Lithuanians in the United States, and has realized to date some two million dollars. The rate of interest is 5 per cent., and date of redemption July 1, 1934.

The sum of 5,000,000 francs is owing to France for locomotives and other material received in 1919. About a million francs of this amount has been reimbursed.

During the occupation Germany advanced merchandise and funds amounting to 100,000,000 marks, but as against this must be set the enormous values of which the country was denuded in foodstuffs and raw material by Germany, besides which, under the Versailles Treaty, Germany forfeits any claim she may formerly have possessed against any of the Border States.

Among internal loans, the first was floated in 1919, for one year, at 5 per cent., and yielded 12,149,200 marks. With the exception of 510,000 marks, this loan has already been redeemed.

A second short-term loan at 6 per cent. was floated June 15, 1921 and realized 42,000,000 marks. It was redeemable in May 1922.

In August 1921 an internal loan in Treasury Bonds, bearing 4 per cent., was issued, and yielded 4,928,200 marks. It falls due in 1928.

In November 1921 an extraordinary loan at 3·6 per cent. was floated for purposes of national defence, and has yielded to date 27,669,250 marks. It matures in 1923.

Before the war there were 300 State credit establishments and 500 private establishments, with a capital of 260,000,000 gold roubles, and savings bank - deposits amounted to 160,000,000 gold roubles. There were also 184 separate co-operative organizations, with 75,521 members, and a capital of 9,000,000 roubles. These organizations also had their own banks. Although the *post-bellum* figures cannot yet vie with the foregoing, a steady revival has set in, the co-operative movement being particularly strong. The following figures bear witness to the recent growth of this movement : In 1919 (from March to December) there were registered 261 co-operatives, composed of 253 consumers' societies, 6 producers' societies, and 2 agricultural societies. In 1920 (January to December) 78 were registered, composed of 59 consumers' societies, 15 producers' societies, 3 agricultural societies, and 1 cultural society. In 1921 42 were registered, viz. 25 consumers', 8 producers', 6 cultural, and 3 agricultural societies. In January 1922 6 were registered, i.e. 5 consumers' and 1 cultural. The total from March 1919 to January 1922 is therefore 387, i.e. consumers', 342 ; producers', 29 ; agricultural, 8'; and cultural, 8. Of the foregoing societies, however, the accounts of only

85 are available at the time of writing with regard to operations for 1919 and 1920.   These show:

	Marks
Various goods	3,776,282
Cash in hand	920,975
Capital	1,435,946
Turnover	17,314,298

The net profit was 1,435,936 marks, out of which 62,877 marks were allotted in dividends to 13,561 members.   The co-operative movement in Lithuania is worthy of serious attention from British business circles, since its ubiquity should afford them the most direct medium for getting into touch with general purchasers.

Several banks have been established since the war, and are rapidly extending their sphere of usefulness. They comprise the following :

Agricultural Bank (Ūkio Bankas), with 10,000,000 marks capital, and deposits totalling 47,000,000 marks.

The Bank of Industry and Commerce (Prekybos ir Pramonés Bankas), capital 12,000,000 marks, and deposits 27,700,000 marks.

International Bank (Tarptautinis Bankas), capital 5,000,000 marks, deposits 16,675,000 marks.

Commercial Bank (Komercijos Bankas), capital 4,000,000 marks, deposits 48,000,000 marks.

Central Jewish Co-operative Bank (Centr. žydu koperacijai remti Bankas), capital 3,010,000 marks, deposits 5,500,000 marks.

Bank of Credit (Kredito Bankas), capital 3,000,000 marks, deposits 5,700,000 marks.

A very appreciable increase of banking investments has followed in the wake of the peace treaty with Russia, and a satisfactory settlement of the Polish-Lithuanian dispute would undoubtedly encourage still further development in this direction.

The project for an Emission Bank, already referred to elsewhere, contemplates the formation of a joint-stock company.   The shares will be nominal, two-thirds being reserved for Lithuanian citizens and the remaining third open to foreign subscription.   The proposed capital is 2,000,000 gold dollars.   The manager of the bank and one of his assistants will be appointed by the Government, while one other assistant and two directors will be elected by the shareholders. One of the directors will be a foreigner. The Council of Administration will consist of nine members, i.e. a managing director, two assistants, and six members elected by the shareholders. Two places will be reserved for foreigners. The bank's monopoly will be for fifteen years. The notes issued are to be guaranteed up to one-third by a reserve of precious metal, and the remainder by foreign securities or merchandise. The right of emission is limited to 3,000,000,000 " auksinas," any extension beyond that requiring parliamentary sanction.

The proposed creation of a national currency to replace the depreciated Ost mark is associated with the foregoing project. The unit will be the " auksinas," equal to 1/200th of a gold dollar. This money will be issued in the near future, as soon as the Emission Bank can be organized. Negotiations were actually begun in March 1922 between representatives of the German Reich and Darlehnskasse Ost, on the one hand, and representatives of the Lithuanian State, on the other, for the liquidation of the Ost currency, but are not yet terminated.

COMMUNICATIONS.

The total railway mileage for all Lithuania is 1,552 miles, of which 1,180 miles are broad gauge and the rest narrow gauge. The roadbeds are generally in good condition, but the ties need replacing. Thirty per cent. of the railway stations were destroyed during the war, but have been provisionally rebuilt, as also the bridges, most of which are wood. Rolling-stock is greatly needed. The Lithuanian railways in 1913 yielded a gross revenue of about £2,400,000 ; net revenue, without deduction for sinking-fund, new equipment, etc., about £1,300,000. Under the terms of the agreement between the Allied Military Mission and the German Railway Administration, Lithuania was to receive 88 locomotives and 1,400 cars from Germany, for damage inflicted by the Bermondt invasion,

but at the time of writing the complement had not yet
been handed over.   The lines in 1921–22 yielded an income
of 114,942,000 marks, but showed a small net deficit in
comparison with outlays.   Any comparison between pre-
war and post-war figures under this head must not lose
sight of the fact that through the Polish occupation of the
Vilnius territory the Lithuanian Government is deprived
of a very important portion of the total railway network.

The system as a whole was bequeathed to the country
by the Russians, and in part was altered during the
German occupation.   When planned by Russia the lines
were intended to serve the needs of Russian export, or
they pursued purely strategic aims.   They are not, therefore, properly adapted to the economic and geographic
requirements of the country.   The Lithuanian Government is now considering a project for a network of broad-
gauge lines better suited to these national needs, supple-
menting the present system with lines of perhaps more
local importance, especially to feed the comparatively
neglected districts, as regards communications, and thus
facilitate the growth of agriculture, commerce and industry
throughout the country.

WATERWAYS.

The Nemunas (Niemen), the country's greatest river,
is 961 kilometres in length, its source being in White
Russia.   Its lower reaches, 112 kilometres in length, form
the boundary between East Prussia and Lithuania Minor.
The Nemunas is open only during four or five months of
the year over a stretch of 200 kilometres from its mouth,
and its navigable portion in Lithuanian territory, from
Jurburg to Kovno, does not exceed 110 kilometres, and
even this stretch is only suitable for the rafting of timber.
Owing to the prevalence of shallows, rapids and sandbanks,
navigation is attended with numerous difficulties.   The
principal tributary of the Nemunas, the Vilija, or Neris, is
navigable for small steamers for 45 miles.   The Nemunas
thus forms the backbone of Lithuania's system of com-

munications. The mouth of this river on the Baltic has hitherto been in the hands of the Germans, whose traditional intention, as I have pointed out in the chapter on the Memel question, has been to control the foreign trade of Lithuania and to debar the country from independent access to the sea.

The economic policy outlined by the new Lithuanian Government is based upon free initiative and free competition. It will be the aim of the Government to afford foreign capital an opportunity to participate in the development of the country's trade, in the case of States which harbour no designs to oppress or crush Lithuania economically.

Under satisfactory conditions, the safeguarding against attack from without, more particularly, Lithuania should be assured a highly prosperous future. Before the war, the Virbalis station (Wirballen), on the Russo-East Prussian frontier, was one of the most important continental customs points for trade between Western Europe and Russia, and as the quickest transit route in this respect, Lithuania should play a leading rôle hereafter in the rehabilitation of economic intercourse between Russia and the outside world.

LEGAL REFORM IN LITHUANIA.

With the substitution of a genuinely native régime for what before the war was a purely Russian administration, in the confines of the present Lithuanian State, and German domination during the period of occupation, the new leaders of the nation had to face the herculean task of effecting transition from one language to the other in every branch of public and official life. It was one thing, and a comparatively simple thing at that, to replace Russian with Lithuanian in the colloquial intercourse of all departments and those having dealings with them; it was another, and an immeasurably more difficult thing, to dispense with the heritage of Russian practice embodied in written laws and regulations applicable to every conceivable official contingency. Indeed, it would have been physically impossible, even if it had been desirable, to do this immediately. With a prudence and wisdom which have been conspicuous throughout the regeneration of Lithuanian nationality, the new Lithuanian leaders preferred to take over Russian law at the outset, but to inaugurate without delay the business of translating the same into Lithuanian, of adapting it to changed conditions, rejecting parts of it no longer in harmony with the principles of a democratic State, and gradually codifying it to satisfy the requirements of a thoroughly scientific system. Concurrently, the setting up of courts for the dispensation of justice has been attended with innumerable difficulties. It had been the consistent policy of the old Russian régime to suppress the Lithuanian tongue by every conceivable means. This has already been shown in previous chapters. Thus it followed that many Lithuanians educated in Russia had a better literary knowledge of Russian than of their native speech. Since the renascence of the Lithuanian people all this is being rapidly changed, but it has not always been easy to find sufficient trained jurists with perfect knowledge of both languages, without which the work of codifying the laws in Lithuanian at the present moment cannot be satisfactorily accomplished.

It appears from information furnished by the Lithuanian Minister of Justice that a great deal is now being done to bring both the courts and the laws in line with modern demands. The appeal machinery is being entirely overhauled. The Constituent Assembly has passed a Bill for the establishment of a court of cassation to which recourse will lie from justices of the peace and the district courts. At the same time the competence of the various lower courts has been largely extended. Formerly justices of the peace had no power to deal with cases involving sums over a thousand marks. Now, by virtue of the law of March 14, 1919, the limit has been raised to five thousand marks, except in cases of horse-stealing, which have to go to the district courts. A Bill has also been introduced increasing the scope of court orders (*sudebnye prikazy*). Hitherto court orders could be issued for fines up to fifty roubles, and detention up to fifteen days. The new Bill proposes to make court orders applicable to offences against the Excise and Customs regulations, secret distilling, illegal felling of timber, non-fulfilment of regulations, etc. In such cases the justices of the peace, after having examined the militia reports and other evidence, and being satisfied of the guilt of the accused, may inflict penalties by court order. Cases of this kind must be dealt with not earlier than twenty-four hours, and not later than seven days from the alleged commission of the offence. The accused in his turn has the right to appeal to the district court. In civil suits, justices of the peace may sit on cases involving movables and immovables up to ten thousand marks.

A reform of great importance is the contemplated introduction of trial by jury, which has not hitherto been in operation. It is now provided that after election of an organ of local administration for a term of three years, trial by jury may be instituted in the district courts. Steps are also being taken to increase facilities for legal education, so that the cadre of candidates for judicial appointments and court pleading may be far larger than at present.

Under the Law of January 16, 1919, special delegates from the Lithuanian Ministry of Justice took over from the German courts (Friedensgericht, Bezirksgericht, Obergericht and Kriegsgericht) all cases, documents and money. This law provides that in the organization of courts, legal proceedings, preliminary hearings and sentences in criminal and civil cases, the laws formerly in operation during the Russian administration must be applied in so far as they do not contradict the Lithuanian Constitution and the changes contemplated by the law in question.

Court proceedings must be conducted in the Lithuanian language, protocols, judgments and sentences are written in this tongue. Judges must be able to express themselves in other local languages (Polish and White Russian) where the percentage of non-Lithuanian-speaking citizens renders this necessary. Knowledge of Jewish is not indicated owing to the small number of lawyers familiar with that speech. Where litigants do not understand Lithuanian, interpreters are supplied.

The Criminal Code and Regulations for Bills of Exchange (Veksel) are already translated from Russian into Lithuanian. In other cases the Russian text may be made use of. The work of preparing the Civil and Criminal Codes is one of immense difficulty, and cannot be finished in a day. The materials necessary for the task are, however, being prepared A good deal depends on the consummation of agrarian reform by the Constituent Assembly, the supply of funds, and the reversion of life to normal channels.

The Minister of Justice is quoted as saying that since the cessation of the German occupation there has been a steady diminution of crime. Stern measures have been adopted to deal with lawlessness, including the introduction of martial law. The militia also have gradually improved and gathered experience, so that they too are better able to cope with crime. Horse-stealing and secret distilling are among the most prevalent offences.

CHAPTER XII

LITHUANIAN TYPES AND CHARACTER

WRITERS like Vidūnas and Šalkauskis have indulged in very acute analysis of the Lithuanian character, but although Lithuanians themselves, they have never written anything more flattering about their own people than foreign investigators, preferably Russian, German and French, who have all been most powerfully impressed by the distinctive traits of this interesting race. In the following pages, therefore, I have drawn largely upon such sources for a brief pen picture of both its intellectual and physical aspects.

Lithuanians and Slavs (says a well-known Russian author, Viatcheslav Ivanov) are two branches of the same family; but the memory of the Aryan cradle is more alive among the Lithuanians than among us. In the intimate life of the village, the thought and tradition of the old, in the living tissue of the language, in the respiration even of that collective being which we call the soul of a people, still vibrate the chords of the antique conception of the world. Above this little people the old mythical oak extends its moving branches, which still put forth an invisible efflorescence and murmur the indistinct whisper of its omniscience, and across the veil where now is hesitating the luminous regard of man, of people of antique calm, contemplate the intense life of nature in its most secret depths.

E. Réclus, in his *Universal Geography*, has attempted to sketch the Lithuanian national temperament in more concrete lines:

A people of woodmen, of waggoners, of cultivators, very much attached to traditional customs, the Lithuanians willingly submit to destiny and do not seek to influence it beforehand by their will. The phlegm of the Lithuanians has become proverbial; no other people accommodates itself with such tranquillity to the vicissitudes of life.

10

Šalkauskis, in his remarkable study *Sur les Confins de Deux Mondes,* finds that the foregoing comment calls for some modification. He adds that when the necessity arises the Lithuanian will deploy his forces and unchain his anger. He who reacts feebly to the ordinary blows and shocks of life, responds suddenly with surprising violence when his patience and his endurance are at an end. Concentrated in himself, more inclined to contemplation than to action, the Lithuanian manifests this temperament in his exterior. " The peasants of Lithuania," writes Réclus, " contrast singularly with the Poles in the simplicity of their costume. They avoid striking colours, daring fashions, lace and fringe. Their sombre clothing without embroidery attests their national modesty ; they do not try to make themselves conspicuous. Michelet, comparing the Lithuanians with the Poles, ' sons of the sun,' calls them ' sons of the shadow.' "

The popular poesy of the Lithuanians has inspired in Réclus the following description of their moral traits :

Their songs or *dainos* reveal their naked soul. They are acute observers, sometimes gently ironical, tender, melancholy, full of the sentiment of nature. Although they have often been obliged to make war and have also possessed great leaders, these debonair people have not preserved the memory of a single hero ; they sing of no exploit of war, they do not boast of any battle won ; they confine themselves to bewailing those who are dead. In this respect they are perhaps unique among European peoples. They are distinguished also from other continental races by the delicate reserve, by the modest discretion with which all their popular songs speak of love.

Such, then, is the Lithuanian as Nature made him. This passive temperament germane to the Oriental excited the curiosity of Réclus, who wrote :

The people, for long oppressed by the forests of the Niemen, are not of those who can compare their share of influence with that which the other civilized peoples of the continent have exercised. One asks oneself even with surprise how a race composed almost entirely of men, refined, intelligent, full of imagination and poesy, " loyal, strong in the consciousness of their personal dignity " (Kant, preface to Milke's *Lithuanian Grammar*), had not been able to give birth to a single great poet or to some eminent genius in the world of mind.

In the opinion of Šalkauskis, much of the seeming paradox in Lithuanian character may be explained by the meeting of East and West on Lithuanian soil. Lithuania has passed through both the active and passive phases. Provoked by the invasions of her neighbours, she, so to speak, emerged from herself and from her passivity to come into contact with diverse nations, above all the Russian, the Polish and the German. Thus she acquired the active temperament hitherto lacking. Then, yielding to the return wave, her national spirit, now capable of creating, enters again into itself and works on the synthesis of the primitive Oriental elements and the Occidental elements thus acquired. " It is in this period," Šalkauskis adds, " that the Lithuanian people find themselves to-day ; their renascence dates from the day when they entered into it."

Further :

> The productions of the Lithuanian national intellect differ as the latter is subjected to the action and influence of one or other of the above-mentioned nations. In relation with Russia and in the domain of Greco-Russian civilization, Lithuania endeavoured to establish between the Orient and Occident a material and political equilibrium. Her external activity expended itself in the struggle against Tartars and Teutons, and her internal activity manifested itself in the legislative function by the elaboration of the famous Lithuanian Statute, superior to anything that the Russian people had attempted till then in that line.

At critical moments in Lithuanian history the Lithuanian temperament has shown itself capable of amazing effort, in the XIth century, for example, when the pressure of neighbouring peoples provoked on the part of the Lithuanians an energetic resistance which, from legitimate defence, soon transformed itself into an expansion of conquest ; and again in the XIXth century, when the crushing weight of an alien yoke stimulated the impetus of the national renascence and gave it an irresistible vitality. When reacting on the first-named occasion the Lithuanian genius prepared the creation of a strong and powerful State ; to-day the momentum of its energy has led it into a path on which it will not stop until it has assured its national independence. Although several centuries divide the two epochs, and although the present-day activity of the Lithuanians is taking a different direction, Šalkauskis detects a very close link between them :

> It is because in their efforts to create for the assistance of the State a national civilization the Lithuanians were obliged not only to give way, but even to submit at first to the influence and subsequently to the domination of the foreigner, that we see them to-day, in order to recover their independence, working with ardour in the acquisition of a superior intellectual culture.

Turning from these more or less philosophical aspects of the question to rather more concrete considerations, I will quote what Vidūnas has written about the physical characteristics of his countrymen and women :

> The true Lithuanian type (he says) is slender and above rather than below the medium height. It has blue eyes, fair hair, a fresh and healthy complexion. To designate this there are in Lithuanian several expressions. It is above all the complexion of young Lithuanian women that particularly strikes one. It is white, delicate, with a beautiful rose colour in the cheeks. The lips are exceptionally fresh. Women in good health, who have not been guilty of excesses, preserve all this splendour till a ripe age, whether they are married or not. . . . Persons with black hair and eyes also possess this white and delicate skin. The stranger is often inclined to think artificial colour has been applied, whereas the true Lithuanian woman, in place of all that, relies upon fresh air, good water and her own clean and pure blood. The face is long, with a broad and prominent brow, the lower part of the face being often small and narrow ; the jaws, on the other hand, are projecting. Here probably is a characteristic resulting from a Mongolian strain. A remarkable thing, which one frequently encounters, is the classic profile with the straight line from brow to nose. The limbs are long and thin, the foot very arched, the Lithuanian having a light and easy step, to describe which the language possesses a series of expressions. He is also naturally skilful in all sorts of work, thanks undoubtedly to a special disposition in muscles and limbs, without which this skill of the Lithuanian would not have become proverbial.

Vidūnas also remarks on the absence of grossness from Lithuanian speech, in contrast to the German of corresponding social position :

> It is, above all, in his relations with Nature that one can note the sensibility of the Lithuanian. Everything alive is for him

connected with man, and he moulds his line of conduct on this idea. In his songs he treats the trees as if they were his brothers. The song of the cuckoo is a greeting from loved beings, so much so that he will even imagine that his mother or little sister has assumed the form of the bird which is fluttering above his head. Among animals the horse is above all the object of his tenderness Preference for the horse is certainly something innate in him. It can be remarked among the children of both sexes. And many persons claim to be able to tell merely by seeing whether horses have been bred and cared for by Lithuanians. The Lithuanian horse is not only an instrument of toil; it is also a friend to man. It gives the impression of having learnt to suffer and rejoice with man.

The idea that Nature is an intermediary between men, that she takes part in their joys and sorrows, is very strong among the Lithuanians The forests and the thickets sigh with him; the flowers and the sun's rays rejoice with him, and the light of the stars accompanies him for consolation.

Particularly marked is the Lithuanian's passion for trees. In his eyes there is something sacred in the forest, and he loves to live in a home surrounded with woods. Practical needs seem a secondary consideration. That is why in his songs and legends he returns constantly to the forest.

That a race possessing these distinguished characteristics should have exercised comparatively so little influence upon European civilization, Vidūnas explains by its relatively numerical weakness, by the lack of a national organization absolutely necessary for the development of internal forces, and above all by the fact that Lithuanian intelligence has been constantly at the service of other nations, and has apparently never had a proper chance of asserting itself. But study of the proverbs and sayings of the Lithuanians, of their popular tales and poems, will convince one of their quite exceptional sagacity.

A very refreshing Lithuanian trait is a freedom of attitude which makes no distinction between classes; a typical Lithuanian will bear himself the same in the presence of a lord or a beggar. The Lithuanian is a man of his word. The head or father of the family gives his orders in the fewest words, but without appeal.

One can have entire confidence in the promise of a

Lithuanian. Even to-day large sums pass from hand to hand on the simple word without written acknowledgment.

Despite centuries of political dependence, the Lithuanian has not lost a certain masterful temperament. This has nothing in common with the wish to enslave others, but is rather a feeling of pure personal dignity. With this is combined another trait less strongly marked in other races. He does not fear solitude, which for him is often a kind of refuge from which perhaps emanates the primitive " atomic " character of the Lithuanian national life, the want of harmony which one may even observe to-day, although the suffering of recent decades has wrought marvels in this direction.

In his intercourse with strangers the Lithuanian is generally reserved and chary of speech. Although the language lends itself admirably to eloquence, the Lithuanian, until he knows you well, is laconic, and rarely disposed to mingle in conversation unless this touches upon a subject interesting to him as a Lithuanian, while a momentary outburst is often succeeded by relapse into contemplative calm.

Other impressive qualities are boldness, tenacity of purpose and an iron will. Once a Lithuanian has resolved to embark upon a given course of action nothing will turn him from his purpose. At the present day these traits, sometimes degenerating into obstinacy, manifest themselves in an inordinate love for litigation which is keeping the newly-established courts decidedly busy.

The Lithuanian considers that his own penetration and decision have a value superior to any money. He will neglect no sacrifice for that which he deems good and just. He gives himself completely to the thing or the person that he honours. If he is deceived he does not take vengeance. His attitude is rather one of shame mingled with contempt—shame for the unworthiness of the erstwhile object of his respect. In one of his stories Wichert has made good use of this characteristic. He does not make the lover slay the betrayer of his fiancée ;

instead the lover himself commits suicide. In real life, however, suicide is very rare among the Lithuanians, who throughout the centuries have remained singularly immune from the phenomena of degeneracy.

Forbearance and a too trusting disposition are typical Lithuanian qualities which run through history. It was thus that Keistutis fell into the hands of Jagellon. It was thus that Vytautas lost his great battle against the Tartars. And this disposition was largely responsible for the fatal union with Poland which the Council of the League of Nations would fain have the Lithuania of to-day repeat. On the other hand, the Lithuanian does not easily forget a betrayal of his confidence, as the Poles are now finding to their cost. The latter's flagrant breach of the Suvalkai agreement has from the first proved a stumbling-block to any *modus vivendi*.

The Lithuanian is temperamentally religious. He is much given to acts of devotion in which singing largely figures. In many homes a verse is sung before every meal. And before the commencement of a religious service, those who have assembled will sing with extraordinary fervour hymns which they themselves have selected. One or two will begin, others will join, and soon the entire company will be singing together. Hymns set to some ancient popular melody are generally preferred.

Among the Lithuanians there still survive numerous superstitions which are generally regarded as heritages of their former Paganism. Belief in the supernatural is very common and in certain of its forms this belief may be an echo of the cult of the dead and of ancestor worship. A rather voluminous collection of materials on this subject has been made by Vilius Kalvaitis and edited by Dr. Basanavičius under the title of *Gyvenimo Vėlių bei Velnių* (Life of Ghosts and Devils), Chicago, 1903. During recent years, too, a large number of religious fanatics and faith-healers of various kinds have made their appearance in Lithuania, as elsewhere. The names of some of these are still remembered. Vidūnas mentions one Piklaps who functioned in the Memel region about

1880 ; also Rodszuweit of Kartsninkai, near Pillkallen, between 1870 and 1880.   In many villages *zinciai*, or persons capable of curing both corporal and spiritual maladies, are held in high esteem and are often consulted in preference to regular doctors.

CHAPTER XIII

IN THE COUNTRY

In past times the inhabitants were distributed in scattered groups dwelling each, so to speak, in a sort of oasis hemmed in by fields and dense forests belonging to nobody. Even to-day in many of the older villages the arrangement of houses on either side of an interminable street, so favoured in Russia Proper, is less in evidence.

Where the older practice prevails, we find each farm absolutely isolated, with its own special entrance. The buildings rise in the midst of a garden which is surrounded with groves of birch, fir or oak and, in sandy regions, pine. That is why these farms are termed "sodiba," which means plantation.

Formerly a Lithuanian farm comprised a row of houses sometimes to the number of twenty. The grouping of these houses around the main dwelling was characteristic. The latter was called "namas," i.e. the home.

Vidūnas thus describes his parents' farm as it was somewhat later than 1850. In the middle of the garden rose the principal building, the "namas." About ten metres to the side of the latter was the "kletis," or store-house, two storeys high, with a large verandah, approached by two stone steps. Around the kletis were clumps of birch and maple. A little farther to the side of the kletis was a building for the storage of all sorts of implements. Beneath was a cellar into which one descended by steps in the wall. By the side of this building was a space enclosed with a hedge made of interlaced osiers. In the centre was a pond surrounded by grass in summer. Here the poultry disported themselves during the day, while at night they took refuge behind in the fowl roost.

On the other side of the main building stretched the larger part of the orchard traversed by a path leading to the spring. Behind the latter, separated by a hedge, extended a large open space covered with turf, forming the farmyard, around which were grouped the various stables and sheds for cattle, horses, sheep, etc.

Near the orchard was a space for hemp and hops; many bee-hives were also kept. By the side of the dwelling house, some distance outside the garden, was the thrashing floor with the baths (pirtis). In the direction of the stables were several additional houses where the families of the servants and other lodgers had their quarters.

To-day this arrangement of buildings is rarely found. The farm in question has been gradually transformed into a typical model of the German farm.

The most interesting building of the Lithuanian farm is the kletis which is also called "svirnas." Although usually styled loosely a storehouse, Vidūnas points out that in reality it is much more than that, as the numerous wooden carvings of the interior should indicate. In popular songs the kletis is always the centre of sentimental life. The girls of the household used to have their bedrooms in the kletis, and on the verandah they were accustomed to pursue their daily manual tasks. Close by the kletis was the flower garden of the daughters of the house where they grew rue throughout the summer. For the Lithuanian the kletis embodies all that he has acquired through the sweat of his brow; it is the spot towards which his thoughts ever turn, whereby the farm, the "sodiba" has its *raison d'être* and from which the farm and family issue and are renewed.

The house, properly speaking, and also the other buildings are for the most part constructed of wood, which is only natural in so heavily timbered a land as Lithuania. Through a large doorway one enters a spacious apartment at the opposite end of which is another door. This room might perhaps be regarded as a sort of vestibule, although its furnishing gives it another signification. The walls are hung with all kinds of household utensils. In the middle of one of the side walls is a huge fireplace surmounted by a chimney—the " dumlakas," from " dumas," smoke, and " lakinti," to cause to fly. Besides the central apartment there are two others which occupy the extremities of the building, and these again are often divided into two. The windows are small, as in nearly all farmhouses of every nation. The frames are generally painted white, the shutters in green or blue, but this again is not peculiar to the Lithuanians.

But originally this division into three apartments did not obtain in Lithuania. Descriptions of past centuries agree in declaring that formerly Lithuanian houses consisted of but the one room, which may help to explain why even to-day the same word is often used to signify both the chamber and the house.

The oldest part of the house divided into three is the " namas," home. It is the site of the hearth or fireplace which formerly was in the middle of the room : a fire was kept constantly burning. This house was the centre of the farm where all the members of the family who had their lodging outside assembled. Vidūnas opines that the old hearth may possibly have been copied from the scene of Lithuanian fire-worship, and adds that certain religious rites used to be practised by the hearth until modern times, albeit not in Russian Lithuania.

The other rooms of the Lithuanian dwelling serve for working and sleep. These were formerly situated in separate buildings but are now united under one roof. The working house, for example, where the women did their needlework and weaving, and the men kept their tools, has become the chamber most frequented by the members of the household. By the side of the stove was a niche in the wall where cooking was done in the winter on a portable hearth, the smoke escaping by a hole through the wall. The former sleeping house in many cases has become a convenient reception room.

A tendency still further to subdivide these rooms may sometimes be observed. The old desire to build many houses has given place to the multiplication of small rooms. To-day the Lithuanian almost always terms his home " namai," the plural form of " namas," probably because several houses are now joined into one.

The interior of a peasant's cottage does not reveal so easily as a more pretentious house its Lithuanian character, because it is often in almost imperceptible details that history manifests itself. The roof and walls are planked, and the earth is flagged. Wooden benches are ranged against the walls, and in one corner is a well scrubbed table. Near the entrance is a large stove surrounded by a ledge or in lieu thereof a bench. From · the ceiling, attached to a branch, hangs an elongated basket made of birch boughs. This is the " lopschis," the baby's cradle. Thanks to the elasticity of the branch this cradle can be very easily rocked. The depth of the " lopschis," as well as the large amount of cord with which it is tied to the branch make it impossible for the child to fall.

Most of the articles in the room are carvings or pictures of various kinds. The Lithuanian has always been celebrated for this sort of work. As far back as the XVIIth century a writer, speaking about the skill of the Lithuanian, quotes the proverb, " The Lithuanian rides on horseback into the forest and returns therefrom in a coach."

Nearly all Lithuanian graves are surmounted by large wooden crosses, though sometimes iron is used for this purpose instead of wood. Frequently the tombstones are of curious shape, which is not without traditional meaning and probably associated with mystical ideas. A reproduction of the human body is often very striking ; similarly birds are occasionally depicted in flight, whilst a triangle finishes off the tombstone. Here also the Lithuanian penchant for lively colours (other than in dress) asserts itself.

A very singular article used in the house was the " žibintas "—a receptacle, very often lavishly carved, which contained the chips and shavings with which the chamber of the spinning women was illuminated. As everywhere in peasants' houses, the spinning room was the hall of songs and stories. And every one of these old žibintas, with its bizarre paintings and motley carvings, has heard almost all of them, while lighting the labours of many generations of toilers.

Another interesting object is the " kanklys," a species of zither, which is also always carved. The kanklys is really an appendage of the žibintas, for it was in the nature of a fête when a " kanklyninkas " performed in the women's spinning room in much the same way as the peripatetic rhapsodist of the ancient Greeks. The kanklyninkas sang or recited to the accompaniment of his instrument.

Dress among the Lithuanians has altered with the times as in every other country ; but throughout certain characteristic features have survived. Old drawings indicate that the principal article of clothing for both sexes was a long garment of white linen resembling a shirt. Over this was worn a robe of various colours, which the wearer adjusted to suit his own fancy. Later, towards the XVth and XVIth century, two of these upper garments were worn. One end would be brought under the arms and fixed to the shoulder with a clasp. The two pieces of material crossed naturally at the back and in front. A belt above the hips gave stability to the whole. Often the upper garments would be simply white instead of coloured.

Colours were worn for joyous occasions, white being usual for graver festivals. This custom has survived to our own day as indicated in Lithuanian popular songs. Engravings of the XVIIth century (Pretorius) show that in place of wearing over the loose white under-garment two large pieces of material, women and young girls often wore two small pieces which descended from the hips at the sides, another in front and a fourth behind. Another garment would also be worn over these, white in hue. Embroidery and ornamentation woven into the white garments have always been popular.

In winter furs were worn. The feminine headgear called " kyka " has been retained till the present day. Young girls had their hair either unplaited, tied with a ribbon and adorned with a crown of rue which was gathered daily in the garden, or plaited and coiffured in different styles. But the last-named usage did not become general until recent times. On the feet shoes of leather or bark were worn. Sabots were unknown among the Lithuanians until the XVIIIth century.

At that date Lepner speaks about two white undergarments, which the Lithuanians wore in the Prussian region. The lower part of the body was covered with several garments already described, but over these was placed a sleeved coat, coloured blue or green, with a broad yellow collar, and cuffs of the same colour on very wide sleeves. For ceremonial occasions this coat was worn longer than in ordinary life. Over this again was put a linen garment entirely white. Shoes or boots, worn instead of bark slippers, were of drab leather.

Male dress has always been simpler than that of women. An upper garment with sleeves formed the man's entire equipment. In summer the upper garment was of white linen, in winter white or brown or grey wool. A belt encircled the body and was fastened with a buckle. Later the men wore an overcoat of grey cloth with a straight collar and wide skirts with black borders. On the head was a felt hat or in winter a leather cap.

In the XIXth century the women generally wore a robe instead of all the pieces of material above described. The name of these garments, which hung from the body or which enveloped the latter, has been transferred to the robe. They were in strips or squares, bright or sombre in colour, and were called " margine " or " inodine." Women now also wear a bodice imported by immigrants, the Salzbourgeois. It is often red or green, though in many places black is preferred. The taste for sombre colours is well developed, above all in the regions where a certain religious spirit drawn from the experience of life prevails, and where there is less belief in the prolongation of that which is essentially Lithuanian.

It is gratifying to be able to state that petticoats are generally short. Young girls and women wear white stockings and low shoes. The story that stockings were formerly unknown to the Lithuanians and that in their stead they were in the habit of wrapping their feet in cloth or linen is devoid of all foundation. The word employed to designate Russian socks, i.e. " autas," which means something which is drawn on like a boot, for example, serves to disprove the older report. But as Vidūnas says, the frequency of such inanities at the expense of the Lithuanians suggests either a deliberate desire to depict the people as devoid of all civilization or is due simply to crass ignorance.

Neither the bodice nor corset has come into general use, though the latter has always been worn in the form of a shirt-waist termed " papetis," which is often richly embroidered at the collar, sleeves and shoulders. Vidūnas denies the allegation that the Lithuanians learned the art of embroidery from immigrants, the Lithuanian language being particularly copious in expressions having to do with needlework. Moreover, it would be impossible to explain the universal inclination for work of this kind by mere imitation. Besides, productions of the seamstress's art are comparatively more numerous in Lithuania than among her neighbours of other nationalities. Embroidery on white material has ever been held in the highest esteem among Lithuanians, whilst embroidery in colours was in fashion for everyday use. It is only during the last dozen years or so that the latter has become somewhat neglected. The upper garment of blue or green mentioned by Lepner was still worn in the XIXth century and was called " pamustine." It was frequently lined with fur, the straight collar of sable and the shoulders adorned with multicoloured embroideries.

Great attention is devoted to the coiffure. The older practice of wearing the hair flowing loose has been entirely abandoned. The hair is now carefully parted and sometimes plaited over the ears. If the hair was not very thick, women until recently would introduce into their tresses, as a sort of " transformation," some wool—red, yellow, green, black or white in colour. On the other hand, if the hair was abundant, a black or coloured band was bound round the head with some white ornament in front called " raistis." In a series of oil paintings Edward Gisevius has shown samples of the Lithuanian costume and headdress. The Lithuanian Literary Society of Tilsit possesses several specimens.

Formerly the Lithuanians did not wear aprons, this fashion having been borrowed from immigrants. But until lately they often wore broad sashes, the long ends of which, ornamented with tassels, hung down at the side. This sash, styled "juosta," was very popular and still is, Lithuanian women spending a great deal of time in its preparation. The juosta also figures largely in love and is a favourite theme of sentimental ditties. The successful swain makes a juosta for his well beloved either as a sash or a collar. The symbols woven into it to form a scheme of ornament are not merely haphazard but until recently bore a special meaning, in this regard recalling Hindu necklaces with their magic formulas of love and healing.

White as a colour for dress enjoyed a great vogue up to about 1890 in the region of Šešupe. Worshippers at church thus attired offered a striking spectacle. The value of one's wardrobe was estimated chiefly by its rich embroideries and artistic texture. It is curious that the older forms of dress have survived longer in Prussian than in Russian Lithuania. As recently as 1907 there was a wonderful display of national costumes on Lithuanian fête days at Tilsit. On one occasion about three thousand persons assembled and prizes were given for the most beautiful Lithuanian costumes.

Turning to Lithuanian habits and customs, here also rural life provides the best field for their study, as it is the peasant who adheres most closely to tradition. "My mother (or father) used to do that," is a remark frequently heard from young Lithuanians. Among the peasantry the apportionment of time is largely determined by the exigencies of agriculture and stock-breeding. Only the more striking details can be mentioned here. The love of the Lithuanian for song everywhere and almost at all times is most marked. In those homes where the religious spirit is predominant the singing of a hymn constitutes the first and last collective act of the day. A verse is sung before meals, before starting out on a journey, or undertaking some difficult task, etc. In those homes where religion plays a less prominent rôle a popular song or an amusing story takes the place of the hymn. This characteristic Lithuanian trait manifests itself especially on important occasions of life—weddings, baptisms, funerals, harvest festivals, common tasks—the building of a house, removal, etc. While no exhaustive description can be given here, it must be repeated that the song enjoys everywhere a preponderant importance, above all at a wedding.

Even during the preliminaries, the demand in marriage by the intermediary called " pirślis," the negotiations usually terminate with a chanted phrase. The celebration, which begins at the place whence one of the two contracting parties sets out, consists of a series of customs always accompanied by a song of greater or lesser length. The old woman of the house, where thereafter the young spouse is to rule, places a bonnet on the latter's head to a vocal accompaniment, and the young wife is installed in her duties in the same musical fashion. Every service rendered the bride on the day of her nuptials is paid for by her with things made by her own hand, such as gloves of various colours, sashes, ribbons, chemises, table napkins, etc. Everywhere and always the song has its place. It might almost be said that a Lithuanian marriage resembles an opera. Indeed one of the best Lithuanian composers of the day, Mikas Petrauskas, has introduced into his operetta "Vestuvės " (The Marriage) actual popular *motifs*, at the same time adhering strictly to traditional usages, so that his work is really an artistic representation of the Lithuanian wedding.

During a wedding there are of course all sorts of games. Dancing is very popular. Among the latter may be mentioned the dance of the hat which is executed only by men ; then the dance of the rue performed only by young girls. There are others in which the two sexes join. At the same time these dances are not simply movements to music, but, as in ancient times, constitute the expression of specific ideas and sentiments. At one stage there appeared some danger of these interesting

11

dances being forgotten, but of recent years they have been revived. I can add from personal observation that the sense of rhythm is innate to the Lithuanian. I recall on one occasion taking a London newspaper correspondent to see a popular ball in Kaunas. The floor was packed with couples who would promenade during the intervals between the dances; but within a few seconds from the resumption of the orchestra every couple had fallen into place, and so perfect was the " tempo " that a huge blanket might have covered the heads of the crowd without losing its surface smoothness. The hideous one-step of Occidental society had not yet gained a foothold, and so the ball was well worth seeing, for many of the popular dances are decidedly graceful and call for no little physical agility.

Vidūnas mentions the custom observed among young girls of decking themselves daily in summer with a garland of rue, to which popular songs have lent a special significance as an emblem of purity. Thus when in song the loss of the rue garland is deplored, this intimates that innocence or virginity has been forfeited.

CHAPTER XIV

LITHUANIAN MYTHOLOGY

Speaking of Lithuanian mythology, O. Schraeder, in his work *Reallexikon der indogermanischen Altertumskunde : Grundzüge einer Kultur-und Völkergeschichte Europas*, remarks : " From the point of view of religions . . . it is above all the names of the gods and the conception of the divinity amongst the Lithuanians which help to penetrate the mysteries of the primitive Indo-European belief."

Lithuanian mythology is attached to the common trunk of Indo-European mythologies. The Lithuanians were the last among civilized peoples to abandon Paganism which survived till the end of the XIVth century as their official religion. Šalkauskis rejects the idea that traditionalism is sufficient to account for this, and favours instead the supposition that Lithuanian Paganism derived its vitality from some degree of perfection as well as the powerful organization of a sacerdotal caste.

During one phase of the national Romantic movement, German, Polish and Lithuanian investigators were wont to compare Lithuanian mythology with classic mythology and the sacerdotal caste with the organization of the Roman priesthood. Later it was recognized that these appreciations were somewhat exaggerated, but it is to-day agreed that in Lithuania the ancient national religion was more refined and better organized than amongst the Germans or the Slavs. The critical study of available data is not yet complete ; but methods of comparative philology, which have latterly been applied to this question with some success, throw an interesting light upon Lithuanian mythological conceptions and Lithuanian religious society.

The sacerdotal caste of ancient Lithuania was not without resemblance to that of the Hindu Brahmins or Gallic Druids. Its influence was great, not only in religious, but also in the entire social life. One can gain an approximate idea of its organization by examining that of the primitive Borussians, a Lithuanian tribe who were conquered and assimilated by the Prussians in the XVIIth century.

They gave their priests the name of *vaidilas* or *vaidilutis,* which we come across in German documents in the form of *Waidelotte.* These words contain the Indo-European root *void* (among the Hindus *veda*) which signifies " to know." The *vaidilas* enjoyed the prestige of science ; they were the Roman *sapiens* or German *Wiste* of the Middle Ages. Vestal virgins, called *vaidilutès,* took an equal part in the sacred ceremonies. In Lithuania properly speaking they employed also instead of *vaidilas* the word *žynys,* of the same origin as the Sanscrit *Jânâti,* the Latin *noscere,* and the Greek γιγνώσκω (*gignosko*) and possessing the same signification.

The ordinary priests were subordinated to a sovereign pontiff, *krivis* or *krivaitis. Krivis* comes from the Lithuanian *kèrèti* (German *zaubern*), and its etymological signification is that of the ancient Hindu *kartar,* in Greek ὄργιος (*orgios*), in Latin *sacrificus.* The dwelling of the *krivis* was called *Ruomuva* (*Romowe*). The etymology of the word *Ruomuva* indicates that it was there that the sacred fire burned, as the Indo-European root *rem,* whence it is derived, signifies in Latin *cremare, ardere.* The inhabitants of the regions a little distant from *Ruomuva* were called *Rikajotas,* which translated literally means " the abode of the lords."

The accidental resemblance of sounds between *Romowe* and *Roma* led the early investigators of the primitive Lithuanian religion to suppose that the two words had the same origin ; this was evidently an error of interpretation. It appears, however, historically indisputable that *Ruomuva* was the cult centre of the Borussians ; that the sacred fire was kept there ; that the sovereign sacrificer *krivis* or *krivaitis* resided there, and that he exercised supreme power over all the sacerdotal caste.

There is every reason to believe that the religious organisation of Lithuania Proper was identical with that of Prussian Lithuania.

As at *Ruomuva* fire worship was practised at Vilnius, the capital of Lithuania, and other places. There were sacred trees and woods, foremost of all the oak, *ąžuolas*, for which great veneration was entertained. It was beneath its shadow that the perpetual fire burned and that the sacrifice of goats and other sacred ceremonies were held.

Primitive religions owed their powers of organization to factors which were equally present in Lithuania. As in all the Orient, the priests here were the scholars, the sages; they participated more or less largely in the exercise of social authority; it was to them that judicial power and doubtless other functions belonged. There is every reason to believe that in Lithuania, as elsewhere, the social organization bore a theocratic impress and that the sacerdotal organization occupied a high rung of the social ladder.

Adam Mickiewicz, the celebrated Lithuanian poet, wrote in this context:

Among the Slavs all religion passed into private life, into domestic life, into the life of the village; among the Lithuanians religion passed also into political life. Among the Slavs superior castes seem never to have existed. Those people were not able to form a political society; they were a composition of partial associations. Among the Lithuanians, on the contrary, the castes of the priesthood, warriors and people were founded together and formed a very compact social and political body imbued with a deeply developed religious life

The word *dievas*, which in Lithuanian signifies God in general, bears the same relation to the physical heavens as the Sanscrit *deva*, Latin *deus*, Greek *Zeus*. In order to form their mythological conceptions the Lithuanians followed the same path as other Indo-European peoples. Struck by the grandeur of celestial phenomena they began to venerate them, then to personify them, and finally passed from the sensible image to the abstract idea of the Divinity.

The King of the Lithuanian Olympus is Perkūnas or God of Thunder. The word itself also means simply thunder and is still used in that sense to-day. In this the Lithuanian mythology offers a certain contrast to that of the Greeks and Romans, who placed in a higher degree of the Olympian hierarchy the god of lightning, Zeus or Jupiter, who became subsequently "father of the gods." The father of the lightning nevertheless exists in Lithuanian mythology ; he was called among the primitive Prussians *zvaigždikis*, which name, like that of the Greek Phœbus, comes from the Indo-European *ghvoigvos*, which means lightning.

Several peoples have venerated a divinity of the earth whom they gave as a spouse to the God of Heaven. This symbolical conception was not foreign to the Lithuanians. They knew a divinity called *Žemyn or Žeminėlė*, a word derived from *Žeme*, " the earth." It is certainly curious to recall that the goddess Σεμέλη (Semele), whose name has the same etymology, held a corresponding place in the Thraco-Grecian mythology.

Moreover the terrestrial divinity among the Lithuanians bore also masculine names like *Žemelukas, Žemininkas* and *Žemepatis*, which indicates that the tendency to create gods in pairs did not generally exist among the Lithuanians, and still less that of imagining sexual relations between gods and men. This it is that sharply distinguishes classic from Lithuanian mythology which latter, however, is far from being indifferent to the sexual problem, albeit tending to solve it in the sense of Oriental ascetism.

The myths of the Sun and Moon from this point of view are instinctive. One can find survivals of them even to-day in popular songs. The moon (*mėnuo* and its diminutive *mėnulis* are of masculine gender) is the husband ; the Sun (*saulė* and *saulutė* are feminine) the wife. In due course the fickle Moon paid court to the Morning Star (*aušrinė*) which so angered Perkūnas, the God of Thunder, that he seized his sword and clove the Moon's face in twain. Another version ascribes this drastic action to the Sun herself. We have here an explanation of the moon's phases and the diminution of its disc. It is also a deeper symbol, since in other songs the Moon represents the father, the Sun the mother of the new generations. The father gives to young people their share of the inheritance and the mother prepares the *dot* of the young daughters ; thus the relations of the Moon and Sun explain the question of conjugal fidelity which may not be violated with impunity.

Like the Slav the Lithuanian loves Nature. The sky, the sun, the moon, the stars, the thunder and all atmospheric phenomena are for him objects of adoration. According to another very old conception, the entire heaven with its constellations was incarnated in the person of a single divinity, Karalunė. Karalunė, the Goddess of Light, is represented as a beautiful virgin whose head is adorned with a sun. She wears a mantle sprinkled with stars and closed at the shoulders with a moon. Her smile is the dawn. When it rains, while the sun shines, Karalunė weeps. But with the development of religious ideas the heavenly bodies form distinct images. The sun is a goddess who rides over the earth in a little coach drawn by three horses, one of silver, one of gold, and one of diamond. Slav traditions speak also of three horses of the sun. The palace of the sun was in the East, in that country whither the souls of the virtuous return after death to enjoy eternal felicity. It was a lofty mountain which the dead had to climb and which represented the vault of the sky in a figurative sense. The two stars, Aušrinė and Vakarinė (the star of morning and the star of evening) ignited the fires of the sun, carried water to the goddess for her bath and prepared her bed.

There was also a god named *Vejopatis* or Lord of the Wind. This god appears in the Rig-Veda under the name of *Vayu*, etymologically related to the Lithuanian *Vėjas*, wind, and to the Greek *Aiolos* or *Eole*. There was among the Lithuanian an *Audras*, God of the Storm and Tempest (*audra* means tempest) and a *Bangputis*, God of the Waves (*banga* means wave and *pūsti* to blow).

The Lithuanians recognized besides a large number of divinities subject to the foregoing who personified more or less clearly the manner of being, acting and thinking of the man himself. The number of these inferior divinities was considerable, and cannot be cited here. It is, however worthy of note that the gods who represent and protect the activity of man are subordinated to the gods of nature. Šalkauskis suggests that these relations may attest the passive resignation of the primitive Lithuanians to the powers of the universe and of destiny. This resignation should not be confounded with an attitude of despair ; it was rather a sort of intimate abandonment which prompted Mickiewicz to say : " The Slavs admire more external nature whereas the Lithuanians have a more intimate and more exquisite feeling for the life of nature." This kind of intimacy reveals the soul of nature to the Lithuanians. It is this soul which impregnates their mythology with so distinctive an animism, which nowhere among primitive mythologies is so universal and sustained as among the Lithuanians, who closely attach religious symbolism to mythical personification. If, as they imagine it, nature is made up entirely of living and animate forces, each inert material object is but an envelope for a hidden life and even sometimes the sign of punishment. For example, the little flints which are present in sand are the breasts of Laumé, a malicious spirit formerly punished by God for her amours with a handsome young man. The rainbow is merely the belt of this same Laumé (*Laumés juosta*). This tendency to allegory was so powerful that it is difficult, when studying the mythology of these people, to distinguish that which belongs to symbolism from that which relates to personification. In this respect it is interesting to dwell upon the fire cult which was held in great honour among the Lithuanians. The question of idols in general in the primitive religion of the Lithuanians is not yet fully explained ; certain authors affirm that idols made their appearance in Lithuania only at the epoch when that country had established its first relations with the neighbouring Christian peoples.

The sacred fire was called *Šventoji ugnis* (in Sanscrit *Spenta*, holy, *agni*, fire; in Latin, *sanctus ignis*). There were two kinds of fire—one which was never allowed to go out, and the other which was lit at fixed times and upon certain occasions, for example, to consume propitiatory victims. In addition to its association with public worship the fire was the object of special veneration even in private life, in the home, shown above all towards what was called the "fire of the ashes" (*peleno ugnis*) which was compulsory in every household. The divinity of the hearth, the Estia of the Greeks and the Vesta of the Romans, was called Gabija; and it is not so long ago that a Samogitian woman, when preparing the embers for the night, would pronounce the formula, *Šventa Gabija! gyvenk su mumis linksma!*" i.e. "St. Gabija, live with us in joy!"

For the Lithuanians fire was the best symbol of the divine and universal spirituality. Converted to Christianity, they have not lost this taste for symbolism, and the cross became with their baptism an object of similar veneration, which shows itself in the richness and variety of the ornamentation of Lithuanian crosses, of which a special architectural art could be made. In this worship the Lithuanians never separate flowers from the cross; such a union of the symbol of joy with that of suffering is a Lithuanian characteristic. We find the same tendency even more strikingly revealed in popular poetry.

The Lithuanians believed in good and evil spirits. One of the latter category named Giltinė is the cause of death, in which we should not see a natural and necessary phenomenon. Another, named Aitvaras, represented in the form of a flying serpent, bore riches to those whom it favoured, since everybody knows that wealth is not always the fruit of a laborious and economical life. The devil, known under various forms (*velnias*, *kipsas*) was incessantly pursued by Perkunas who tried to overtake him in order to strike him with a thunderbolt. There were spirits everywhere under the earth (*kaukas* or *nanis*), in the waters of the rivers and lakes (*Undines* or nymphs), etc.

Naturally the Lithuanians did not neglect the cult of the dead. Says Mickiewicz: " The cult of the dead is common to the Lithuanians as to other peoples of antiquity; but nowhere has it remained more deeply rooted and so pure as in this race."

It has been more than once observed that the Lithuanians are particularly sensitive to telepathic phenomena. Perhaps, Šalkauskis opines, this may be accounted for by their fidelity to ancestor worship. Their popular literature is rich in tales of the life led by souls after death (in Lithuanian *vėlės*). The curiosity of scholars has already explored this field of investigation; the International Congress of the History of Religions held at Leyde, in Holland, in 1902, heard a very detailed paper on this subject by M. R. van der Meulen.

The Lithuanians have at all times observed a very elaborate ritual in their celebration of funerals. A special feature of popular poesy is the funeral chant known to this day as *Raudos*. Professional " weepers " accompanied the cortège, and without doubt they took their office to heart, since there were also in use lachrymatory urns.

Nor was the idea of metempsychosis alien to the Lithuanians. On this subject Mickiewicz says :

The soul, according to the ancient religion of the Lithuanians, after death of the individual, can take different forms, either of animals or plants and sometimes of men, according to the moral quality. The soul of the best developed passes into heaven by the Milky Way, and the seat of these privileged souls is located amongst the stars north of the Milky Way. When a man is born a new star always appears on the horizon. The stars of children or of men who will not live long are very small and last a few years only in the sky. The stars of men who die a violent death are the shooting stars, whilst the fixed stars are attached to the destinies of gods and heroes.

The same author observes :

This race could only adhere to a religion which excludes none of the great problems which occupy mankind.

Legends of giants are as common as they are to all Indo-European peoples. These gigantic forms, which many scholars have declared are the arbitrary creation of the popular imagination, will not seem at all surprising when we realize that according to their original signification they give meaning to the irresistible strength of physical nature. In the Lithuanian legend of Water and Wind these are giants who devastate the earth. In the Mohilev government people tell how the giants' heads reach the clouds, how the giants seize the summit of the mountains in their hands and toss them like grains of sand to another spot, while they move with the swiftness of the wind. The tradition of two children of the race of giants is also preserved here. When one of them blows, the wind roars round the peasants' huts ; when the other spits, he makes a bottomless lake. When a violent tempest tears up century-old oaks, and the horizon is illumined with lightning, the peasants say that the giants are at play. In the epic poetry of the Greeks and Scandinavians, the Finns and other nations, giants have always had the same supernatural character. Later, they fell to the rank of heroes, but nevertheless retain many traits of their old mythological character. The peasant believes that there actually was an epoch when giants of incredible strength and amazing size fought on the earth. " To-day," say the peasants, " the earth is not as it was formerly ; a curse hangs over it. To-day the trees do not grow so high and the stones are almost without life. But formerly rye grew as high as the vine. In olden times men were of greater stature, the trees extremely strong, and they bore such fruit as one can hardly describe. But afterwards all people became smaller and weaker from year to year, and we shall yet come to such a pass that men will be transformed into dwarfs and will require half a dozen to lift a single straw."

Popular superstitions and beliefs are innumerable and cannot be dealt with at all exhaustively here. Again natural phenomena play an important rôle. To succeed, any enterprise should be implemented at the time of a new or full moon. If a peasant on the way to his field or the town meets a woman carrying an empty cask, the omen is a bad one. Equally so if an animal runs across the road before the wayfarer. If a peasant suddenly thinks of a wolf on the road, it is a sign that danger threatens the domestic herd. The language of grain is interpreted by soothsayers. Great importance is ascribed to dreams which are also interpreted by specialists. The belief prevails that dreams go by contraries. Thus if you dream you are going to become rich, you may be sure you are destined to become poor ; or if you dream you are very well, that you will soon fall sick.

Generally it may be said that Greek, Hindu, and Persian influences can be traced in Lithuanian mythology, and anything like adequate treatment of the subject would require a special volume.

In olden times a temple dedicated to the god Perkunas stood near the royal palace at Vilnius, but this gave way to a Catholic church when Lithuania became Christian.

CHAPTER XV

LANGUAGE AND LITERATURE

THE Lithuanian language is not, as is often supposed, a Slavonic idiom, but, together with Lettish and Old Prussian, constitutes the Aestian or Baltic linguistic branch which is parallel to the Slavonic and German groups. Belief in the existence of a primitive Balto-Slavonic idiom is due simply to the neighbourhood of the two races and the presence in Lithuania of a large number of words borrowed from Russian and Polish and vice-versa. The philologist Brugman, in his Précis of Comparative Grammar, enumerates seven distinctive characteristics of the Baltic or Aestian idiom, which give it an independent place in the Indo-European linguistic family.

Among Baltic languages Old Prussian is already extinct, the Borussians having been for the most part Germanized by the XVIIth century. Lithuanian has many points of contact with Lettish, which is spoken to-day in Kurland and Livonia. It may be safely affirmed that the two idioms originally formed one language of the Aestian or Baltic linguistic branch.

Lithuanian comprises two main dialects—High and Low Lithuanian. The former is spoken in the eastern part of the country (Vilnius and Kaunas governments). It embraces four-fifths of the Lithuanian linguistic territory. The second is the idiom of the west and north (governments of Kaunas and Prussian Lithuania), and embraces only about a fifth of the Lithuanian-speaking people. The essential phonetic differences of the two dialects are the following : The *uo* and *ie* of High Lithuanian are *u* and *i* in Low Lithuanian. Thus High Lithuanian *duona* (bread) becomes *duna* in Low Lithuanian, and High Lithuanian *pienas* (milk) becomes *pinas* in Low Lithuanian. The sounds *tj* and *dj* of Low Lithuanian becomes *c* and *dz* in High Lithuanian. The zones of the two dialects are separated by a straight line which from the Kurland frontier passes through the towns of Vezenai and Krupiai ; thence almost forty-eight kilometres in a north-westerly direction through Šiauliai, the postal station of Bubiai, thirteen kilometres from Šiauliai, Raseiniai, and thence towards the south-west through Tauragė, across the Prussian frontier, and thence following the course of the Nemunas arrives at the Kurisches Haff. East and south of this line High Lithuanian is spoken ; west and south of it Low. These two principal dialects are subdivided into other minor dialects. Low Lithuanian has dialects of the south-west, north-west and east. High Lithuanian has dialects of the west and east.

From many standpoints, especially the phonetic, Lithuanian appears to be the most archaic of all living Indo-European languages. Lithuanian words bearing resemblance to corresponding Latin and Greek words are numerous. The following is but a partial list :

Latin.	*Lithuanian.*
Vir (man)	Vyras
Deus (God)	Dievas
Ignis (fire)	Ugnis
Vinum (wine)	Vynas
Dies (day)	Diena
Sol (sun)	Saulė
Jocus (joke)	Juokas
Senis (old)	Senas
Dare (to give)	Duoti
Duo (two)	Du
Trahite (pull !)	Traukite
Tres (three)	Trys
Jungus (yoke)	Jungas

Nor are these special cases laboriously sought for, to prove the similarity of the two languages ; on the contrary, they could readily be increased. The resemblance between Lithuanian and Greek is also very striking. Both have a dual number; they are further alike in their use of the instrumental, vocative and locative cases. The following Greek and Lithuanian words suggest a common origin :

Greek.	Lithuanian.
Mêter (mother)	Motina
Vespatis (despot)	Viešpatis

Later borrowings from German, Russian and Polish have less philological interest; nor do they affect the essence of the language which remains Lithuanian. The national existence of Lithuania is bound up with her language; for a Lithuanian State in which a foreign tongue was spoken would be an impossible anomaly.

Very characteristic of Lithuanian is the use of the nominative with the infinitive, the dative with the infinitive, the dative absolute, and particularly the quite special use of variable and invariable participles. The participle is almost always used in a subordinate clause following the conjunction. For example, the phrase, " He says that he sees," in Lithuanian would be rendered, *Sako, kad jis matąs*, i.e. " He says that he (is) seeing." This construction runs through all the tenses with different forms of the participle. Another peculiarity of the language is the use of the verb " to be " as the auxiliary for both active and passive constructions. Thus in Lithuanian we say for " I have turned," *Esu sukęs*, meaning literally, " I am having turned." I can say from personal experience that this peculiarity is at first more than a little puzzling. The difference, however, is shown by the participle itself which has distinct forms for both moods. As in Russian the Lithuanian participle proper (not the gerund) is declined as an adjective with seven cases—viz. nominative, genitive, dative, accusative, vocative, instrumental and locative.

Like Sanscrit and Greek, the Lithuanian verb has a reflexive or medium voice which is constantly employed. It is formed very simply by adding an *s* to the ending of the active voice or, if the verb is a compound one, the syllable *si* is inserted between the verbal stem and prefix. Thus *suku*, "I turn," becomes *sukuos*, "I turn myself." *Sukalbame*, "we agree or speak together," becomes *susikalbame*, "we understand each other," etc.

The use of *s* and *si* for the reflexive voice suggests the Russian *sya*, but in Russian this syllable, a contraction of *sebya*, meaning "self," is used only as an ending, and cannot be inserted between a verbal prefix and stem, as in Lithuanian.

As in Russian, there is a feminine form for family names. But Lithuanian goes even farther in this respect and provides special forms of the family name for various members of the family. Thus the wife of Mr. Svelnas is Svelniene ; the girl daughter is Svelnyte ; the grown daughter Svelnike ; the boy son Svelnytis ; the grown son Svelnukas, etc.

Sentences are usually laconic, as in antique languages. For example, the genitive attributive is freely placed between the adjective and the substantive—*Antrasis Žydų Bendruomenių Suvažiavimas* (literally, Second of the Communes of the Jews Congress). The auxiliary is often omitted. After all declarative verbs the subjunctive is invariably used. Prepositions are comparatively seldom employed. The subordination of the subsidiary to the principal clause is stricter than in German or English. Co-ordination is rather determined by the sense of the phrase than by conjunctions.

In its rhythm Lithuanian is probably unique in our day. It submits itself to the tension of parallel rhythms which, as it were, oppose each other. The fundamental rhythm is that of the mutation of syllables or sounds, short and long, to which must be added the change between the acute and grave sound. The acute tone is often given to the short vowel, i.e. in some isolated words, *sūnus*, son ; *upė*, river ; but in the greater number of cases of declined words, the tone changes from one syllable to another, though always between the same two. Nevertheless the tonic accent has merely secondary importance. In fact, in good Lithuanian, the tone should never be too strongly accentuated. A very marked accent would threaten the existence of the case endings. This tendency, indeed, is already noticeable in Low Lithuanian, where the stress is often fixed on the first syllable.

The Lithuanian language is rich in vowel sounds, above all in *a*; among diphthongs the sound *uo* is notable. Lithuanian proper lacks the *f* and *h*, which are used nowadays only in words of foreign origin. The Lithuanian for France, for example, is " Prancuzija."

It may well be doubted whether any other known language possesses so many diminutives and caressive forms as Lithuanian. Certainly in this respect it surpasses Russian, Italian, or Spanish. One example will suffice. *Brolis* is the simple form for brother; but the following variations are all in use : *Brolelis, brolaitis, broluźis, broliukas, brolúlis, brolutis, brolytis, brolaitėlis, broleliukas, brolutėlis, broluźėlis, broluźaitis, brolytukas, broliukelis, brolytuźis,* etc.

R. Bytautas, in his *Philosophy of the Lithuanian Language,* writes : " Lithuanian possesses an incalculable richness of expression, as it has in abundance all the essentials for an extension of its vocabulary. With the aid of various prefixes and terminations, while slightly modifying the radical of the words, it forms with remarkable facility a multitude of new expressions which can be derived from every part of speech." In this regard Lithuanian recalls the Greek; there is the same natural richness, the same suppleness, the same adaptation to the most varied nuances of thought; but its brevity and construction are more akin to Latin.

To illustrate the foregoing contention Šalkauskis gives the following example. The idea of " to eat " receives a different expression according to the subject of the action. For a man one says *valgyti*; for animals in general *ėsti*; but if one speaks of certain species one must again use a special word. Thus for a dog or cat *lakti* is used; for domestic fowl *lesti*. Further, to feed a man the verb *valgydinti* is correct; but to feed a child is *penėti*; a horse, cow or other horned animal, *šerti*; a pig *liuobti*, a cat or dog *lakinti*; domestic fowl *lesinti*. A man's food is called *valgis*, a child's *penas*, a horse's, etc., *pašaras*, a pig's

12

jovalas, a dog's or cat's *lakalas,* and domestic fowl's *lesalas.*
In this manner the Lithuanian distinguishes between a
collection of similar phenomena, giving to each one a
special designation, thanks to the richness of derivative
forms, and this not only in the domain of concrete ideas,
but also in that of abstractions. The idea is expressed
by different terms according to the object, the quality,
the quantity, the position, the relation, etc., under which
it is envisaged.

From the verb *sakyti,* " to say," are derived : *Sakytojas*
and *sakytoja,* the person who says, male and female ;
sakymas, the action itself, the " saying " ; *sakinys,* the
object of the action, that which is said, the " proposition " ;
pa-saka, the result, the story ; *sakykla,* indicating the
place from which one speaks, the chair or tribune, etc.

Judging from the remarkable progress made by the
literary language during only about thirty-five years of
the renascence movement, in spite of the persecution to
which it was formerly subjected by Russia, it is not
unreasonable to expect that a few decades from now,
if its evolution proceeds at the same rate, it will take a
very high place among civilized tongues by virtue of its
antiquity, its richness and purity, and its philosophical value.

Before becoming an object of study by the Lithuanian
intellectuals themselves, the popular poetry of the country
since the second half of the XVIIIth century had begun
to attract the attention of eminent German writers.
Philippe Ruhig inaugurated the movement by reproduc-
ing in his essay on the language, entitled " *Betrachtungen
der Litauischen Sprache* " (Königsberg, 1745), three Lithuanian popular songs with favourable comment. This work
evoked in Germany powerful interest in Lithuanian popular poetry. The moment, too, was opportune, because
a reaction against pseudo-classicism had just set in
headed by Lessing and Herder, who were the first to
appreciate the distinction of Lithuanian poetry which,
in many respects, satisfied the æsthetic exigencies of
the time.

In his *Litteraturbriefe* of 1759, Lessing thus expressed
his enthusiasm for the Lithuanian songs, or *dainos* :

You should learn also that poets are born in all latitudes and that the vivacity of impressions is not the privilege of civilized populations. In turning over the pages of Ruhig's Lithuanian dictionary recently, I found after preliminary considerations on the language some precious rarities which gave me extreme satisfaction ; they were the *dainos*, i.e. chansonettes, such as are sung by the young girls of the people. What naive pleasantries ! What charming simplicity ! The frequent use of diminutives, the great number of vowels mingled with the *l*, *r* and *t* give extraordinary grace to the language of these songs.

After Lessing, Herder supported the vogue of Lithuanian poesy. In his " *Stimmen der Voelker in Lieder*," he reproduced a tasteful translation of eight Lithuanian songs. One of these so pleased Goethe, that he introduced it in his *Singspiel*, under the title of " Die Fischerin."

The publicity thus given to Lithuanian popular poetry by Germany evoked also among Polish writers a certain amount of interest in Lithuanian culture and history. As elsewhere, Polish Romanticism in its reaction against pseudo-classicism was seeking for less remote themes in the history of the Middle Ages, and was, therefore, not loth to find inspiration in the national culture of Lithuania. But whereas German authors were attracted by the ethnic side of popular poesy, Polish-Lithuanian mentality turned more to mythology. In the doings of personages like Gediminas, Algirdas, Keistutis, Vytautas, etc., or the battles of the XIVth century against the Russians, Poland, and the Order of Cross-Bearers, Polish writers discovered an inexhaustible storehouse of literary material. In this regard the intellectual classes of the country, who derived their spiritual pabulum from Vilnius, differed from the masses of the people, who were comparatively indifferent to these concrete historical themes, their mental activity manifesting itself rather in tales and fables drawn from the lives of animals or based upon moral conceptions. Such a rupture with the past had been deliberately fostered by the Cross-Bearers in East Prussia, where the official use of the Lithuanian language had been forbidden, and whence, together with the Bohemians and Jews, the Lithuanian bards, called *vaidilas*, the sole popular repositories of historical traditions, had been expelled. Even in Lithuania when Christianity had penetrated the country, and the use of the Polish language had spread, the ancient priests and the national tongue were included in the same oblivion. The people, fallen into servitude and attached to the soil, forgot the glorious lays of olden times or recalled them but fitfully in the privacy of the home. The upper classes, indifferent to their national duty, gradually lost contact with the people and thenceforth were incapable of furnishing popular poesy with the elements of an epic. In these circumstances the population fed on cosmic images A surprising predilection was shown for animal personification, the lion being quite a favourite. More interesting, however, are the proverbs, adages, riddles, and conundrums attached to moral tales. This class of literary output is especially suited to the genius of the language, with its conciseness and distinctive rhythm. The result is seen in a wide range of little masterpieces which well repay study.

Nevertheless, the gems of popular literature are unquestionably the *dainos* or songs, already mentioned. We have already seen (*vide* Chapter XIII) how largely song bulks in the life of almost every Lithuanian; analogously he distinguishes in his songs almost as many forms, shades and varieties as there are in life itself. Juska's dictionary gives more than thirty expressions for what in English we should be content to render through the single verb " to sing "; and he gives fifteen names for different songs. Šalkauskis, however, classifies Lithuanian songs into three main divisions, viz., religious hymns or *giesmés;* funeral dirges or songs of farewell, *raudos;* and general songs, *dainos;* whence the corresponding verbs *giedoti, raudoti, dainuoti.* The Lithuanian uses the words *giesmé* and *giedoti* to designate the song of the birds as though he wished to emphasize its religious character.

Šalkauskis says of the *dainos:*

They certainly constitute the richest efflorescence of Lithuanian lyricism; remarkable above all are those which owe their inspiration to family life. The family was always the most solid basis of Lithuanian national existence, the vitality of which is due in great measure to the purity of morals which is maintained at the domestic hearth; one can realize this in those *dainos* in which the family finds the faithful expression of its joys and of its daily vicissitudes, and in which the problem of love is set and then solved with a breadth and depth of view which does not fail to astonish. They are so characteristic, both from the moral and artistic standpoints, that it behoves us to dwell upon them for a short time.

The question of love and purity is presented under an allegorical form which must date back to a remote antiquity. The symbolism of the *dainos* is apparently attributable to the same stock as the mythological songs. Vidūnas remarks in this context :

> The interest of the Lithuanian songs and stories rests not only in the profound and tender sentiments which they express ; one recovers therein the last rays of a sun which has long since set, and the trace of ancient events of the history of these people.

The *dainos* give to the young girl the epithet of " beautiful white lily " (*balta graži lelijėlė* is in Lithuanian of the feminine gender) ; the young man is described as " beautiful white clover " (the Lithuanian *baltas gražus dobilelis* is masculine). This is a guarantee of happiness. Adolescent the young girl devotes her time to the culture of a garden ; but in the midst of flowers which there abound, the green rue (*žalia rūta*) occupies the place of choice. Its freshness, its bright colour symbolize virginity. It is upon this plant that the young girl bestows her greatest care, and it is from this that the garden takes its name (*rūtų darželis*). Often by the side of the rue grows the " shrub of God " (*diemedėlis*), which has the same meaning for the young man. While under the eye of her mother the young girl tends her garden, the young man takes care of his brown bay horse (*bėras žirgelis*), the image of a virile temperament. The young girl appears in the world crowned with rue (*žalių rūtų vainikėlis*). A ring of gold and silk ribbons complete her toilette, but the crown of green rue, symbolizing her purity, is her most beautiful ornament. " As in the dark night a little star sparkles in the heavens, so shines the young girl under her green aureola."

> Kaip tamsioj naktelėj
> Danguj žiba zvaigždelė,
> Taıp mergelė zibejo
> Kol vainiką turėjo.

But, whatever the subject-matter of the *dainos*, one is ever struck by the absence of grossness. In this connexion a Lithuanian commentator has observed :

Lithuanian folklore is remarkable for its absolute purity; all allusion to sexuality, even to sensuality, is rigorously banned. What freshness and what innocence after the grossness, the violence and, sometimes, the unbridled bestiality of the Slav folklore ! The Lithuanian song does but confirm that which legend and tradition teach us of the purity of morals of ancient Lietuva, happily conserved in modern Lithuania, despite the solvent influence of the dynastic union with Poland and of its result, the degrading Muscovite domination. It is impossible, when questioning the soul of ancient Lithuania, not to associate with the cult of the Sun and Fire the adoration of Virginity. . . . When social and economic order has been re-established in our hierarchical republic, recently resuscitated, we shall invite the artists, the poets, the thinkers—all the bruised heroes of our stupid and ugly epoch, all the intellectual pariahs of the plutocratic and materialistic Occident, to come and enjoy a long rest of body and spirit on the hills where our ancestors fed the pure Fire and which bear even to-day names of the spiritual world : Rambynas, Alexota. There, in the immense solitude of the Nemunas, they will refresh their heart and their spirit with the inspiration of Druidical times, effacing from their memory the hideous recollection of modern concepts of love.

The most ancient historic chant extant is one dating from 1282, which celebrates the glory of Prince Daumantas of Pskov. A later chant describes the sad end of 300 heroes, who in 1362 defended the fortress of Kaunas against the attacks of Winrich of Kniprode, and preferred to perish in the flames rather than fall into the hands of their enemies.

Belles lettres proper date from the XVIIth century in Prussian Lithuania. The earliest known author is Christian Duonelaitis, who wrote six fables and five idylls, famous for their style and vigour. Perhaps the best known name abroad is that of Adam Mickiewicz (1798–1845), professor of the academy of Lausanne, where the hall in which he lectured still bears his name. In 1840 he became professor in the College de France. It is true that Mickiewicz wrote in Polish, but the inspiration and subject matter of his verse are almost exclusively Lithuanian.

Among his masterpieces are, *Sonnets of the Crimea, Konrad Wallenrod, Sir Thadeus or Lithuania, Grazyna, Dziady* and others. It is conceded by experts that Mickiewicz ranks among the greatest poets of the XIXth century. Among his contemporaries were Ignatius Chodzko, Poska, Daukantas and Valančius.

The result of the tyrannical Tsarist prohibition of Lithuanian books from 1864 to 1904 was to drive Lithuanian literary effort abroad, chiefly to Prussia and America. In Prussian Lithuania Tilsit was the principal centre of Lithuania's intellectual life. Here were printed books reviews, journals, etc., which were smuggled over the border into Lithuania Major. In these circumstances the language found the most favourable conditions for development in Lithuania Minor, where writers like Kuršaitis, Jacobi, Vidūnas, Sauerwein and others flourished. The last-named was a German, but he possessed such a mastery of the Lithuanian language, that nobody could suppose from internal evidence of his Lithuanian writings that he was other than a Lithuanian. W. St. Vidūnas, born in the district of Heydekrug, East Prussia, in 1868, is still very much alive and justly regarded as one of the most distinguished of all Lithuanian scholars, poets and philosophers. In his youth he wrote in German, but later devoted himself solely to Lithuanian. He is famous as a dramatist. Among his works the trilogy entitled *The Eternal Fire* has had great success. In his play, *In the Shadow of the Ancestors*, he shows himself fully conscious of his Lithuanian nationality. He is the author of numerous tragedies, comedies, mysteries and legends. From 1911 to 1914 he engaged in editing a monthly review entitled *Youth*, and in 1916 he published his book *Lithuania in the Past and Present*. Vidūnas is further celebrated as a choir leader and as a public speaker. He is also the author of a Lithuanian grammar in German.

In Lithuania Major, notwithstanding the Russian persecution, a certain number of poets continued to cultivate the Muse in secret. The name of Maironis, really the pseudonym of Jean Maculevičius, is famous in this connexion. Mention should be made of the valuable contribution to Lithuanian literature of the Jesuits who entered the country in 1569. In 1608 they were detached from the Polish province and formed an independent Lithuanian province, where they established the colleges of Kražiai and Niesviž and in Prussian Lithuania the academy of Braunsberg and the college of Poessel. In these various institutions the Jesuits promoted theatrical representations by their pupils. The plays were actually performed in Latin, but for the benefit of the auditors, few of whom were familiar with that tongue, scenarios were printed in Lithuanian. These performances attracted thousands of spectators of all classes and covered a vast range of subjects, both sacred and secular.

Immediately before the war tremendous literary activity was displayed throughout Lithuania. Among lyrical poets should be mentioned Putinas, Gira, Gustaitis, Vaitkus ; among epic poets Puida, Šeinius, Krėvė ; among dramatists, besides Vidūnas, Vargšas, Keturakis, and others. The authoresses Ragana, Bitė, Kymont-Čiurlionis and Lazdynų Pelėda have written admirable novels. Prominent among modern Lithuanian historians are Daukantas, Mathieu Valančius and Maironis.

CHAPTER XVI

ART AND MUSIC

I DO not propose to trace Lithuanian art and music back to pre-historic times, relics of which bear a general family resemblance to similar survivals discovered in the Scandinavian Peninsula. Instead, I shall try to interest the reader in comparatively contemporaneous exponents of these branches of national culture. And without further preliminary, I wish to introduce him to perhaps one of the few known men of our own day who have achieved a great reputation both as artists and musicians. Yet such was Mykolas Čiurlionis, who died prematurely in 1914 at the age of thirty-nine, in the full flush of his creative genius. Comparatively unknown, I fear, in this country, Čiurlionis before his untimely demise had already achieved an otherwise European reputation, more especially in Russia, where he was acclaimed a genius of the very first rank.

He was born in 1875 at Druskinikai, Vilnius government. When five years old he already displayed musical talent, and at nine entered the musical school of Prince Michael Oginski where he remained till 1888. It was then that he made his first attempts at composition, which attracted Prince Oginski's attention and patronage, thanks to which he was able to enter the Warsaw Conservatoire. At the close of his studies he made a considerable reputation as a composer of distinction, but his true vocation lay elsewhere, and in 1902, still at Warsaw, he was initiated into the principles of painting and speedily became an independent artist. Soon he quitted Warsaw for Vilnius, where he took an active part in the Lithuanian renascence movement. His sojourn at Vilnius was for Čiurlionis the most fruitful period of his short life, and it was there that he painted his most remarkable canvases. The two last years of his life he spent at Petersburg, where death came suddenly, doubtless as the result of overwork. He bequeathed to posterity some four hundred pictures and studies produced for the most part during the last five years of his career.

It is primarily in Russia that the art of Čiurlionis has evoked the liveliest general interest, and the best monographs on his work are from Russian pens. One of these—that of Chudovsky—says in part :

> To-day that he is dead, the authors of the spiritual renascence of Lithuania present Čiurlionis as a national artist. It is not for us to judge of that ; nevertheless his extraordinary independence of all contemporary art leads one to suppose that he actually was inspired by the secret forces of his people. It is well to believe that this strange genius was not a fortuitous caprice of Fate, but the precursor of a future sublime Lithuanian art. . . . When I think of him, of the Lithuanian, a single idea impresses itself upon my mind ; these people have not had their Middle Age ; perhaps they have conserved till the twentieth century, much more than we other Russians, the giant energies of the mystic life received from the Aryans and which our brothers of the West lavished on the Middle Ages in such grandiose abundance. And then Čiurlionis acquires a strange meaning and a strange grandeur.

The same critic recognizes the acuteness of vision peculiar to Čiurlionis : " His pictures bear testimony to the faculty which he had, like primitive man, of perceiving at the bottom of living phenomena the very essence of life," because " he had a conception of the world as rich as himself," which may explain why, although educated in the atmosphere of Occidental culture, he always felt drawn to the mystical visions of the ancient Orient.

Another Russian critic, Leman, observes :

> The marvellous harmony of the celestial mechanism which reveals all the real infinity of the universe ; the pitiless logic of natural selection, the theory of Laplace with his tourbillions of fire which are reflected, so to speak, in the atoms of Descartes, these it was that beguiled his soul for ever by the imposing verity of a rigorous concatenation. The cult of the sun, that flaming centre which carries us into the unfathomable spaces of creation ; the magnificent idea of a single principle, link and soul of the system which is subject to it, conduct Čiurlionis to the study of

ancient Persia and of Egypt, and sweep him still farther to the sources of thought and to the six religious and philosophical systems of India

All this partly explains why, as Chudovsky puts it, " the work of Čiurlionis is a visual revelation of the world of beauty, and of harmony, of the eternal and illimitable life."

Speaking of the method adopted by Čiurlionis in order to express his æsthetic feelings, Šalkauskis says :

A traveller is crossing the arid spaces of a desert. Suddenly his gaze discloses in the distance a peaceful vision ; the sensation is real and corresponds also to a reality. But the traveller has need of all his experience to recognize that this reality which appears before him exists, but is situated at some other spot than where he seems to see it. The mirage interposes itself between a real object and the perception, real also, which the traveller has of it. It serves as intermediary ; it can also serve as symbol. The penetrating eye of Čiurlionis, without calling in question the reality of the sensations which it receives, sees in the phenomenal world a mirage across which it endeavours to seize the true reality of things. That which it has thus succeeded in discovering he depicts in his pictures.

This symbolic sense of the work of Čiurlionis has been magisterially explained by Viatcheslav Ivanov, to whom we owe the best study of our artist, entitled, *Čiurlionis and the Problem of the Synthesis of the Arts.* " The inspired art of Čiurlionis," he writes, " borders upon divination. This seer is above all interesting and persuasive when he undertakes a task foreign in itself to painting, when he abandons himself without reserve to his gift of second sight. Then the objects of our sensible world generalize their forms and become diaphanous. Matter seems to pass to a second plane of creation and permits us to perceive only the rhythmic and geometric principle of its being. Space itself seems invaded by the transparency of forms which do not exclude neighbouring forms but permit themselves, so to speak, to be penetrated by them. This geometrical transparence appears to be an attempt to expose to the view the spectacles of a contemplation in which our three dimensions of space no longer suffice." The artist seems therefore to have found a fourth in time. " How, by what laws can the vision of this remote and sublime material arise from the pitiful material that surrounds us ? " demands the same critic. " To answer this question is to describe the method of Čiurlionis, the novelty of which justly determines the extreme originality of the artist. In our opinion his method is the pictorial elaboration of the elements of his vision according to a principle drawn from music. . . . In a certain sense this work is an attempt at synthesis of painting and music ; an attempt undoubtedly unpremeditated, naïve, yet none the less executed with a semi-conscious application which is always the attribute of genius. These two sisters are opposed one to the other ; painting knows only space ; music admits only time. Their synthesis is conceivable in reason as a harmony of the spheres, as the parallel march of two worlds whereof one chants in colours and the other sparkles with tones, but in art it is unrealizable. Čiurlionis has not attempted to realize it ; but he has been able at least to describe it ; he had to consider time and space as a homogeneous whole. But yet again, in art he was born to indicate this conception. He has given us the sensation of being in a space which contains simultaneously time and movement, a space which is the basis of a chatoyant play of colours. . . . And the musical method for our artist has been the sesame which has opened for him the inviolate sanctuaries of the universal mystery. He has seen the music of phenomena and has made use of it to lift the veil of Isis. He has tried to penetrate the secret of forms issued from the divine seed of the primitive, forms of realities ; his pictures are attempts to explain the world."

Such is the judgment passed upon Čiurlionis by one of the ablest men of contemporary Russia.

One of the ideas which Čiurlionis loves to express with a visible predeliction is that of the living unity of the world, as also of its march to perfection. Hence his taste for cycles of pictures which he terms sonatas. V. Chudovsky, who sees in the sonata a tendency " to show the æsthetic theme by way of improvement in successive moments of its movement towards final beauty," considers that the cycle which Čiurlionis entitled " La Mer," and which he divides according to the dialectic Triad, into thesis, anti-thesis, and synthesis, is that which corresponds the best to the ideal essence of the sonata.

Says Šalkauskis :

The delicious vertigo of infinite spaces, the swell of the ocean of life, the seductive face of evil, the union of earth and heaven in the signs of the constellations, the birth of the world after the *fiat lux*, the profound truth of fantasy and of myth, the eloquent silence of the desert, the apocalyptic sense of urban agglomerations, the nostalgia of the terrestrial Paradise—such are some of the subjects which have inspired Čiurlionis.

Some titles of the pictures of Čiurlionis, chosen almost at random, are suggestive of his penchant, viz., "Rex," "The Recital," "The Sonata of Beethoven," "Fantasy," "Paradise," "The Paladin," "Spring," "Sign of the Zodiac," "The Virgin," "Andante of the Sonata La Mer," "Conte fantastique," etc. In living artists like Sileika, Kalpokas and Varnas, Čiurlionis has found disciples and imitators who not unworthily maintain the tradition of his unique art.

Antanas Žmuidzinavičius is by many considered the most remarkable painter of the Lithuanian Renascence. He pursued most of his studies in Western Europe, and from 1904 to 1907 attended the School of Fine Arts in Paris. On returning to Lithuania he there founded the Society of Fine Arts, to which have belonged most of the leading Lithuanian artists including Čiurlionis himself, Petras Rimša, Šlapelis, Kalpokas, Šileika, Ulianskis, Varnas, Zikaras, etc. Žmuidzinavičius also did much to organize expositions. The first, which contained the works of one hundred and fourteen artists, had immense success, and had to be removed from Kaunas to Riga in deference to an insistent demand. Among his paintings "The Tomb of the Heroes" and "The Vision" merit special mention. The first depicts an old man seated on the tomb of dead warriors and narrating to a child the glorious past of Lithuania. "The Vision" represents the Vytis, the Lithuanian Knight on his charger, brandishing his naked sword; in the background of the picture dawn is beginning to touch the horizon with crimson. This work, which was exhibited at Vilnius in 1912, provoked tremendous enthusiasm. Žmuidzinavičius is the author of numerous landscape paintings very finely executed.

Among sculptors Rimša and Zikaras are conceded the first place. I have already referred to Rimša as the author of the group entitled "The Lithuanian School," which represents a Lithuanian woman seated at her spinning wheel and teaching her child its mother tongue. This scene is the symbol of the Lithuanian school oppressed under the Russian yoke, of the epoch when only in the privacy of the family dared one speak the national idiom. Another

work by the same artist shows the Lithuanian Knight
fighting against the Polish eagle ; this work was one of
the most admired at the Vilnius exhibition of 1914, and
it clearly characterizes the national tendencies.

Zikaras is one of the best known of the younger genera-
tion of Lithuanian sculptors. He attended the School
of Fine Arts at Vilnius, and subsequently the Academy
at Petersburg. He soon made a name for himself with his
ceramic productions. A very typical piece of statuary
shows a Lithuanian woman quarrelling with a Russian
policeman who wishes to confiscate goods which have been
smuggled across the Prussian frontier.

Aleksandravičius has done honour to the Lithuanian
name in America, having pursued his early studies at the
Chicago Fine Arts Academy. In 1912 he returned to
Lithuania and successfully directed the School of Fine
Arts at Kaunas. The monument to the Lithuanian
philologist, Dr. Jaunius, is his work.

Jusaitis represents Lithuanian art in France and
Germany, having studied at Paris and Munich. He works
in marble and has produced groups which have attracted
flattering attention in many salons of Paris and of
expositions in Vilnius.

Other names that occur to one are Ulianskis, Antokolski,
Velioniškis, and Vivulskis, the three last of whom have
followed their career almost entirely abroad, but are none
the less Lithuanian by origin.

It is noteworthy that, with few exceptions, the most
distinguished of modern art exponents in Lithuania are
drawn from the ranks of the people. This remark holds
specially true of the sculptors.

Before leaving the subject, a few words should be said
about a more humble but very interesting category of
Lithuanian art production, in the shape of the peasants'
handicrafts in wood and amber which are beginning to
attract attention beyond the confines of Lithuania. Wood-
carving, more particularly, has attained a high pitch of
excellence as exemplified in everyday articles like walking-
sticks, culinary utensils, boxes, sabots, etc. Motives
drawn from the animal and vegetable kingdom are popular

and often executed with astounding fidelity. In domestic architecture, which remains to-day very much what it was centuries ago, we find the same principles applied. Many Lithuanian farm-houses are ornamented with elaborate carvings, heads of animals being a favourite theme. The implement used is often an ordinary saw, and the pains bestowed upon the task are considerable. The Lithuanian peasants are very proud of these master-pieces. Weaving is an artistic occupation which the Lithuanian people practice with success. For centuries women and girls have applied themselves assiduously to the work. Much taste and fancy are devoted to various articles of feminine wearing apparel, which are designed in brilliant colours. Swaddling clothes for infants, ribbons to decorate musical instruments, scarves, hat-bands, tablecloths, gloves, and so forth, are all items of this domestic industry. Crosses are another characteristic product of Lithuanian popular art. These Catholic people love the symbol of their faith, and one finds it almost everywhere, on the roads, in silent cemeteries, in front of houses and churches. These crosses usually measure five to six metres in height, and are always very carefully made. They are adorned with images of Christ, the Virgin, and the Saints, and often reproduce entire scenes from biblical history. Frequently, too, these crosses are painted in lively colours. Every farm has its large crucifix, which is reverently tended and occasionally surrounded by a flowerbed. Many of these specimens of Lithuanian popular art were destroyed in the war, and it will be one of the tasks of the New State to preserve the residue. Exhibitions of peasants' handicrafts are now regularly held at Kaunas, and well repay a visit.

In the churches one may observe the decisive influence which Christianity has exercised over Lithuanian art. These structures are so numerous that Lithuania is some-times called the land of churches. They are usually erected on an eminence, those built on the lofty banks of the Nemunas enjoying a wonderful situation. Originally the churches were built of wood, which is the most easily procurable building material in Lithunia. The earliest structures were small. In course of time they grew more spacious and artistic, the interior being adorned with wooden pillars. The belfry was formerly separate from the main building, and usually higher, in two stories. In many places the churches are enclosed with a high wall. The style of these wooden churches has hardly varied for centuries.

On the other hand, stone churches, found chiefly in the towns, have had an interesting development. The first churches were built of brick. Several specimens may be seen at Vilnius; the churches of St. Peter and St. Paul, and the church of the Franciscans at Kaunas date also from this epoch. They are of Gothic architecture and several, viz., St. Bernard and St. Anne at Vilnius, are regarded as amongst the most perfect monuments of that style. With the counter-Reformation, directed above all by the Jesuits, the Italian cupola was introduced into Lithuanian architecture. Thereafter specimens of the Italian renascence and the baroque style predominated. Towards the end of the XVIIIth century and at the beginning of the XIXth, Greek models came into favour at Vilnius, but these were succeeded again by a wave of Gothic influence manifested in the churches of Vilki and Janov among others. Many of the church altars belonging to the counter-Reformation period are magnificent, affording striking proof of a rich imagination. Images of the Madonna are common in Lithuania. The most celebrated is that of "Aušros Vartai" (Ostrabama) at Vilnius, which is regarded as a national sanctuary. Even the Russians, in their most iconoclastic mood, never ventured to interfere with this emblem.

The Lithuanians are essentially a music-loving people. Here again, a distinction must be drawn between popular music and the art of musical composition. In the former sphere, melodies for the dainos are most common. These *motifs* have never been fixed on paper, but have been transmitted from ear to ear and mouth to mouth. They are generally as old as the words. Recent investigation has proved that these chants were composed according to the Greek musical system, in the diatonic style proper to Hellenic music. Thus the connexion between the Greek and Lithuanian peoples is verified not only in the ethnographic and philosophical domains, but also in that of music. The resemblance to the music of the Ionians and Dorians is most striking in the finale of Lithuanian popular songs. It consists in this, that the final note gives the pitch of the piece. An interesting example of this similitude is the finale of the Hymn of Homer to Demetrius, which is preserved almost intact to this day in the region of Trakai. Even the rhythm of Lithuanian songs recalls Greek melodies. Occasionally we find the bar of two or four time suddenly interrupted by a bar of three time. Very often also in a piece of 4/4 time appears a bar of 5/4. It is not uncommon to encounter a melody which begins with a bar of 2/4 and ends with one of 5/8.

The dainos to-day form an essential part of the Lithuanian musical art. The people consider these melodies their own and are deeply devoted to them. The sailor on his raft which carries him down the Nemunas to the sea times his poling to the elegiacs of the dainos. The peasant wields his scythe to the same accompaniment. Lithuanian girls and women while weaving invoke in their dainos a more beautiful world, a life replete with the joys of spring. These melodies are a national heritage which neither Russian nor Polish gendarmes could destroy.

Among musicians of the Lithuanian revival one of the best known abroad is Mikas Petrauskas, who studied at Petersburg and Paris. Several years before the war he established himself in America, where he opened a Lithuanian conservatoire. Petrauskas is known as a composer of operettas, and his works have been produced with brilliant success on the stage of the United States. He is also a noted tenor, and for some time sang at the Russian Imperial Opera. His younger brother Kipras Petrauskas is even better known as a tenor for the most part connected with the Russian opera, both before and since the Revolution. He has constantly been associated with the famous Shalyapin who regards him as perhaps the greatest tenor in Russia, and therefore in the world. The younger Petrauskas recently returned to Lithuania, where he is working hard to develop Lithuanian opera, and that too with no small success. Native talent is extraordinarily rich in that country and only needs encouraging. Other well-known Lithuanian musicians are S. Šimkus, Talat-Kelpša, T. Sasnauskas, Brazys and Naujalis.

Šimkus, like Petrauskas, is a pupil of the Petersburg conservatoire. He has set to music a series of dainos and composed many choruses which are widespread in Lithuania.

Sasnauskas is also a well-known composer who studied at Petersburg. His cantatas have achieved a signal success, and have been performed on numerous occasions in Russia and America. The Lithuanians abroad frequently organize musical seances in order to cultivate the national sentiment of the members of the colony and maintain amicable relations among them.

Brazys is one of the most eminent authorities on musical theory in Lithuania. He was formerly director of the choir at the Vilnius cathedral, and is the author of numerous scientific works on the Lithuanian popular songs. His most recent publication entitled *Melodies of Lithuanian Dainos* appeared a few years ago.

Naujalis is best known as a church composer. He pursued his studies at the conservatoire of Ratisbonne; later he became organist of the cathedral at Kaunas. His principal works belong to church music, his hymns and religious songs enjoying a high reputation. Naujalis also composed melodies for the patriotic poems of Maironis. Founder and professor of the conservatoire at Kaunas, he has made a name for himself in the teaching of music.

The most characteristic Lithuanian national instruments are the kanklys, truba, and a kind of kettledrum. Formerly the kanklys was widely used to accompany the dainos, but to-day is less popular. The truba is a kind of flute. Violins and concertinas are also in common use among the peasantry.

The love of music in all its forms is deeply ingrained in Lithuanian character. The Lithuanian soldier, like the Russian, invariably sings on the march, and I shall always associate my life in Kaunas with the sound of these military chants given forth by deep-chested infantrymen in the early hours of morning, as I lay half waking, half sleeping, in my comfortable bed at the British Mission in Keistučio Gatvé.

LITHUANIAN NATIONAL HYMN

I append here for reference the text of the Lithuanian national hymn, together with an English metrical rendering, for which I am indebted to Miss A. C. Sawers, a member of the staff of the Lithuanian Legation, London:

Lithuanian Text.

Lietuva, tevyne mūsų,
Tu didvyrių žemé !
Iš praeities tavo sūnūs
Te stiprybę semia.
Tegu tavo vaikai eina
Vien takais dorybės,
Tegu dirba tavo naudai
Ir žmonių gerybei.
Tegu saule Lietuvos
Tamsumus prašalina,
Ir šviesa ir tiesa
Mūs žingsnius telydi,
Tegu meile Lietuvos
Dega mūsų širdyse !
Vardan tos Lietuvos
Vienybė težydi !

English Version.

Lithuania, land of heroes,
    Thou our Fatherland that art,
From the glorious deeds of ages
    Shall thy sons take heart.
May thy children, day by day,
Labour in the narrow way,
May they strive,
            While they can,
For the greater good of man.

May the sun of Lithuania
Pierce the darkness of the night,
And the light of truth and honour
    Guide our steps aright.
May the love of our dear land
Nerve and strengthen heart and hand,
We will strive,
            While we can,
For the brotherhood of man.

CHAPTER XVII

THE PERSONAL EQUATION AND CONCLUSION

I HAVE mentioned in earlier chapters the manner of my introduction to Lithuania through the British Commission for the Baltic Provinces (*sic*).

But my association with the Lithuanians themselves ante-dates my modest activities with the British Commission and subsequently as British Vice-Consul in Kaunas and Vilnius. It goes back indeed to spacious days in Russia Proper, early during the war when I was working at the then Petrograd, now again happily Petersburg, as assistant correspondent for *The Times*. There in my scanty leisure I foregathered with the new sportsmen as a member of an athletic club yclept " Sanitas "—somewhat reminiscent of a fashionable tooth-powder, but a worthy institution none the less—where I knew Pozhela, a young Lithuanian, the amateur champion middle-weight wrestler of Russia in the Græco-Roman or French style. He was, I well recall, a wonderful physical specimen, as are many of his countrymen, with his black hair, rosy cheeks, retroussé nose and ever-ready smile. Allowing for the limitations of the French system, Pozhela was one of the most naturally gifted mat-men I have ever seen, and had he taken up the infinitely superior Japanese art of Judo, would certainly have become a top-notcher. He was absolutely tireless and his good nature and high spirits never flagged. He came back from the Dvina front badly wounded in the right arm, but soon recovered and wrestled as hard as ever. When I asked him if the war had affected his nerves he seemed tremendously amused. Nerves did not worry him.

It is, therefore, some slight moral satisfaction to realize

MEMBERS OF BRITISH MILITARY MISSION AT KAUNAS.

that even in those days I was fully aware that the Lithuanians were not Russians, but a distinct race with a distinctive language.

My resumption of Lithuanian ties was with a gentleman who has achieved a high reputation in a walk of life somewhat different from that so successfully cultivated by young Pozhela. I refer to Mr. T. Naroushevitch (Narusevičius), at the time of writing the popular Lithuanian Diplomatic Representative in London. I returned from Russia to Japan shortly before the Revolution of March 1917, and it was at Tokyo that I first met Mr. Naroushevitch, who, then an official in the Moscow municipal administration, had come to Japan on business, and invoked my services as translator from Russian into English. Four years or so later we met again quite unexpectedly at the Lithuanian President's residence in Kaunas, and were not long in recognizing each other and in renewing our former acquaintance.

I journeyed down from Riga to Kaunas at the end of August 1919 in charge of a heavy motor-lorry laden with preliminary supplies for our branch mission. With me was Mr. S. W. Powell, now British Vice-Consul at Kaunas. In addition we had two Lettish chauffeurs and two Lettish soldiers as armed guards, both decidedly " hefty " lads, who apparently would have welcomed nothing more heartily than a chance for a scrap with the detested Germans, who at that date were still in occupation of the territory south of Riga, and without whose " Ausweis " passage through those regions would have been impossible. This was on the eve of the outrageous Bermondt adventure, and we frequently passed machine-gun posts where German "non-coms" carefully scrutinized our papers before allowing us to continue our journey. On more than one occasion we had the privilege of giving a lift to sturdy specimens of the famous Iron Division which figured largely throughout the sporadic fighting with Latvia and Estonia, which preceded the armistice so ably arranged a short time before by Colonel S. G. Tallents, the British Commissioner, at Strasdenhoff, on the Aa River.

I well remember that this motor-lorry trip of about

150 miles was no joy ride, despite the magnificent weather which favoured us throughout. The going was quite good as far as Shavli, but after that we were constantly hitting sandy stretches into which the heavy wheels of the lorry deeply sank, stopping further progress till we had descended and shoved behind with all the beef at our disposal. Not only that, but we were continually compelled to excavate loads of sand from under the wheels and lay down tree branches as rails for the wheels to pass over until the ground grew firmer. Tiring work, this was, in a temperature nearer 90 than 80 in the shade.

In due course we reached that festive little health resort known as Radzivilishki, where we decided to stay the night. The place was full of German troops, and while we halted our limousine to let our guards seek out appropriate quarters, we found ourselves the cynosure of many a sinister Teutonic eye. Two of these belonged to a stocky red-faced unter-offizier whose broad deep chest was adorned with an iron cross. He seemed more than ordinarily interested in us, but did not ask for an introduction. The motive of his curiosity was revealed later.

After a good deal of reconnoitring, we put up for the night at a luxurious caravansery styled the Bristol, if my memory serves me rightly. It was a two-bedded room into which we were ushered, so Powell took one bed and I the other. The motor-lorry meanwhile had been run round to a neighbouring garage. Although severely assailed during the night by a species of wingless mosquito, we were so weary in the wake of our strenuous exertions that we soon fell asleep. We were aroused, however, about midnight by the abrupt entry of a small posse of German soldiers, headed by none other than our rubicond friend of the iron cross, who, with profuse apologies, explained that we were suspected of smuggling lethal weapons in our lorry, and must therefore accompany the posse to the Military Commandant for interrogation.

Having protested in the best German I could muster at such short notice, I as O.C. Lorry rose, dressed myself, and did the bidding of these burly myrmidons. One of our Lettish chauffeurs went with me as guide for the return trip, because the night was black as pitch, and I should never have been able to find my way back unaided. Luckily the ensuing ordeal did not prove very terrible. With my Ausweise and my winning way I was soon able to convince the commandant—a very worthy fellow— that my intentions were strictly civilian and that my lorry freight was harmless, wherefore we shook hands with considerable éclat and parted for ever.

Resuming our ride the next morning we finally ran into Keidany. As we were ambling bumpily over the cobbled streets a young and handsome man in the uniform, as I subsequently discovered, of the Lithuanian aviation corps, bounded out of a wayside house and clambered up behind. Turning to me in German he explained that he had been piloting Colonel Robinson, Head of the British Military Mission at Kaunas, down from Riga, but had run out of petrol, and had therefore landed in a neighbouring field and would be vastly obliged by a loan from our stores. We soon came upon the machine, an L.V.G., near which stood Colonel Robinson himself, a fine soldierly figure in uniform. While the young pilot was filling up, I asked Colonel Robinson who he might be. The Colonel placed a hand to his mouth and in a loud aside remarked, " Don't say a word, but he's a genuine Boche ! " We learned afterwards that his name was Rother, and that he was acting as a flying instructor in the Lithuanian aviation corps.

We all grew to love Rother, for he was a sunny cheerful character and, what is more to the purpose, a first-class airman. So cordial were our relations that we quite regretted his sudden departure for Germany some months later in very dramatic circumstances which I communicated at the time to the British Press, including *The Aeroplane*. This incident was connected with the capture by the Lithuanians near Dvinsk of a German Junker monoplane, which was flying to Moscow with two Turks, one of whom was subsequently known to be the famous Enver Pasha. They had descended too soon, thinking they were already in Russian territory, and the Lithuanian military had taken them into custody. For the time being the German pilot, named Hans Hesse, also a famous war airman who had flown from Berlin to Bagdad, and participated in many raids on English towns, and the two Turks were interned in a local hotel at Kaunas. Then one fine day the startling news was bruited abroad that the Turks had escaped. The manner of it was this.

Young Rother had taken out a machine from the aerodrome, ostensibly on a practice flight, with one of his best pupils, as far as an outlying fort. Here, through some collusion, the two Turks with a military guard were enjoying a stroll. As the machine landed, they approached it, whereupon Rother whipped out a spare automatic and deftly threw it to them, whilst with another he covered his pupil and made him re-start the propeller. The two Turks, threatening the guard in their turn, then got into the cockpit and Rother carried them safely off to Germany. The following day he had the nerve to telephone the General Staff from Tilsit to say that if they would pay him his arrears of salary he would return the stolen aeroplane. It was reported that he received something like a million marks for this daring rescue, and he certainly deserved it. I never met anybody who did not cordially admire Rother for his skill and courage, which particularly appealed to our British officers then at Kaunas.

To resume after this digression. Colonel Robinson told me that, not trusting Rother, he had sat behind him all the way from Riga with a drawn revolver in his hand, but fortunately Rother had played no tricks. From Keidany my companion Powell, not being very well, left the motor-lorry and flew with Colonel Robinson to Kaunas, which they reached in twenty minutes. Powell had himself been an air cadet towards the end of the war and was therefore quite at home in a plane. Less lucky, we spent a good many hours on the road before arriving at our destination, thanks to more sand, and at one spot a regular bog into which the front wheels of the lorry sank after breaking through what had seemed a perfectly firm road surface. It took the united efforts of many able-bodied men from an adjacent village, and more than an hour's hard work, to extricate us from this impasse, but after

that our luck changed for the better and we dashed down
the Ukmerge chaussée, and the Laisves Aleja of Kaunas
at dusk, in really fine style, and I was able to join my chief,
Colonel R. B. Ward, and Powell at supper in the Metropole
Hotel, where we had our temporary quarters, before turning
in for a well-earned rest.

From the very outset we made the acquaintance of
Polish intrigues, for a Polish plot had just been unearthed
and the town was under martial law, all street traffic
being suspended from 9 p.m. I remember that we had
to send a wireless message to Riga the same evening and
that Powell and I were challenged at least six times in the
course of a hundred yards' walk from the hotel to the wireless station and back.

The retrospect of my more than a year's sojourn at
Kaunas, unbroken save for a few trips to Vilnius, including
our ill-starred removal thither with the Lithuanian Government in the autumn of 1920, shows that we did not fare
at all badly. Excellent premises, with all the comforts
of home, were found for us at No. 19, Keistučio Gatve,
where we spent many pleasant, if strenuous days, for we
were pioneers on the job, and had to do all the rough spade
work for our professional successors.

Food is good and plentiful in Lithuania, and we lived
on the fat of the land, thus gradually filling out the con-
cavities bequeathed by war service and increasing our
neck and waist measurements.

Colonel Ward was essentially an open-air man, and out
of office we were constant companions, during the summer
months on morning rides with our Lithuanian liaison
officer, dear old Colonel Tomašauskas, on the bracing,
beautifully timbered uplands ; as members of boisterous
bathing parties in the swift waters of the Nemunas, or
motor-boat trips thereon ; on occasional motoring jaunts
to the famous Red Chateau and other neighbouring estates ;
sometimes with Colonel Ward as pilot in an aeroplane
flight over Kaunas ; and, last but not least, as ill-matched
opponents in the classic game of clock golf in our back
garden ; while in the winter we skated and tobogganed
together.

Our household pets comprised a couple of goats, several rabbits, a cat, and the Colonel's own personal possession, a delightful polizei-hund named Jim. In summer meals were taken in the garden, under a tree, where good digestion waited on appetite, thanks largely to the hilarity provoked by the pup's harmless persecution of the two goats. We in turn were persecuted by wasps which apparently had established a nest somewhere near our table, because although we must have slain hundreds in the course of the summer, we were never able to exhaust the supply. Fortunately none of us got stung.

The story of our Vilnius experiences has been told in Chapter XIX. But while in reminiscent mood I may say that I first visited Vilnius, then Vilna, in the summer of 1915, shortly before its capture by the Germans, when travelling through to Warsaw as a war correspondent. Again, I had paid the town a visit during the Polish régime in the winter of 1919-20, in bitterly cold weather which froze the oil in our Crossley overnight. My presence synchronized with that of Marshal Pilsudski and the Papal Nuncio, Cardinal Ratti, now Pope of Rome, who were attending special service in the cathedral at the time. Large bodies of Polish cavalry and infantry were paraded in the wide open space fronting the cathedral, where, despite a temperature which menaced my toes with frostbite after remaining stationary for even a few minutes, these poor fellows were compelled to stand for upwards of an hour, in terrible physical discomfort, to satisfy the Polish love of " swank " and puerile military display. I then had an opportunity to confirm the previous impression gained from my second visit to Warsaw not long before, that the Poles had succumbed badly to the imperialistic spirit. Officers formed virtually a privileged class to whom precedence was granted everywhere, notably on the railways, where the mere civilian had to be content with such accommodation as was available after my lords the officers had been served. The practice of saluting on the smallest provocation had been restored in all its pristine glory. No officer entered a restaurant, hotel lounge or other public place, without looking anxiously around for some brother officer to salute, and one felt instinctively that his failure to find a victim would involve severe disappointment. Other less showy, but more useful qualifications of an officer's calling, especially solicitude for the comfort and welfare of one's men, and technical knowledge, were not cultivated with anything like the same enthusiasm.

I should like also to add a few words about the brief Bolshevik régime in the city prior to the entry of the Lithuanians in the summer of 1920. I hold no brief for the Soviet, but seeing that it was my duty to enter Vilnius with Captain Baring Gould, then British Military Attaché, immediately after the withdrawal of the Red Army and the assumption of authority by the Lithuanians, I feel entitled to refer to the preposterous reports of Bolshevik atrocities which were sedulously printed by a certain section of the West European Press. It was stated, for instance, that something like 1,500 persons had been shot. As a matter of fact, the most painstaking investigation by the Lithuanian officials could not verify more than thirty of such executions, and the majority of the victims were Polish soldiers. Incidentally, I myself examined one of the graves in which several bodies had been buried in the outskirts of the town. It may be taken for granted that for every person shot by the Bolsheviks the Poles had similarly taken toll of adherents of the Soviet, so the account was perfectly squared. I allude to the matter just to show what monstrous exaggerations are apt to gain a start of the truth when the inspiration is tendencious.

The Rother incident was not our only aeroplane adventure. It is well known that German machines maintained regular communication with Moscow, though as a rule they flew so high as to be scarcely discernible. Once more, however, as in the case of the Junker monoplane, luck deserted a German pilot who was carrying the famous Swiss Communist Von Platen in a Gotha from Moscow to Germany in the spring, I think, of 1920. Von Platen had with him his newly-wedded wife, who, besides being herself a convinced and fervent Bolshevik, was a celebrated Russian soprano. The machine ran out of petrol owing to a leak, so the story ran, and had to land in Lithuanian territory, not far from Kaunas. Von Platen himself was detained some time in prison, but his wife was allowed to live at an hotel, where I made her acquaintance. We also met on several occasions at the home of a mutual friend, where I had the good fortune to hear her sing. She certainly had a wonderful voice, perfectly trained, and I thoroughly enjoyed these few meetings. I can well believe that the lady made a very able propagandist of Communist principles. She spoke with obvious sincerity about the proletarian love of music in Russia and declared that no artist could wish for a more attentive audience than one composed of the working classes, who did not attend in order to exhibit their clothes but to listen. Both Von Platen and his talented wife were eventually released and went, I believe, to Switzerland.

During our stay in Kaunas we naturally met most of the Lithuanian leaders, notably Smetona, the first President, Slezevičius, Naruševičius, Stulginskis, Galvanauskas, Dobkevičius, Dr. J. Šliūpas, M. P. Klimas, M. Yčas, Balutis, Kairys, the able Social Democratic chieftain : Baron Šilingas ; Professor Šimkus ; Professor Voldemaras, and others. The last-named was the head of the first Lithuanian Cabinet in November 1918, but besides his connexion with politics is a distinguished scholar who, before that date, had taught history and classic philology at the Universities of Petersburg and Perm. He reads, writes and speaks fifteen languages, including English, which he knows almost perfectly although he has never been in England. As a raconteur I have rarely met his equal, and on many occasions he kept the table " on a roar " with his amusing anecdotes drawn from every walk of life. But the gift of tongues is common enough among the Lithuanians. The servants at our consulate nearly all spoke four, i.e. Lithuanian, Polish, Russian and German.

In the course of our official duties, it was our privilege to announce to the Lithuanian Government Great Britain's *de facto* recognition of Lithuanian independence, which resulted in a popular ovation in our honour outside the Metropole Hotel, where we were then quartered, in the autumn of 1919. It is to be regretted that we had to leave our post without being permitted to convey an intimation of *de jure* recognition, to which Lithuania was long ago entitled.

While we thus waver and procrastinate, France and Poland are perfecting their plans for the political and military domination of Eastern Europe, the essential prelude in their case to the hoped-for economic stranglehold. If they cannot achieve their entire programme in Upper Silesia they will leave no stone unturned to involve both Lithuania and the Memel region in their toils. The Franco-Polish policy of alienating the Memel region from the rest of Lithuania at all costs has led to an anomalous situation which I have already attempted to describe elsewhere. If we are not careful we shall wake up one of these days to belated realization that the Poles, in collusion with their French patrons, have carved out another " corridor," this time from the south through Lithuania along the Nemunas River to link up with the Memel region. Whether or not before then Memel had received the nominal status of an independent State, France would see that in practice Poland possessed the port she covets in fee simple, regardless of the national susceptibilities of the Lithuanian majority.

With the mass of data available to substantiate the foregoing anticipation, it seems strange that British statesmanship can continue blind to what is going on or so callous to British economic and political interests as to connive at it. Granted that Lithuania herself would never voluntarily sign her own death warrant by accepting any such solution of her difference with Poland as that so blandly proffered by M. Hymans, it would be childish in the light of facts to imagine that Polish " diplomacy," fertile in underhand expedients, will not eventually succeed in precipitating another *fait accompli* in Western Lithuania, on the familiar lines of the Zeligowski and Korfanty adventures in Eastern Lithuania and Upper Silesia respectively. Poland will act thus, as she has acted in the past, with the open or secret approval and backing of the Quai d'Orsay.

Confession is good for the soul. The special and peculiar bane of the *post-bellum* situation here and elsewhere has been and is the refusal to recognize facts, and the habit of repeating parrot-like the thing that is not. The thing that is not, so far as Poland and Lithuania, and Poland and Upper Silesia are concerned, is a community of Franco-British interests, and one very salient fact we refuse to recognize is the necessity for a change of British policy to meet the lack of such community. We have seen from the first that so long as the Polish-Lithuanian dispute is entrusted to the tender mercies of the French and Belgian members of the League of Nations, there can be no settlement save by *force majeure* and the stultification of every principle for which the war is supposed to have been fought. France is irrevocably bound to Poland by special pacts, and to imagine that either her representatives or those of Belgium, who shares France's Welt-Politik, will ever sanction a decision running counter to Polish wishes and ambitions is too feeble for words.

If it is too late in the day to appeal to justice, then let me appeal at least to self-interest to elicit from all classes of the British public, who have to work for a living, a plainly-worded demand that political reactionaries shall no longer be permitted to penalize an entire people whose friendship and pro-British orientation may in the near future prove an invaluable asset to this country.

APPENDIX

ANNEX I

SUVALKI AGREEMENT

The Delegation of the Government of Lithuania, composed of :

(1) Representatives of the Lithuanian High Command, Lieut.-General Maxim Katche and Commander Alexander Šumskis,

(2) Representatives of the Ministry for Foreign Affairs, Messrs. Bronius Balutis, Voldemar Carneckis, and Mykolas Birziška,

and the Delegation of the Government of Poland, composed of :

(1) Representative of the Polish High Command, Colonel Mackiewicz,

(2) Representative of the Ministry for Foreign Affairs, M. Jules Lukasiewicz,

met at the Conference of Suvalki, on September 30–October 7, 1920, and, after having presented their credentials, which were recognized in good and proper form, concluded the following agreement.

CHAPTER I

On the Line of Demarcation.

(a) A line of demarcation, which does not decide beforehand what are the territorial rights of the two contracting parties, is fixed in the following manner :

From the frontier of East Prussia to the confluence of the Tcharna-Hantcha with the Niemen, i.e. the line fixed by the decision of the Supreme Council on December 8, 1919 ; then along the Niemen to the mouth of the Greva ; then ascending the Greva to the line Noretch-Rotnitsa ; then in a straight line to the confluence of the Scroblis with the Neretchanka ; then along the Neretchanka to the mouth of the Derechnitsa, leaving the village of Salovertsy on the Lithuanian side and the village Holodubno on the Polish side ; along the Derechnitsa to the spot where it is crossed by the Vilna-Orany railway, almost 2½ kilometres to the east of the Orany station ; then along the road through Bartelé Kuice, Novy-Dvor, Eishishki, Podzitwa, Horodenka, and the station of Bastouny, leaving this road and the Bastouny station in the hands of the Polish authorities.

(b) In proportion as hostilities between the Polish troops and Lithuanian troops cease, the above-mentioned line throughout its extent, in conformity with Chapter II of the present agreement, must not under any pretext be passed by the troops of the two contracting parties. However, this line shall not prevent the peasants from cultivating their fields which are situated on the other side of it.

(c) The establishment on the spot of the line of demarcation on the ground of the old government of Suvalki in the portions that are contemplated by the decision of the Supreme Council of December 8, 1919, shall be referred to the Control Commission of the League of Nations.

CHAPTER II

On the Cessation of Hostilities.

(a) In confirming and completing the cessation of hostilities between the Polish army and the Lithuanian army, which have been accepted during the present Conference, and which have only a provisional character and relate only to certain places, the two contracting parties undertake to cease all hostilities on the entire length of the line of demarcation described in Chapter I, para. (a), of the present agreement, i.e. from the frontier of East Prussia to the southern line which passes through Potourse, almost 9 kilometres to the south-east of Eishishki.

The Soviet troops having been removed to the east of the Vilna-Lida railway, military actions shall be stopped between the Polish troops and the Lithuanian troops on the sector of the line of demarcation between the southern line of the village of Potourse and the station of Bastouny inclusively.

(c) *As regards the cessation of hostilities and the establishment of the line of demarcation between the Lithuanian troops and the Polish troops in the region to the east of the southern line of the village of Bastouny, these questions shall be regulated by a special agreement when the Soviet troops are removed from there. In case of failure to arrive at this agreement, the two contracting parties, in order to determine these questions, reserve the right to appeal to the League of Nations.*

CHAPTER III

On the Station of Orany.

(a) The Polish authorities undertake to allow to pass freely through the station of Orany, Lithuanian trains which are proceeding from Olita to Vilna and return, except troop trains and trains with war material, and guarantee to the Lithuanian trains at the Orany station all help and all technical conditions necessary for their free movement in either direction.

(b) As an exception, the Polish Government consents to allow to pass without difficulty through the Orany station trains with troops and war materials which are proceeding from Olita to Vilna, on condition that there are not more than seven of them ; that there shall not pass more than two trains a day, and that the passage of these trains through the Orany station shall take place between seven and 17 o'clock Polish time.

(c) Supervision of the strict execution of the decisions described in paragraphs (a) and (b) of the present Chapter shall be entrusted to the Control Commission of the League of Nations.

CHAPTER IV

On the Exchange of Prisoners.

The two contracting parties declare reciprocal consent in principle to begin the exchange of all prisoners made by either contracting party. The order and date of exchange shall be decided separately.

CHAPTER V

On the Duration of Agreement.

The present agreement comes into force at noon of October 10, 1920, this date, however, not affecting the cessation of hostilities already accepted, and remains in force until all litigious questions between the Poles and the Lithuanians shall be definitely settled.

During re-drafting of the present agreement the two contracting parties have made use of the map of the German General Staff on a scale of 1 : 100,000.

The present treaty is drafted in two equivalent copies, in Lithuanian and in Polish, and is signed at Suvalki, on October 7, 1920.

For the Lithuanian Delegation.—Lieut.-General Katche, Bronius Balutis, Voldemaras Carneckis, Mykolas Birziška, Majoras Šumskis.

For the Polish Delegation.—M. Mackiewicz, Colonel ; J. Lukasiewicz.

ANNEX II

ENQUIRY

Into Military Events of the Polish-Lithuanian Conflict from July 1920 to October 9 of the same year, the date of the occupation of Vilna by the Polish Troops of General Zeligowski.

Attached is an Explanatory Note from the Chief of the General Staff of the Lithuanian Army, Colonel KLEŠČINSKAS.

JULY.

6th.—In consequence of the Bolshevik offensive, the Polish army began the evacuation of the region situated between Dvinsk and Turmont.

14

7th.—The Chief of the 3rd Lithuanian Division received orders to advance and occupy the region evacuated by the Poles. An encounter has taken place between Lithuanian and Russian detachments near Lavkes. A detachment of Bolshevik cavalry arrived at the Turmont station and demanded a free passage through the Lithuanian lines in view of an attack of Polish forces in the rear. A categorical refusal was opposed to this demand. Major Koscialkovski arrived from Vilna at the Lithuanian Headquarters with a proposal that the Lithuanian Command should withdraw all its forces from the line of demarcation and dispose them between Dvinsk and Lake Drisviaty, with absolute prohibition to cross the demarcation lines. To this proposal was joined one for the elaboration of a general plan of military operations against the Bolsheviks.

A refusal was given to this unseasonable proposal of Major Koscialkovski.

8th–11th.—The Lithuanian armies successively occupied the localities evacuated by the Polish troops.

12th.—The Lithuanian troops extinguished a fire caused by Poles in the region of Lakes Golodus (Suvalki) and Meischagoly.

14th.—News to hand of a complete evacuation of Vilna by the Poles and of the approach of the Bolsheviks. Orders at once given to the Chief of the 1st Division to entrain his troops and put them *en route* in order to occupy Vilna. At the same moment, a report arrived from the Lithuanian liaison officer with the Poles, according to which Colonel Rylski had been sent to Kovno with a proposal to the Lithuanian Government to send its troops by rail to Vilna and to occupy that city.

This proposal did not prevent the Polish troops from directing a violent fire on the Lithuanian *echelons* 6 kilometres from Vievis, which gave rise to a fight lasting three hours. The Lithuanian losses were several dozen killed and wounded.

This fight had the effect of retarding by 24 hours the advance of the Lithuanians and permitting the Bolsheviks to occupy Vilna.

15th.—The Lithuanian troops enter Vilna.

16th.—Lithuanian forces occupy Rudzischki, Orany and Marcinkance.

17th.—A Polish brigade having penetrated into Lithuanian territory is interned in Lithuania.

18th.—Lithuanian troops occupy Druskiniki and Rotnitza.

19th.—In consequence of the demand of the inhabitants of Suvalki to come to their help against the Bolsheviks, orders are given to the 1st Battalion of the Reserve to occupy the region evacuated by the Polish troops. The battalion occupies the line of villages Bobcy, Vizainy, Tschaplichki, Slobodka, as far as Lake Seivy and Kadych.

20th.—The Poles precipitately evacuate Suvalki and Augustovo.

21st–29th.—The Lithuanian troops progressively advance.

29th.—The Poles have definitely left Suvalki.
80th.—At 20 o'clock the Lithuanian forces enter Suvalki.

AUGUST.

2nd.—The Lithuanian troops at Suvalki have advanced as far as the line Ratchi, Plotitchno, Lake Vigrus, Tscharna, Gantcha, Vysoki Most, Boudvietce.

6th.—An agreement is signed with the representatives of the Bolshevik High Command, according to which the Bolsheviks pledge themselves to evacuate Lithuanian territory before August 24th.

8th.—The Lithuanian troops have advanced as far as the line of the Augustovo Canal.

11th.—The Bolsheviks arrive at Rotnitza with a view to organizing a " Revkom " (Revolutionary Committee), but are driven from this locality by Lithuanian soldiers.

16th.—At Vilna, Lithuanian soldiers guard the public buildings from which the Bolsheviks have been expelled.

21st.—Armed Bolsheviks made their appearance in the region of Sopotzkine. After an armed collision with the Lithuanian troops the Bolsheviks retired.

Representatives of the " Revkon " of Augustovo demanded from the Commander of the 1st Reserve Battalion the surrender of Sopotzkine and received a categorical refusal.

22nd.—The Commanders of the 1st Division and the Mariampol Group received orders not to allow the Bolsheviks to cross Lithuanian territory.

23rd.—News to hand of a Bolshevik check. The Bolsheviks demand passage through Lithuanian territory for their wounded. This has been refused.

Delegates from the 15th Bolshevik Army present themselves at Seiny to the Commander of the Mariampol Group, authorized to conduct negotiations with the Lithuanian authorities concerning a passage into Lithuanian territory for the 15th Bolshevik Army. The Commander of the Mariampol Group receives orders to refuse the said passage to the Bolsheviks, and the Mariampol Group is reinforced with two regiments and two batteries.

24th.—An order is given to the Lithuanian armies to occupy the second demarcation line against the Bolsheviks.

The Commandant of Vilna is charged with the administration of that town.

Lithuanian detachments destroy the railway between Orany and Olkeniki with a view to preventing Bolshevik forces in retreat from proceeding to Vilna.

A delegation arrives from Grodno at Druskeniki demanding the occupation of Grodno. In consequence, the Commander of the Mariampol Group receives an order to send scouts to Grodno and to occupy, if possible, the line Grobovo–Augustovo–Shtabin, and the remainder of the Lithuanian State frontier, in conformity with the treaty concluded with Russia.

The Commander of the Mariampol Group reports as follows : In his region considerable Bolshevik forces penetrated into Lithuanian territory, but were arrested, disarmed, and sent to the rear under Lithuanian military escort.

25th.—Order given to the Commander of the 1st Division to intern the " Revkom " of Landvarovo.

26th.—Order given to the Commandant of Vilna to demand from the Bolsheviks an immediate evacuation of that town.

A Polish delegation arrives at Kovno. It is composed of Colonel Matzkevitch and Captain Romer, who propose a plan of combined action against Soviet Russia.

27th.—A delegation arrives from Grodno demanding that Lithuanian troops should occupy that town.

28th.—The Lithuanian Government sends to the Polish Government a Note in which it declares that Lithuania will observe strict neutrality in the Polish-Russian war. It proposes to the Polish Government to give an order to its troops not to pass the Lithuanian frontiers and, as regards the region of Suvalki (where the frontiers of Lithuania have not yet been fixed), to establish a provisional demarcation line Grayevo–Augustovo–Shtabin, in order to avoid sanguinary collisions.

Polish forces composed of a regiment of infantry, a battery and a squadron penetrate into Augustovo.

The Commander of the Mariampol Group receives an order : (1) Not to allow the Poles to approach the line occupied by us ; (2) To inform the Poles that, owing to our neutrality, we cannot permit them access to our territory, and that should the Poles undertake a forward movement, we shall be obliged to offer them armed resistance.

30th.—Having reinforced their troops at Augustovo and begun guerilla warfare against the Lithuanians, the Poles drove the Lithuanian detachments from Domorovo. Several Lithuanians were killed, wounded, and taken prisoners.

At 20 o'clock the Poles launch an offensive against the Lithuanians on the whole Suvalki front.

A French officer arrived at Suvalki, leaves for Augustovo with the Commander of the 10th Regiment of Infantry (Lithuanian) in order to confer with the Poles. The result of these pourparlers is the liberation of the Lithuanian company stationed at Augustovo.

31st.—The French General, Manneville, arrives at Seiny to inform the Chief of the 2nd Lithuanian Division that the Poles are advancing to occupy the Foch line. The Chief of the Lithuanian Division declares to the French General that he has received no instructions on the subject. He adds that in the event of a forward movement by the Poles, he would be compelled to offer them armed resistance.

The same day the Chief of the General Staff of the Lithuanian Army, Colonel KLEŠČINSKAS, had a telephone conversation with the said French General. The latter confirmed his communication on the subject of the intention of the Poles to occupy the Foch line. By order of the Commander-in-Chief of the Lithuanian Army, Colonel KLEŠČINSKAS begged the General to transmit to the Poles a demand to halt at the points which they occupied at the moment, other questions to be elucidated by means of diplomatic negotiations. The French General replied that he had already advised the Polish Command thereof, but that it was impossible for him to demand from the Poles a stoppage of their advance, such a demand having no chance whatever of being taken into consideration by the Poles.

Colonel KLEŠČINSKAS declared, in the name of the Commander-in-Chief, that if the Poles, notwithstanding this proposal, continued their advance, the Commander-in-Chief would reserve for himself entire freedom of action.

In spite of these pourparlers, the Poles continue their movement.

Several hours later, the Poles, after a lively engagement, occupy Seiny and demand a withdrawal of the Lithuanian troops beyond the Foch line, for September 2nd at noon.

SEPTEMBER.

2nd.—The Lithuanian armies have reinforced their resistance to the Poles with a view to arresting their advance on Lithuanian territory. They have also occupied the line Farm of Yasinowska–Seiny–Lipsk.

5th.—The Poles have counter-attacked and the Lithuanian detachments were obliged to retire on the line Lipsk–Rudavka–Rigalovka.

The Chief of the Mariampol Group has received orders to defend the line Rigalovka–Lipsk–Bogatery–Rudovka–Czarna–Gansza–Lake Vigrey–Lake Perty–Kaletniki–Lipina–Fornetka–Lake Vizainy–Lake Vichtinietz.

6th.—In reply to a proposal of the Polish Government to open "direct negotiations with the object of finding an amicable solution," the Lithuanian Government sends its consent, and proposes the town of Mariampol.

7th–8th.—Fighting on the entire front with varying success. The Lithuanians lose Seiny once more.

9th.—The Polish Government proposes for direct negotiations the town of Kalvaria instead of Mariampol.

12th.—The Lithuanian Government, while acquiescing in the proposal for negotiations at Kalvaria for September 14th, proposes to the Polish Government a suspension of hostilities on both sides on September 13th at midday. Without taking this proposal into account, the Poles continue their operations.

13th.—At 10 o'clock, continually repulsing Polish attacks, the Lithuanians occupy Seiny, and in conformity with the order of the Commander-in-Chief, at noon suspended their action on the entire front, with the exception of the village Giby where, as the Poles pursued their attacks, the Lithuanians were obliged to defend themselves.

14th.—Fighting is stopped on the entire front.

At 5.30 a Polish parlementaire arrives at Kalvaria, with a letter for our delegation. He informs us that at noon on the 13th news was received at Warsaw of the consent of the Lithuanians to negotiations with the Poles, and that on the evening of 13th September orders were given to the Polish troops to suspend their operations.

15th.—A Polish delegation has arrived at Kalvaria with Colonel Matzkiewicz as president. The Lithuanian delegation, with General Katché, arrived at Kalvaria on the 14th.

16th.—At Kalvaria, negotiations. On the front, scouting encounters.

18th.—At 19.30 o'clock at Kalvaria, the negotiations are broken by the Poles, who refuse to establish along the line of 8th December 1919 the neutral zone proposed by the Lithuanian delegation. Truce on the 19th till 6 o'clock.

19th–21st.—The Poles renew the action against the Lithuanians on the entire front.

There is sent from Vilna by rail, via Orany, the 7th Regiment, to occupy the Niemen to the south of Goza.

The Poles having concentrated considerable forces, launched an offensive against the centre of our army and, after violent fighting we are thrown back on the line Lake Galadous–Dousnitsa–Jopse–Gruchi–Kopcivo–Biala–Ganja.

The Lithuanian Government informs the Polish Government that as direct negotiations have given no result, it has decided to submit the settlement of the dispute to the League of Nations.

23rd.—Detachments of the Polish army are moving towards the Niemen with the object of crossing that river. The rest of the enemy's forces continue to harass the Lithuanian troops on the line Pazerniki–Jivulchichki–Niemen.

At 22 o'clock the Poles cross the Niemen at Druskiniki after having cut off several detachments of the 7th Regiment stationed at the Martsinkancie station. Polish cavalry has destroyed the bridge over the Oula, which prevents the *echelons* (rolling-stock) of the 7th Regiment from opening a way to the north.

24th.—On the front, encounters between scouts.

25th.—The Poles who crossed the river at Druskiniki have attacked the rear of the Lithuanian detachments established ·to the south of the Martsinkancie station and in the neighbourhood of the village Natcha, forcing these detachments to retire to the east, the roads to the north being cut off by the Poles.

26th.—Important local engagements on the entire front. Some

detachments of the 1st Infantry Regiment, under Polish pressure, are obliged to withdraw to the line Yurkchancie–Mistuny–Pulstoki–Kuze. Order given to the Lithuanian army to concentrate in the region of Vilna.

The Polish Government proposes fresh direct negotiations for September 29th at Suvalki.

27th–28th.—The Lithuanian Government accepts the proposal for negotiations at Suvalki, and proposes the cessation of hostilities from the 29th.

On the front, scout encounters. Orders are given to the armies to cease hostilities against the Poles on the entire front at noon on the 29th.

29th.—Negotiations with the Poles have begun at Suvalki. The Poles declare their consent to a truce, but only in the region of the highroad Kalvaria–Suvalki between 16 and 18 o'clock.

30th.—Owing to the insistence of the Lithuanian delegation, the Poles agree to a suspension of hostilities, but only west of the Niemen. They will not, however, agree to one east of the Niemen, ascribing their refusal to their ignorance of the whereabouts of our armies and that of the Bolsheviks, and, indeed, while the negotiations are proceeding at Suvalki, the Poles, after concentrating forces south of the river Oula, assume the offensive along the Martsinkancie–Orany railway.

OCTOBER.

1st.—With the help of a Lithuanian armoured train, the Poles were repulsed. Notwithstanding their promise to cease hostilities, the Poles, to the west of the Niemen, have attacked our positions and driven back our detachments.

2nd.—The Poles renew the attack and occupy the villages Juratchichki (to the south of Orany) and Jirvine.

3rd.—At 6 o'clock considerable Polish forces launch an offensive against Orany, and at 9.30 occupy the town of Orany and the station of the same name.

The Chief of the 3rd Division receives orders to dislodge the Poles from Orany, and drive them back beyond the river Oula.

4th.—The detachments of the 3rd Division succeeded in driving back some of the Poles, but the station and town of Orany remain in their hands.

5th.—Intermittent fire on the front. The order is given to the armies to entrench in their occupied positions and avoid all action. The Chief of Aviation receives orders not to bomb the Polish armies, and to suspend all machine-gun fire.

6th.—At the Suvalki Conference it is decided to suspend hostilities in the region of Orany (from the Niemen to the meridian of Poturtche).

Along the Vilna–Lida railway the Poles, assuming the offensive, have occupied Gervichki, Potchebuty, Pocholie and Beniakonie.

A delegation has left Vilna for Yachuny, composed of the English

Major Pargiter, the French Captain Pujol, and the Lettish Colonel Ozol, in order to obtain from the Polish Command (nearest to Vilna) explanations of the reasons for the movements of Polish troops. At the same time the Poles at Suvalki declare that they have no intention of occupying Vilna.

The result of the Suvalki Conference is as follows : An agreement is signed according to the terms of which a demarcation line will be established between the Lithuanian and Polish troops. commencing from the German frontier to the east, passing through Orany, and terminating at the railway station of Bastuny, to the south of Vilna.

The Allied Delegation, returned to Vilna, reports that the Poles have declared that they have received no orders relative to the suspension of hostilities, and await instructions.

8th.—Superior Polish forces have launched an offensive from the south to the north against Vilna, which is defended by two battalions of the 4th Regiment, a battalion of the 9th Regiment, and one battery.

Owing to the clearly ascertained intention of the Poles to occupy Vilna, the order for evacuation of this town is given, which order is executed on the night of 8th–9th October. During the whole day of the 8th and the night of the 9th a violent engagement developed south of Vilna.

9th.—Fighting continues with unequal forces (the Poles have about five divisions) till noon, after which the Lithuanian army receives orders to cross the Vilija and Vaka. At that time the evacuation of Vilna had already terminated.

The Poles occupy Vilna.

The foregoing summary has been compiled from data furnished by official documents and the War Diary of the General Staff of the Lithuanian Army

---

EXPLANATORY NOTE.

The following appears from a rapid examination of the Polish-Lithuanian conflict between July 6th and September 9th :

1. While the Polish army was sustaining a series of reverses and at a time when the most feeble pressure by the Lithuanian army against the rear of the Polish army would have caused the latter a veritable catastrophe, the Lithuanian Government and army observed a perfectly correct attitude towards the Polish army (which had occupied Lithuanian territory since 1919), and perfect neutrality, categorically refusing Bolshevist troops passage through the Lithuanian lines and not hesitating to intern them.

2. When the Lithuanian Government and its army, owing to the failure of the Polish army, were endeavouring to occupy Lithuanian territory and the capital Vilna as quickly as possible and liberate them from the Bolshevist administration, the Polish Government

and its army on the contrary were obstinately resolved to prevent the Lithuanians from occupying that town and those territories. Even at the time of the disorderly retreat of the Polish armies before the Bolsheviks, any forward movement of the Lithuanian army encountered the resistance of Polish forces. The consequence of this attitude was that the consent of the Polish Command to the occupation of Vilna by the Lithuanians was obtained only when the Bolsheviks had already occupied that town. With the object of retarding the occupation of Vilna by the Lithuanian troops, an action was also provoked at Vievis by the Polish army which attacked a military train transporting armoured motor-cars.

3. Notwithstanding the Bolshevik successes, the Lithuanian Government and its army made every effort to free Lithuanian territory, while threatening the Bolsheviks.

4. Considering that at the time of the gravest Polish military reverses, the Lithuanian Government and Command refrained from opening negotiations with the Bolsheviks regarding co-ordination of their operations against the Poles, one can only deem ridiculous the Polish assertion relative to the concentration of Bolshevist forces in the rear of the Lithuanian army, as well as the co-operation of the Lithuanian and Bolshevik armies at the moment of the failure of the latter. This assertion is contrary to the truth and common sense.

5. Faithful to their declaration of strict neutrality, the Lithuanian Government and Command issued a series of orders relative to the prohibition of no matter what military force from penetrating into Lithuanian territory, not hesitating to disarm and intern the Bolsheviks, which actually took place, and at the same time transmitting the settlement of the Polish-Lithuanian conflict to diplomatic negotiations and to the League of Nations.

6. The occupation of Suvalki by the Lithuanian armies was decided on in the wake of urgent and repeated demands from the local population imploring succour from the horrors of the Bolshevist administration.

7. Notwithstanding many proposals from the Lithuanian Government regarding a peaceful settlement of mutual relations, the Polish Government preferred a settlement of this question by arms and was the first to begin military operations from August 28th to August 30th.

8. As regards the negotiations which had just opened, the Polish Government raised a series of obstacles to them which, on the one hand, showed clearly the insincerity of its desire to reach a pacific settlement and, on the other, denoted a tendency to delay matters with the object of putting its secret projects into execution. This manœuvre is confirmed by facts. While peace negotiations were taking place at Suvalki, Polish attacks were launched in the region of Orany with the evident object of occupying the railway junction and preventing the transfer of our troops from Suvalki to Vilna.

In occupying Orany the Poles attained their object, after which the negotiations at Suvalki developed with more success. In order to have their hands free in the region of Orany, the Poles consented to suspend military operations only to the west of the Niemen. As soon as their end was attained and the Orany station was in their hands, they consented to conclude a suspension of hostilities in the region of Orany, but only as far as the meridian of Poturtché, leaving the region to the south of Vilna exempt from all obligation, and clumsily ascribing their refusal to complete ignorance as to the whereabouts of our forces and those of the Bolsheviks. It is useless to insist on the absurdity of such an explanation. How indeed could one suppose that the victorious Polish Command did not know what troops were before it ? The object was perfectly clear ; by drawing away in the region of Orany our troops on the march from Suvalki to Vilna for the purpose of defending that city, the Poles facilitated the occupation of Vilna for the so-called rebel troops.

9. The negotiations of the Allied Delegation, which had left Vilna on October 6th, and the reply of the Polish Command, clearly show the nature of the " chivalrous conduct " of the rebel General who did not scruple to employ any means to dissimulate his real " noble intentions."

At the same time let us not forget that through the intermediary of the English Colonel Ward, the Polish Minister for Foreign Affairs, Sapieha, solemnly affirmed that the Poles did not even think of occupying Vilna.

On October 7th at Suvalki was signed the agreement regarding the establishment of the line of demarcation, and the same day the Poles attacked Vilna.

10. From the attached statements of officers of the General Staff of General Zeligowski's Army [1] it is clearly disclosed that Zeligowski was never for a single instant a " rebel " General, and that everything was and is directed from Warsaw.

ANNEX A

The Chief of the Organization Section of the General Staff of the Army of General Zeligowski, Lieutenant Grodski, deposed as follows :—

1. On October 1–2, 1920, a conference took place at Grodno in the train of Marshal PILSUDSKI, at which were present Generals PILSUDSKI, RYDZ SMIGLY, BERBETSKI, ZELIGOWSKI, ZHANTKOVSKI, Colonel KOTZ, officers of the General Staff, including Lieutenant

---

[1] Captain Buczynski, Chief of Armament Section ; Captain Engineer Javorsky, Lieutenant Slovikovski, Attaché to the Commissariat Bureau ; Lieutenant Edmund Gegendorf Grodski, Chief of Organization Section (who fled from the Polish army of General Zeligowski for political motives).

GRODSKI. At this meeting a plan drafted by Colonel KOTZ, Chief of the Volunteer Division, was finally adopted for the occupation of Vilna, and General ZELIGOWSKI was appointed to direct the operation instead of General ZHANTKOVSKI, who had been proposed. The composition of troops assigned for the occupation of Vilna was as follows : 1st and 3rd Divisions of Legionaries, 1st and 2nd Lithuanian-White Russian Divisions, the Volunteer Division of Colonel KOTZ, a total of five Divisions of Infantry with a corresponding quantity of Cavalry and Artillery. At this time negotiations were proceeding at Suvalki between the Lithuanians and Poles on the suspension of military operations and the establishment of a demarcation line.

2. On October 6, 1920, Marshal PILSUDSKI near Lida carried out an inspection of the troops assigned for the occupation of Vilna. On that day the Poles began an offensive along the Lida-Vilna Railway.

3. After the Geneva Conference on the Polish-Lithuanian question, where the subject of disarming General ZELIGOWSKI's troops was raised, the following plan was drafted. To save himself from disarmament, General ZELIGOWSKI with a division would ostensibly flee to Kovno. Two divisions assigned for his disarmament would march on his flanks. On General ZELIGOWSKI's arrival at Kovno, however, he would overthrow the Lithuanian Government, while the divisions assigned for his disarmament would go over to his side.

4. On the third day following the occupation of Vilna, electric generators with munitions and arms for General ZELIGOWSKI's army arrived in the town. In order to conceal the carriage of these munitions to the warehouses from the observation of the French officers attached to General ZELIGOWSKI's army, the General Staff appropriated a large sum of money for a dinner in the Hotel St. George to the foreign officers, which was given. During this dinner all the munitions and arms were conveyed on carts and motor-cars to the Schmidt factory.

5. Subsequently, the task of rationing General ZELIGOWSKI's army and supplying it with ammunition and clothing was effected in the following manner : In order to conceal transport from the observation of the Control Commission everything was conveyed from Central Poland in trains. Before reaching Lida everything was unloaded from the trains and carried in carts and motors, past Lida, to Beniakone and Vilna.

6. In December and January, ZELIGOWSKI's army was re-armed with French rifles and machine-guns brought from Warsaw.

7. The Information Bureau of General ZELIGOWSKI's army derives its financial resources direct from the Information Bureau of the General Staff in Warsaw.

Officer GRODSKI gave his deposition on April 14, 1921, in Kovno, in the presence of the Minister of War, Professor ŠIMKUS, the

ex-Minister of War, Colonel ŽUKAS, Colonel KLEŠČĪNSKAS of the
General Staff, and General KATCHE, Chief of the Officers' Course.

Analogous depositions were given by the Chief of the Armament
Section of Zeligowski's General Staff, Captain Buczynski, his
assistant Engineer-Captain Javorski, and Chief of the Commissariat
Section, Lieutenant Slovikovski.

ANNEX B

Statement of the Polish Officer, Lieutenant Edmund Gegendorf Grodski.

On April 8, 1921, I went over to the Lithuanian army with some
comrades of the army of Zeligowski (which is only a part of the
Polish regular army), the Chief of the Armament Section, Captain
Buczynski, Captain-Engineer Javorski, and the Attaché to the Commissariat Bureau, Lieutenant Slovikovski.   Being in Lithuanian
territory I wish to furnish absolutely authentic information on the
organization of the P.O.W. operating in Lithuania.   I know from a
certain source that the centre of this organization is at Warsaw, and
that at its head is Section No. 2 of Information of the Polish General
Headquarters, the chief of which is Lieut.-Colonel Matczynski.
The latter's substitute, Major Kieszkowski, is the Commander-in-
Chief of the entire P.O.W. organization.   This organization is
directly connected with the 2nd Information Section, which in its
turn is subordinated to the Chief of the General Staff.   The P.O.W.
organization possesses at Vilna its sections P.P.S. and P.O.W.,
equally directed by the 2nd Section of Warsaw.   The Chief of the
2nd Section of Vilna is Major Koscialkowski, ex-Commander of the
Sharpshooters of the Niemen.   At Kovno it is an old Starosta
of the Troki district, Lieutenant Staniewicz, who is entrusted with
the organization of the P.O.W.   To the direction of Staniewicz
are confided the sharpshooters of the Niemen and the " bojowki "
(a preparatory fighting organization in Lithuania).   At the head
of each bojowka is a Polish officer.   At Kovno there are 100 members
of these bojowki, of whom none is inferior to the rank of non-
commissioned officer.   All these men have done their six or seven
years of gymnasium, and have followed special courses of military
instruction.   The chief of these bojowki at Kovno is an ex-officer
of the Russian army, Antzierovitch.   As for the Commander of
the Sharpshooters of the Niemen, he is a Lieutenant of the name
of Staniewicz.   This organization is divided into local comman-
datures, and into " obwody " (districts).   The names of the commanders of these obwody are not known to me, nor the division
of these districts.   With reference to the opinion of the Polish
Government on Lithuania, I can affirm that it has been decided
to overthrow by all possible means the Government of Kovno,

and it is to this end that it is deemed necessary to give a solid organization to the P.O.W. Important funds are actually devoted to this end; an unlimited credit exempt from all control is guaranteed; also to the chiefs of the bojowki. The entire organization is directed by Lieut.-Colonel Matczynski, who has at his disposal unlimited credits, which he transfers to Major Kieszkowski, who in his turn sends money by couriers to the chiefs of the bojowki. The Chief of the 2nd Section proposes to unite all the organizations, i.e. the P.O.W. and the P.P.S., Ordodzenie (Renaissance) and Straz Kresowa (Guard of the Borders), into a single " organization of the Niemen." I cannot, however, say whether this project has been realized. All the other officers confirm these allegations. The signatures follow.

GRODSKI, STANISLAV JAVORSKI,
SLOVIKOVSKI, and Captain BUCZYNSKI.

The enquiry was conducted by Captain Uzupis,
Kovno, April 13, 1921.

ANNEX C

Deposition of Captain Buczynski.

I. To the question regarding the original armament of the Zeligowski army and the renewal of the same, he replied :

After the occupation of Vilna by General Zeligowski's army, all the regiments of that General were armed in the most defective and heterogeneous manner. Machine-guns were completely lacking and there could be no question even of establishing uniformity of armament. I was appointed Chief of the Armament Section the fourth day after the occupation of Vilna, and from that moment I had no other concern than to improve the equipment of the entire army of Zeligowski as speedily as possible.

Nevertheless, the engagements in progress did not permit me to realize my project. It was in the second half of January that I completed the effective equipment, with the help of the Director of the Arsenal, Engineer Javorski. At present, each infantry regiment of General Zeligowski possesses 30 French " Hotchkiss " machine-guns, and 20 to 24 automatic rifles of " Chassau " pattern. As regards the rifle regiments 5 and 9, they are armed with rifles of the French system.

Artillery.—72 Russian light guns of 3 cm., 8 French long-range pieces of 185 mm., 8 heavy mortars of 105 mm., 5 Russian pieces of 48 lines (i.e. 4 in.).

Cavalry.—The cavalry regiments are armed with hand carbines of various systems ; as regards machine-guns, each squadron has 2 light ones ; the 6th squadron has 8 heavy ones of Schwerlass pattern.

The rear-guard detachments and communications, as also the female legion, are armed with French carbines. The residue which remained after this transformation was sent to Warsaw.

II. To question No. 2 he replied : I know that the project for the occupation of Vilna and the creation of a Central Lithuania was conceived in the Siedlec market town in the environs of Warsaw at the moment when the Polish army repulsed the Bolsheviks under the walls of the capital. Marshal Pilsudski, with his new General Staff, was at Siedlec at this time. The original plan of appointing General Zhantkovski head of Central Lithuania was abandoned on the arrival of Marshal Pilsudski at Grodno, from Lida, owing to the origin of General Zhantkovski, born in Poland, and not in Lithuania.

I assisted at the meeting of officers summoned to Marshal Pilsudski to receive explanations regarding the relations of this newly-created Central Lithuania with Poland.

III. Money and armament (arms and munitions) arrived in Central Lithuania solely from Warsaw. All settlements of accounts were effected direct with the Ministry of Military Affairs of Warsaw.

IV. As far as I know, Poland did not send new recruits to Central Lithuania. On the contrary, the reserve battalions of Division I, L.B., viz. of Novogrodek (previously in garrison at Vlotslavek), of Grodno (stationed formerly at Czenstochova), of Minsk (stationed at Plock), lastly of Vilna (stationed at Skierniewice), were composed each of 1,500 men furnished by mobilization throughout the territory of Poland. The soldiers belonging to these battalions were distributed among the various regiments.

Independently of the aforesaid forces, two recruiting offices functioned permanently at Warsaw, those of Captain Perhawicz and Captain Kucharzewski, whose object was to discover officers and men who were natives of Central Lithuania.

CAPTAIN BUCZYNSKI.

ANNEX D

Statement by Captain Javorski.

No. 4.

The following reply was given in answer to the question, whence came the funds devoted to the organization and maintenance of Zeligowski's army :

The Paymaster's Office attached to the General Staff Armament Section of Zeligowski's army was directly connected with the Armament Section of the Warsaw High Command. Similarly, the funds for the arsenal and munitions factory of Zeligowski's army were obtained from Warsaw.

The payments were approved by the Armament Section at Warsaw (General Gliniecki, of the Headquarters Staff).

Finally, General Norwid, ex-Quartermaster-General, was the chief administrator of Central Lithuanian affairs in Poland.

ANNEX E.

Statement by 2nd Lieutenant Slovikovski.

No. 5.

The following reply was given in answer to the question as to whence came the funds devoted to the organization and maintenance of General Zeligowski's army :

The money was sent from the Ministry of War at Warsaw.

The supplies were partly provided by the Commissariat of the Second Army at Lida, but not entirely, as some of the supplies and forage were obtained from the local population in return for ready-money, and also by means of agreements with contractors who imported them from the " Kingdom " (Poland), Germany and America.

Uniforms were furnished by the Commissariat of the Second Army at Lida. They were partly made at newly-built factories at Vilna. The cloth came from the town of Lodz.

ANNEX F

No. 6.

Warsaw D.O.G.

General District Command,
Warsaw.
February 9, 1921

Secret Order No. 20.

(2) *Treatment of soldiers belonging to the Lithuanian-White-Russian Division.*

Supplementary to Order 5.1.21.25.1., it is commanded, in virtue of the Commander-in-Chief's order, and is proclaimed to all soldiers sent back from General Zeligowski's army for various reasons, that the Lithuanian-White-Russian Divisions are placed under the orders of the Commander-in-Chief of the Polish army by the same right as all the other divisions of this army.

ANNEX IIa

Telegram from Colonel Chardigny, President of the Military Control Commission to the Council of the League of Nations.

Colonel Chardigny to the Council)
War—Paris.

No. 15. For the League of Nations.

As the results of events at Vilna, the Commission begs to forward by telegram, for your information, statements made by the Minister for Foreign Affairs at Warsaw on the 3rd, and by the Marshal Commanding-in-Chief at Bialystok on the 4th, contained in its report No. 1, dated October 5th. The Minister definitely declared that the Government would not cause Vilna to be occupied, and expressed himself in favour of a settlement of the frontier dispute between the two countries by a plebiscite of a summary and speedy nature. The Marshal also assured the Commission that a march against Vilna was not intended, but that he could not answer for his troops in the event of provocation by the Lithuanians. He declared that a division composed of officers and soldiers from the Vilna district is operating in the Lida district, and that the feelings of these troops might lead them on to unforeseen acts ; he added that if he were not Chief of the State, he would, as a soldier, have occupied the town a week ago.

COLONEL CHARDIGNY

INDEX

Adaptation of Russian law, 142
Aestian origin of Lithuanian race, 37, 38–9, 40
Agrarian law, operation of, 132
Agrarian reform, 129
   central office of, 130
Agreement of Suvalki, 207
Agricultural exports, 125
Agricultural holdings, area of, 127
Agricultural societies, 74
Agricultural statistics, 124
Agriculture, Department of, 131
Agriculture, Ministry of, 128
Algird threatens Moscow, 15
Allies' treatment of Lithuania, 115
Altitude of Lithuanian hill ranges, 34
Amber industry, 133
Analogies of language with Latin, 174
Ancestor worship, 170
Animals, statistics of, 125
Appeal Court, formation of, 142
Ardvila, Grand Duke, 41
Area—
   of forests, 30
   of Lithuania, present, 17, 20, 123
   under cultivation, 30
Assembly, Constituent, election of, 18
Associations—
   secret, 62
   student, 64

Balt, or Aestian origins of race, 37, 38–9
Baltic languages, 173
Banks, 137, 138
Basanavičius, Dr., 65–7
Battle of Vorksla, 1399, 45
Berne Conference, 1915, 86
Biruté, vestal virgin, 43
Bolshevik advance on Lithuania, 17, 93
Bolshevik occupation of Vilnius, 99–100
Bolshevik propaganda, its ineffectiveness, 95

Books, output of, 72
Building materials, 128
Buildings, arrangement of, 153–4

Calvinism, rise and fall of, in Lithuania, 51
Catholic Church, oppression of, 69
Catholic renascence, 52
Character of people, 145–152
Chaucer, reference to Lithuania, 17
Christianity—
   coming of, 50
   under Gediminas, 42
Churches—
   decoration of, 191–2
   destruction of, 77
Cities, principal, pre-war population of, 124
Čiurlionis, musical composer, 185–8
Climate of the country, 33
Code Napoléon, 60
Codes, civil and criminal, 144
Coiffure, Lithuanian, 160
Committee, central, "Lithuania," 80
Committee, Lithuanian, for war refugees, 79
Communism, unpopularity of, 96
Conference of Berne, 1915, 86
Conference of St. Petersburg, 90
Conference of Stockholm, 1918, 91
Confiscations—
   by Germans, 82
   by Russians, 75
Congress of Vilnius, 1905, 67
Constituent Assembly, election of, 18, 94
Convention of Vilnius, 1917, 16
Co-operative Societies, 138
Council, National—
   election of, 91
   formed, 89
Crime, diminution of, 144
Crops, principal, grown, 124
Cultivation, systems of, 73
Currency, 122, 135, 139
Customs of people, 160

15

Dainos, or national songs, 146
Dairy farming, 126
Dancing in Lithuania, 161
Debt, foreign, 136
Demarcation lines violated by Poles, 93, 111
Democrats—
 Christian, 94
 Social, 95
Department of Agriculture, 131
Deportations of population during war, 75, 78
Devastations caused by war, 74–6
Dialects of the language, 173
Dioceses, XVIth century, 49
Diseases caused by war, 78
Divinities, pagan, 166
Dreams, belief in, 172
Dress—
 festival, 157
 Lithuanian national, 157–160
Drought of 1921, 126

Economic development, 173
Edict of 1894, secret Russian, 56
Education—
 in the Constituent Assembly, 94
 statistics of, 69
 under Russian rule, 56, 57
Election of Constituent Assembly, 18, 94
Election, Polish, in Vilnius, 111
Embroidery, prevalence of, 159
Ethnographic limits of Lithuania, 20
Export statistics, 134
Exports, agricultural, 125

Farms, number of, 131
Festival dress, 157
Finance, 135
Fine Arts, Society of, 72–3
Finns, influence of, 39
Fire worship, 164, 169
Fiscal policy, 122
Flax weaving industry, 132
Food products, manufacture of, 132
Foreign debt, 136
Forests—
 depletion of, 128
 of the country, 127–8
Fortresses of Kaunas, etc., 75
Frontier line fixed, 111
Funerals, 170

Gardinas—
 climate of, 34
 province of, 31
Gediminas, Grand Duke, 41–2
Geology of Lithuania, 36

German administration, 80–1
German claims in regard to Memel, 117
German confiscations of property, 82
German headquarters at Vilnius, 81
German language made compulsory, 83
German newspapers, 83
German occupation of Lithuania, 16, 80
German recognition of Lithuania, 92
Giants, legends of, 171
Grand Duke Rimgaudas, the first, 41
Grand Dukes of Lithuania, 41–7
Grodski, Lieutenant, of Zeligowski's staff, 218
 statement by, 218

Headgear in Lithuania, 157
Hills, ranges of, 34
Houses—
 building materials used in, 128
 construction of, 154

Independence—
 attempted, 1655, 53
 proclamation of, 17, 92
 ratified, 94
Industries—
 of the country, 132
 peasant, 133
Iron foundry of Kaunas, Tillman, 132
Iron, use of in early times, 40
Isenburg, Prince, German Administrator, 81, 84

Jagellon—
 attempts conquest, 44
 made King of Poland, 44
Janusevičius demands independence, 86
Jewish Co-operative Bank, central, 139
Jewish preference for Lithuanian Government, 104
Jews, centred at Plungé, 28
Jury, trial by, 143

Kaunas—
 captured in 1352, 43
 climate of province, 33
 province of, 26
 town of, 27
Keistutis, Grand Duke, 43
Kudirka, Vincas, poet, 66

Lakes, 30, 35
Land—
    appropriation of by State, 129
    area of holdings, 127
    distribution of, 61, 129–30, 131
    peasant holdings of, 73
    seizure of, 60
Language—
    dialects of, 173
    Latin analogies, 174
    origin of, 37, 173–182
    records of, 25, 30, 37–8
    suppressed by Russian order, 57
Lausanne, Lithuanian representatives at, 87
Law—
    administration of, 59, 141–4
    Russian, adaptation of, 142
League of Nations, intervention by, 107–9
Legal codes in use, 59, 60
Legends—
    of the country, 171
    of giants, 171
Lettish separation from Lithuanians, 39
Literature, 183
"Lithuania" Central Committee, 80
"Lithuania Day" organized in U.S.A., 79
Lithuania Major and Minor, distinction between, 20
Lithuania Minor, record of, 32
Livestock of the country, statistics, 125, 126
Loans—
    internal, 137
    "Liberty Loan," 137
Lublin Union, effects of, 52
Lyda, town of, 26

Manufactures, 132
Marriage ceremonies, 161
Memel—
    administered by French, 120
    area of, 117
    district of, 117
    German claims regarding, 117
    Germanized, 120
    Lithuanian in character, 117, 119
    particulars of, 32
Memorandum of Vilnius, 1905, 67
Mindaugas, Grand Duke, 41
Mineral resources of the country, 133
Mineral springs, 134
Monasteries, suppression of, 60

Moscow—
    Lithuanian Society in, 71
    threatened by Algird, 15
Muraviev—
    persecutions by, 58
    retards progress of Lithuania, 89
    Russian Governor, 58
Musical character of the Lithuanians, 146, 151, 192
Musical composers, 185, 193–4
Mythology, influences on Lithuanian, 172

Name of the country, first use of, 40
Napoléon, Code, 60
Napoleon signs treaty of Tilsit, 33
Naroushevitch, Mr., statement by, 109
National Council—
    election of, 91
    formed, 89
National Hymn, Lithuanian, 195
Nemunas, river, 34, 141
    affluents of, 35
Newspapers, 71
    German, 83

Odessa taken by Vytautas, 45
Origin of Lithuanian race, Aestian, 37
Ost currency, 122, 135

Pagan customs, 163–172
Pagan sanctuaries destroyed, 44
Painters, Lithuanian, 189
Palanga, port of, 28, 29
Peace Treaty with Russia, 1920, 98
Peat, use of, 128
Percentage of different races in Lithuania, 17, 21, 124
Periodicals, revolutionary, 62
Philology, Lithuanian, 37
Pilsudski directing Zeligowski, 106
Plays, performance of, 72
Poland—
    association with, 17, 32
    partition of, 1793–5, 53
Polish election in Vilnius, 111
Polish-Lithuanian conflict, diary of, 209
Polish occupation of Vilnius, 17
Polish offensive launched, 102
Polish pogrom in Vilnius, 112
Polish treacherous attack on Lithuanians, 99
Polish violations of line of demarcation, 93, 111
Population statistics, 17, 20, 123
    pre-war, 124

Poets, principal Lithuanian, 183-4
Police agents, Russian, 72
Policy, fiscal, 122
Pope contributes to Lithuanian relief, 80
Ports of Palanga and Šventoji, 28
Press of the country, 71
Prices of various commodities, 126
Priests, pagan, 164
Primitive cottages of Lithuania, 156
Primitive religion of the country, 163-72
Proclamation of Independence, 17, 92

Radvila Family, home of, 28
Radvila, Nicolai (the Black), 52
Radvila, Nicolas-Christopher, 52
Railways, 140
Ratification of independence, 94
Recognition *de jure* denied, 113
    by Germany, 92
    by U.S.A., 19
Reform, Agrarian, 129
    central office of, 130
Relief, measures for, in war, 79-80
Religious degeneration, 49-50
Religious history, 49, 163-72
Religious reform, 50-1
Religious temperament of Lithuanians, 151
Rimgaudas, first Grand Duke, 41
Russia—
    advance of 1914-5, 75-6
    appropriates provinces of Lithuania, 53
    revolt against, by Lithuanians, 64
    tyranny of, 55-61, 74
Russian deportations during war, 75
Russian edict of 1894, secret, 56
Russian law, adaptation of, 142
Russian police agents, 62
Russian Proclamation of Freedom, 67
Russian requisitions during war, 75
Russian schools in Lithuania, 56-7
Russo-Lithuanian Peace Treaty, 17

Schools—
    closed by Russian order, 56
    opened by educational societies, 70
    Russian, in Lithuania, 57
Sculptors, Lithuanian, 190
Secret associations, 62
Secret Russian edict of 1894, 56
Social democrats, 95
Social Populists, 95

Societies—
    agricultural, 74
    co-operative, 138
Society—
    Lithuanian, in Moscow, 71
    of Fine Arts, 72-3
Songs, folk—
    of Lithuania, 146, 151, 192
    of the poet Kudirka, 66
Speech, suppression of Lithuanian, 57
State Council, formation of, 93
Statistics—
    agricultural, 124
    educational, 69
    industry, 132
    trade, 134
Stockholm, Conference of, 1918, 91
Student associations, 64
Superstitions of the country, 151
Suvalki—
    agreement of, 17, 207
    climate of, 33
    province of, 30
Šventoji, port of, 28, 29, 30

Tartars influenced by Lithuania, 45
Taryba proclaims independence, 92
Taxation, 127, 135
Telepathic phenomena, sensitiveness to, 170
Temperament, Lithuanian, 147
Temperance work, 70
Teutonic Order, struggles with the, 42-43
Tilsit, Treaty of, 33
Timber, 127-8
    rafting, 141
Topography of the country, 20
Towns, principal, 21-32
Trade statistics, 134

U.S.A.—
    Lithuanians in, 85
    organizes "Lithuania Day," 79
University of Vilnius closed, 56

Vestal virgin, Biruté, 43
Villages destroyed by war, 77
Vilnius—
    area of province, 21
    as German headquarters, 81
    Bolshevik occupation of, 99-100
    climate of province, 33
    Congress of, 69
    Diet of, 1905, 85
    evacuation of, 93
    fire worship at, 105
    history of town, 21-25

Vilnius (*continued*)—
    memorandum of, 1905, 67
    Polish election in, 111
    Polish pogrom in, 112
    seat of Lithuanian Government, 100
    university closed, 56
    university of, 88
Vitenis, Grand Duke, 41
Vytautas—
    ceded Memel, 32
    defeated by Tartars, 45
    extension of Lithuania under, 45
    reign of, 44–6
    restored ports of the country, 29

War—
    devastations caused by, 74–6
    Lithuania during the, 75–9
    refugees, Lithuanian Committee for, 79

Waterfalls, 134
Watershed of Lithuania, 34
Waterways, 141
Weaving—
    flax fibre, 132
    peasant, 133
Women and national development, 74
Wood, use of, for building, 128
Writers, Lithuanian, 145

Zeligowski—
    captures Vilnius, 17
    establishes Central Lithuanian Government, 103
    instigated by Polish Government, 106
    organization staff, statement, 218
    proclamation defining Government, 105
    supplied from Warsaw, 106

Printed in Great Britain by
UNWIN BROTHERS, LIMITED
LONDON AND WOKING